The Emotional Development of Young Children

Building an Emotion-Centered Curriculum

Marion C. Hyson

with a Foreword
by Edward Zigler

 Teachers College,
Columbia University
New York and London

Published by Teachers College Press, 1234 Amsterdam Avenue
New York, N.Y. 10027

Library of Congress Cataloging-in-Publication Data

Hyson, Marion C.
    The emotional development of young children : building an emo-
tion-centered curriculum / Marion C. Hyson.
        p.   cm. — (Early childhood education series)
        Includes bibliographical references (p.) and index.
        ISBN 0-8077-3355-5 (alk. paper). — ISBN 0-8077-3354-7
(pbk. : alk. paper)
        1. Early childhood education — United States — Curricula. 2.
Child psychology — United States. 3. Emotions in children. 4.
Curriculum planning — United States. I. Title.   II. Title: Emotion-centered curriculum.   III. Series.
    LB1139.4.H97   1994
    372.19 — dc20   94-3936

ISBN 0-8077-3355-5
ISBN 0-8077-3354-7 (pbk.)

Printed on acid-free paper

Manufactured in the United States of America

01   8 7 6 5 4 3

Contents

Foreword

For decades, child development specialists and educators have seen theoretical trends come and go. At one time, during the era of John Dewey, the emotional development and adjustment of the child were viewed as a central aspect of democratic education. Subsequently, an emphasis on the child's cognitive ability far overshadowed any concerns for the social and emotional spheres of a child's life; we spent many years debating whether her IQ could be increased, and if so, by how much (see Bloom, 1964; Jensen, 1969; Spitz, 1986; Zigler & Seitz, 1982; Zigler, 1988). Now the pendulum seems to have swung back, and once again the importance of emotion is recognized. The publication of this book marks a restoration of emotion to our perception of the "whole child" and represents the best of our current thinking with regard to the role of emotions in very young lives.

Without an appreciation of a child's complexity, we cannot be effective in fostering his development. Clearly, a child is made up of far more than cognitive capacities, and it is not a failure of those capacities that brings about the violence and social decay that increasingly trouble this nation. Thus it is becoming more and more critical to focus our efforts on interventions that address the social, emotional, and motivational structures within a child (see Zigler, 1970). In my own work with the Head Start program, the child's emotional development and overall mental health have always been a central concern. However, these are aspects of development that affect all children alike, not only the disadvantaged, "high risk" individual. All children need assistance in forming a positive self-image, in learning to interact in relationships, and in experiencing emotions as an integral part of daily life. Whether such emotions can become for the child a rich, life-enhancing source of experience or a frightening, incomprehensible array of feelings may depend on how well parents and schools can impart a healthy understanding of emotions and emotional self-regulation.

Recently, displays of physical affection and emotional connection in early childhood settings have become suspect, in part because of a rise in reports of abuse in these settings and in society at large. However, an undue emphasis on formal academics in early childhood programs contributes also to a decline in emotional "warmth" in classrooms. Teachers and other professionals need expert assistance in learning how to modify classroom practice to overcome the effects of these trends. These changes in preschools, primary schools, and other early childhood settings are distressing when we consider the diminishing opportunities young children have to establish warm, continuous and friendly relationships in their young lives. Today's children are spending less and less time with their parents, who are forced by economic necessity to work longer hours and to place even their very young children in preschool settings (see Boyer, 1991; U.S. Bureau of Labor Statistics, 1990; Willer, Hofferth, Kisker, et al., 1991). Thus the nature of the early childhood curriculum, its developmental appropriateness, and the emotional tone its practice creates, are becoming increasingly important.

The children in early childhood settings are just beginning to construct their personal social universes; they are experiencing for the first time many of their own emotional responses and those of others. Marion Hyson has done a splendid job of bringing together the present state of our knowledge of child development and the best of early childhood practice, and combining these with her own creative ideas to help today's educators design an "emotion-centered" curriculum. Her volume is comprehensive, insightful, and highly readable; early childhood professionals should find it invaluable.

Edward Zigler
Yale University

REFERENCES

Bloom, B. (1964). *Stability and change in human characteristics.* New York: Wiley.

Boyer, E. L. (1991). *Ready to learn: A mandate for the nation.* Princeton, NJ: Carnegie Foundation for the Advancement of Teaching.

Jensen, A. R. (1969). How much can we boost IQ and scholastic achievement? *Harvard Educational Review, 31,* 1–123.

Spitz, H. (1986). *The raising of intelligence: A selected history of attempts to raise retarded intelligence.* Hillsdale, NJ: L. Erlbaum.

U.S. Bureau of Labor Statistics. (1990). Marital and family characteristics of the labor force from the March, 1990 Population Survey. Unpublished raw data.

Willer, B., Hofferth, S. L., Kisker, E. E., Divine-Hawkins, P., Farquhar, E., & Glantz, F. (1991). *The demand and supply of child care in 1990: Joint findings from the National Child Care Survey 1990 and a profile of child care settings.* Washington, D.C.: National Association for the Education of Young Children.

Zigler, E. (1970). The environmental mystique: Training the intellect versus development of the child. *Childhood Education, 46,* 402–412.

Zigler, E. (1988). The IQ pendulum. (Review of H. Spitz, *The raising of intelligence*). *Readings, 3* (2), 4–9.

Zigler, E. & Seitz, V. (1982). Social policy and intelligence. In R. Sternberg (Ed.) *Handbook of human intelligence* (pp. 586–641). New York: Cambridge University Press.

Acknowledgments

Writing about emotions is an emotional process. I feel deeply grateful to those who have helped bring this book into print. As is evident to the reader, my theoretical perspective on emotional development has been strongly influenced by Carroll Izard's work; less evident but no less important have been his generosity, good will, and collaborative spirit. Elizabeth Foster Stonorov has exerted a quietly inspiring influence on my beliefs about emotion-centered programs for young children. Feelings of fascination and delight surround my memories of visits to many excellent early childhood settings. I especially acknowledge and honor the contributions of master practitioners Jane Davidson, Nancy Edwards, Nadine Heim, Charlotte Holden, Colleen Katzman, Faithe Koser, and Judy McGlothlin. Numerous colleagues, especially those in the University of Delaware's Department of Individual and Family Studies, have contributed empathy, sincere interest, and practical suggestions. Student research assistants Jennifer Adams and Tonya Fleck were diligent and accurate even under deadline pressures. Linda Granger guided the manuscript through multiple revisions with care and dedication. Finally, John, Jeff, and Dan have never allowed me to forget where emotional development finds its true center.

Introduction

Although set in the world of early childhood education, this book is not about early literacy. It is not about mathematical reasoning. It is not even about social competence or about effective instructional practices. And yet it is about all these things, because it is about emotions—the joy, surprise, sadness, fear, interest, anger, shame, and surprise that color and motivate children's early development, learning, and relationships.

Many early childhood professionals have always believed that children's emotions are central to their lives and should be central to the curriculum. However, in recent years these beliefs have been eroded. Early childhood programs have felt pressured to adopt an academic curriculum accompanied by formal teacher–student relationships and focused exclusively on mastery of cognitive skills. Adults avoid affectionate touch out of fear of unfounded accusations of sexual abuse. In this climate, early childhood professionals who continue to advocate for an emotion-centered curriculum may sound apologetic or defensive.

Ironically, during this same period, developmental psychologists have taken a different path, one that is more consistent with the deep-seated beliefs and preferences of many early childhood professionals. The last decade has witnessed a remarkable revival of interest in the study of emotions and of early emotional development, subjects that had been virtually ignored for several decades in favor of cognitive theory and research. Using innovative research methods and building on earlier theoretical models, a new generation of emotion researchers has documented emotions' importance as organizers of children's behavior and learning. This knowledge base can provide a solid foundation for rebuilding an emotion-centered early childhood curriculum.

DEFINING "EMOTIONS" AND "EMOTION-CENTERED CURRICULUM"

The book's use of the words *emotions* and *emotion-centered curriculum* may need some clarification. As the first chapter will show, emotions have been the subject of much interest throughout the history of early childhood education. However, people have used the word *emotion* in different ways or have used other words like *affect, feelings,* and *mood* to describe similar phenomena. Like many of life's most important features, emotion is easier to experience than to define. For several reasons, this book will use the definition offered by developmental psychologist and emotion researcher Carroll Izard (1991): "An emotion is experienced as a feeling that motivates, organizes, and guides perception, thought, and action" (p. 14).

Izard's definition emphasizes several critical features that will be especially important in our discussion of emotions in early childhood programs. An emotion is something that a person feels inside; in fact, human lives contain a continuous stream of emotions. Everywhere that children and adults are awake and functioning, emotions are always present. Even more important, emotions have a purpose: They "motivate, organize, and guide" our "perception, thought, and action." Each emotion appears to have specific motivational properties. Throughout this book, we will see many examples of the power of emotions such as joy, interest, anger, sadness, and fear to guide children's behavior, color their expressions, and stimulate or discourage their learning.

Emotion, Affect, Feelings, and Moods

In this book, the terms *emotion, emotional,* and *emotional development* will generally be used in preference to *affect, affective,* and *affective development.* This usage is more consistent with current terminology within the field of child development. Some writers use *affect* as a broad category that includes drives like hunger and sexual urges together with emotions like joy, shame, and sadness. Others see emotions and affects as synonymous but prefer to use the term *emotion* because of the narrower association of affect with psychoanalytic theory. In this book, I will follow current usage in developmental psychology, using *emotion* most frequently but occasionally substituting the term *affect* for the sake of variety. Likewise, the term *feelings* will sometimes be used as an approximate but less precise synonym for *emotions.* Finally, the term *moods* will be reserved for relatively enduring (but not permanent) emotional states.

Emotional Development and Socioemotional Development

Like the connection between emotion and affect, *emotional development* is related to but not exactly the same as *social development.* Many texts have traditionally combined these two developmental domains, devoting chapters to *socioemotional* or *social-emotional* development. It is certainly true that social and emotional development are closely intertwined. An important theme throughout this book will be the social context of emotional development. Today, however, researchers emphasize that emotional development is worthy of study in its own right. Combining "emotional" and "social" development in the global phrase "socioemotional" obscures the strong connections between emotion, cognition, and other developmental domains.

Emotion-Centered Curriculum and Affective Education

This book will urge early childhood programs to adopt an "emotion-centered curriculum." Is this the same as "affective education" as it was proposed in the 1970s? "Affective education" had to do primarily with teaching children *about* feelings, helping children to understand their own feelings and those of others, and encouraging open yet appropriate expressions of emotion. These are important goals, and they form one part of what this book will call the "emotion-centered curriculum." However, the concept of an "emotion-centered curriculum" goes beyond the more specific goals of 1970s-style affective education. As we will see, current theory and research support the belief that *all* behavior, thought, and interaction are in some way motivated by and colored by emotions. As young children (and their adult companions) talk, play, plan, write, and argue, emotions are constantly present, helping to focus their attention, influence their interpretation of events, and direct their facial expressions and body language. If this is so, then every early childhood curriculum is emotion-centered. The task of the early childhood professional is to build on this foundation, using current knowledge and professional insight to make the curriculum *appropriately, explicitly,* and *thoughtfully* emotion-centered.

Emphasizing emotions does not mean ignoring other areas of development. A particular goal of this book will be to help break down the artificial separation between the emotional and cognitive domains. Thinking is an emotional activity, and emotions provide an essential scaffold for learning. In fact, children's feelings can support or hinder their involvement in and mastery of intellectual content. An emotion-centered curriculum can be at least as intellectually challenging as any curriculum that is labeled "cognitive" or "academic."

ABOUT THIS BOOK

This book is written for early childhood professionals, including teacher educators, students, caregivers, classroom teachers, or administrators working in programs for young children. The book follows the National Association for the Education of Young Children in defining "early childhood" as spanning the years from birth to age 8. Therefore, the early childhood program settings referred to in this book include day care centers and family day care homes, part-day and full-day preschools, kindergartens, and primary grade classes. Similarly, the young children in the book represent the rich spectrum of age, ethnicity, family environment, and individual temperament that early childhood professionals encounter and welcome in their work. Finally, young children with disabilities are integrated into the book as they are—or should be—in early childhood programs.

The book does not attempt to provide specific guidance in working with children who have serious emotional difficulties. The classroom examples and research summarized in later chapters emphasize typical developmental and individual patterns. However, practitioners may consider adapting many of the book's recommended strategies to the special needs of children with major affective disorders.

This book was written with six specific aims in mind.

1. To convince the reader that emotions can and should be the center of the curriculum in early childhood education.
2. To provide the reader with an historical and theoretical background on current controversies about the place of emotions in early childhood education.
3. To show that current research in child development provides a sound base for an emotion-centered early childhood curriculum.
4. To offer the reader a set of specific, research-based goals for emotional development in early childhood education.
5. To provide suggestions and examples of strategies teachers can use in achieving these goals.
6. To offer resources for early childhood professionals to use in extending their own understanding of the place of emotions in early childhood education, and in reflecting upon their own practice.

ORGANIZATION

This book is written as a professional resource using a mix of theory, research, and anecdotal material, with many specific applications for practitioners. The book is organized into two major sections. Part I introduces the reader to old questions and some new answers concerning emotions in early childhood programs. Chapter 1 traces historical changes in the profession's thinking about where emotions fit into young children's programs. This chapter ends by describing contemporary challenges to an emotion-centered curriculum, including academic pressures and concerns about sexual abuse.

The next three chapters provide an overview of recent theory and research concerning early emotional development, and they discuss the relationship between this work and Piagetian, psychoanalytic, and learning theory perspectives on early development. Chapter 2 reviews theoretical discussions of the importance of emotions in development and describes the key ideas in today's study of emotions. Chapter 3 describes what we know about young children's emergent "emotion skills." The chapter includes normative descriptions of children's emotional repertoire at different ages. Chapter 4 reviews the many factors that influence children's emotional development, including temperament, family, and culture.

Part II applies this theory and research to specific issues in early childhood education. Chapter 5 begins by providing an overview of the emotion-centered curriculum, including the teacher's role, the place of academic subject matter, and adaptations for different age groups, settings, and individual needs. After this overview, the remaining chapters in Part II present specific teaching goals and strategies for an emotion-focused early childhood program.

Chapters 6 through 11 discuss six program goals: creating a secure emotional environment; helping children to understand emotions; modeling genuine, appropriate emotional responses; supporting children's regulation of emotions; recognizing and honoring children's expressive styles; and uniting children's learning with positive emotions.

MEETING THE PRACTITIONERS

Throughout the book, current research on emotions is enriched by the images and voices of children and teachers. Each chapter begins with a vignette that is later interwoven with theory, research, controversial issues, and suggestions for practitioners. Seven early childhood professionals—Christine, Denise, Hope, Ilene, Leslie, Natalie, and Terry—are featured in the chapters to follow. Although descriptions of their backgrounds, programs, and teaching styles combine features from several sources, and although details have been changed to protect adults' and children's privacy, these portrayals are based on real people.

Christine now teaches kindergarten children in a university laboratory school, after several years of working in an urban alternative elementary school. Her class includes children with identified disabilities. Many of her children have parents who teach or hold staff positions at the university, and a number are from other countries.

Denise teaches two-year-olds in an urban child care center that serves predominantly African-American families. Many of the children's families have limited incomes and are single-parent families. Her center has an active foster grandparent program and a strong emphasis on parent involvement.

Hope is a teacher in a public elementary school located in a rural area. She teaches a multi-age primary grade class with a wide range of developmental levels. Hope has also taught in kindergarten and in a public school prekindergarten program. Her multi-age class has been the focus of much community interest this year.

Ilene teaches four-year-olds in a Head Start program and is actively involved in staff development. Her many years of experience in this program were preceded by work in a parent cooperative preschool. Ilene is known for her careful observations of children's behavior and for her commitment to fostering pretend play in her classroom.

Leslie is a family child care provider in a suburban community. Many of her children have stayed with her from the first months of their lives through their transition to elementary school. Leslie has a background in nursing and has become a leader in promoting the professional development of family child care providers.

Natalie also teaches in a laboratory school, where her children include two- and three-year-olds. Each year children with disabilities are included in her program. Natalie has also worked in early intervention programs and in infant child care, and she continues to involve herself in training for infant/toddler caregivers.

Terry is a family child care provider in a suburban/rural area. With the help of her sister-in-law and, occasionally, her husband, she cares for 11 children ranging from 6 months to 4 years in age, including two-year-old triplets. Several of her children are members of racial and ethnic minorities, and one of the triplets has a chronic medical condition.

The practitioners featured in this book are diverse in every way but one: They are all women. In this respect they represent the overwhelming majority of early childhood professionals. However, this gender bias should not be considered a desirable state of affairs, and this book's recommendations are not gender-specific. Both men and women nurture young children's emotional development, in families and in early childhood programs.

Entering their profession with diverse backgrounds and working in diverse settings, Christine, Denise, Hope, Ilene, Leslie, Natalie, and Terry represent a uniformly high level of commitment to excellent early childhood programs with a strong emphasis on emotional development. However, their approaches to teaching are not intended to serve as a "cookbook." I hope, instead, that readers will reflect upon and construct from these materials, their individual experiences, and their personal values, their own understanding of the emotion-centered curriculum.

PART I

Emotions and Early Childhood: Old Questions and New Answers

Chapter 1

How Important are Emotions in Early Childhood Education?

It's Monday of the second week of preschool. As the three-year-olds arrive with their parents, Natalie greets each of them at the door.

"Hi, how are you, Adam?" (accompanied by a quick stroke of Adam's hair; then Adam is off to investigate his new love, the bathroom sink). "Hey, Zach, how are you?" "You're going to stay and play with us today, Felicia." "Sarah! How *are* you? Oh, look at that!" Most of the children come in holding large sheets of paper, to which are pasted photographs with printed captions. (The week before, each child had made an individual "me and my family" poster using pictures that parents had sent in. The posters had been sent home over the weekend for the children to share with their families.) As the children hand their posters to Natalie, she carefully places each one in a growing stack on the radiator.

One child is clutching his poster especially tightly. Natalie says, "We'll put your name on this, Ben, so we'll know it's yours."

As the children enter, many of them spontaneously find things to do. Simple activities have been set out: easel painting, play dough, doll beds with dolls and accessories, Legos and little cars. Natalie walks over to the play dough table. "Michael found the play dough. Where are your fingers, Michael?" she says playfully. "Are your fingers hiding underneath there?"

Natalie moves back toward the doorway. Jessica is standing halfway into the room, leaning against her mother. Tyrone approaches Natalie with a dishpan full of Legos. Natalie says to Tyrone, "I think Jessica really likes to do that. Maybe she would do it with you."

In a nearby kindergarten, the children have just finished a free-choice time like the one in Natalie's class. Now Christine's kindergarten children are sitting in a circle. A book lies on the rug in front of each child. The children have been talking about the books they selected. They have been describing the pictures on the covers and speculating about what stories might be inside them. Lowering her voice intriguingly, Christine says to the children, "You see lots of different things about your books. Here's another question: "What's the *same* about books?" After a few false starts, Brian offers, "They all have pages!"

As the discussion proceeds, Aaron is the only child who does not pay any attention. Seated beside Christine, Aaron has been gazing at his fingers, wiggling his hands, and twisting around looking at the ceiling and at the bulletin board behind him. Christine has occasionally touched his arm or gently rubbed his back. Now Aaron flops over and waves his legs in the air. Christine leans toward him and says in a quiet, friendly tone, "Aaron, please sit up and give Brian your attention and respect."

The discussion of book characteristics continues. Maria looks around at the books on the rug, thinks for a minute, and says, "All books have covers." Christine's face takes on an expression of surprise and pleasure. She looks impressed. "Did you all hear what Maria said? She said books have covers!"

The group meeting ends and the children prepare to go outside. As Christine goes around the circle, collecting a book from each child, she looks each child in the eyes and manages to create a brief personal contact.

Several children are still paging through their books.

"Jameela, would you like me to put that book on the bookshelf for you next week?" Christine asks one reader. Jameela nods enthusiastically. Laughing with delight, Christine comments to the class as a whole, "We *like* books! I think books are our *friends!*"

Both Natalie and Christine show that they value children's expressions of emotion. They respect children's feelings and design activities to engage children's emotions as well as their cognitive processes. The teachers also express their own feelings sincerely and directly. Emotions have a high priority in their classrooms.

Although each of these teachers has her own individual style, and although they teach children of different ages, they share the values of many past and present teachers in high quality early childhood programs. This chapter will begin by outlining the elements of this emotion-centered "core tradition." We will see that some unique historical circumstances have contributed to this emotional emphasis, and we will examine some examples of this emphasis over the years, including psychodynamically influenced programs, open education, and affective education. Despite these persistent patterns, we will also find recurring criticisms of the emotion-focused tradition. Turning to the status of emotions today, I will summarize several studies that show an apparent decline in the traditional emphasis on emotional development and that portray some negative consequences of this shift in emphasis. The chapter will conclude by citing urgent reasons for a renewed emphasis on emotions in early childhood programs.

THE EMOTION-CENTERED CORE TRADITION

The history of early childhood education can be reconstructed from many sources: oral histories, manuals and guides for practitioners, influential theoretical works, contents of professional journals, descriptions of past and present teacher education programs. As summarized in several comprehensive historical accounts (Braun & Edwards, 1972; Spodek, 1993; Weber, 1984), programs for young children have varied greatly in their philosophical foundations, curriculum content, and teaching practices. Within this variability, however, certain patterns have recurred over the field's long history, forming what might be considered a "core tradition" in early childhood education. One aspect of this tradition has been a long-standing concern with young children's emotional development.

Elements of the Emotion-Focused Tradition

Traditionally, early childhood programs have emphasized (1) the emotional nature of teacher–child relationships; (2) the selection of activities to meet children's emotional needs; (3) open expression of feelings by children and adults; (4) the development of positive affective states and dispositions; and (5) awareness of children's emotional responses. As Christine and Natalie begin the new school year, they seem to incorporate all of these elements into their programs.

Emotional Bonds Between Teacher and Child. Early childhood programs have traditionally placed special value on the affective relationship between children and their adult caregivers. Natalie's actions suggest that, like many of her fellow early childhood professionals, her first priority is to build a trusting, emotionally positive bond between herself and the children. Natalie makes certain that each child's basic needs are met promptly and lovingly. Children are touched, held, and helped to feel valued and needed. Natalie skillfully bridges family and school by encouraging parents to stay for a while during the first week and by giving parents and children tasks to complete together, pictures that can then be brought to school and proudly shared. The class "book" that will be made from these posters will literally bind together home and school experiences, as well as individual and group feelings, in a concrete and emotionally meaningful way.

Christine, too, is forging personal emotional links with her kindergartners as they begin the new year. Creating an intimate atmosphere, Christine gets physically close to the children, even during an "academic" activity such as this mini-lesson about books, titles, and authors. Her manner is warm and friendly as she begins to construct individual relationships with the children, sharing small jokes and gently teasing those who enjoy it. When she has to remind a child of the classroom rules, she does so in a personal way. Her words and behavior suggest that she will be a resource, an enthusiastic cheerleader, and a supportive guide for the children as they embark on learning in the kindergarten.

Activities to Meet Children's Emotional Needs. The history of early childhood education shows that practitioners have often selected activities for their value in meeting children's emotional needs. Natalie offers the three-year-olds materials and activities that assist in all areas of development. However, emotional development is always a high priority, and it takes on special significance at this point in the year. Natalie's activities seem designed to heighten children's positive attitudes about coming to school, to help children master separation-related feelings, to provide sensory enjoyment, and to offer opportunities for pleasurable social interaction. For example, Natalie had rigged a long cardboard tube so that it hung from ceiling hooks and could be tilted at various angles. During the first week of school, many children were drawn to the tube, tipping it, peering into it, and placing small cars in the openings, gleefully watching them emerge at the other end. In addition to its obvious cognitive value, the tube activity afforded rich opportunities for children to re-experience disappearance and reappearance, which is an emotionally charged issue at the beginning of the year.

Like Natalie's cardboard tube activity, Christine's book-sharing activity seemed designed to be emotionally as well as intellectually satisfying. The children selected their books individually and were invited to share things about their books with other children. The children's careful handling of the books, and their eagerness to tell about their own selections, showed that they were beginning to develop a personal connection with books and the reading process. Christine structured the activity to meet the kindergartners' need for recognition and acceptance by the group. She explicitly directed children's attention to "good ideas" and interesting comments made by their classmates, encouraging children to admire one another's abilities.

Encouraging Open Expression of Feelings. Another persistent theme in early education has been the encouragement of emotion expression. Children's feelings, even "negative" emotions, are accepted and respected.

Several three-year-olds cried during the first week of school. Tears and sobs came when their parents left and at transition times during the day. Natalie acknowledged children's sadness and offered hugs, soothing words, and tissues as needed. Natalie also encouraged and reflected children's expressions of happiness, curiosity, and surprise, as they explored the play dough, the cardboard tube, and other activities in the room.

With the kindergarten children, Christine's priority seems to be to encourage children to express positive feelings about learning. Christine creates an emotionally expressive environment in which learning activities become sources of curiosity, excitement, and sometimes frustration. Open in her own expression of feelings, Christine models a lively affective style that begins to permeate the classroom.

Developing Desirable Emotional States and Dispositions. In addition to valuing the expression of feelings, the core tradition in early childhood education has included an emphasis on "emotion socialization"—

helping children to learn desirable ways of expressing feelings and helping them to develop healthy patterns of understanding and regulating emotions.

Natalie's selection of activities and materials, and her involvement with the children during this brief observation, suggest some of her priorities. She encourages the development of trust, independence, warm friendships, and a sense of unity and fellowship among the children. At one point, a child, upon hearing the name of another child in the class (Jessica), said she had a sister named Jessica. Hearing this, Natalie commented, "Now you have a *friend* Jessica *and* a sister Jessica."

Like Natalie, Christine encourages positive feelings about school. More specifically, she works on developing feelings of interest and joy about the increasingly challenging cognitive tasks the children will encounter over the next few years. Christine's comment that "books are our friends" made this theme explicit. On a commercial poster, these words might be an empty cliche. However, Christine's spontaneous exclamation served to throw open the door to a year of literacy experiences filled with joy, effort, surprise, and emotional satisfaction.

With her kindergarten children, Christine expects more self-regulation of emotion expression than Natalie expects from the threes. Christine's interaction with Aaron typifies the way she begins to establish class norms about listening to other children, showing respect for classmates, and being kind to others.

Awareness of Children's Emotional Responses. Emotional development has held a strong fascination for many early childhood practitioners and researchers. Children's emotional reactions are frequently the subject of teachers' conversations, observations, and informal study.

Natalie supervises several student teachers, with whom she talks over classroom events after the children leave each day. Topics in these "post-sessions" are broad-ranging, but they often emphasize emotion-related issues such as children's reactions to separation, their interest in activities, or their formation of emotional attachments to adults and children in the class.

Christine takes obvious pleasure in watching how her kindergartners react to the new activities and tasks of the first few weeks of school. Her eyes continually dart around the room as she seeks information about children's responses. When one talks with Christine about the children in her class, it is evident that she thinks of them in highly individual terms. She knows her children's abilities in the cognitive domain, but she integrates that knowledge with perceptive observation of each child's unique affective engagement with social and academic tasks.

Unique Historical Features

These examples from Christine's and Natalie's programs illustrate the key elements of a persistently emotion-focused tradition. This concern with emotions goes beyond early childhood education, of course; teachers and researchers in elementary and secondary education have certainly not ignored emotional development. However, the history of early childhood education contains several unique features that help to account for the field's emotion-focused character.

Early Philosophical Roots. While acknowledging competing philosophies and influences, historical accounts of early childhood education find its strongest philosophical roots in the European Romantic tradition (Kohlberg & Mayer, 1972; Weber, 1984). In literature as well as in life, Romanticism viewed "feeling" as the wellspring of human endeavor and valued spontaneous expressions of natural impulses. Froebel, generally regarded as the father of early childhood education, developed a set of mystical beliefs that had strong links with the idealistic, Romantic philosophies of his time. His educational approach encouraged the outward expression of the child's inner feelings and thoughts; by this means, Froebel thought, the child would be brought into a fundamental sense of unity with the divine.

Independent Origins of ECE Programs. Another factor that may have contributed to the field's emphasis on emotion is that programs for young children originated apart from formal systems of public education. Child care, nursery schools, and kindergartens began independent of bureaucratic institutions and responded to needs broader than the acquisition of academic skills (Shapiro, 1983; Weber, 1969). Although kindergartens became integrated with public elementary schools by the 1920s, several writers have argued that their early history allowed them to be more open to new psychological ideas (Katz, 1971; Weber, 1969). Beane's (1990) historical review of the rocky path of "affect" in public education offers convincing evidence that emotion issues were more easily accepted in early childhood settings than in elementary and secondary public schools.

Psychological Underpinnings of ECE. Beginning in the 1920s, psychoanalysis made a significant impact on the thinking of early childhood practitioners through its emphasis on the power of subconscious emotions to motivate behavior and learning. Gesell's normative picture of child development also may have contributed to this emotion-focused tradition. Many early childhood educators began to adopt a belief in allowing free expression to children's "natural" behavior as it unfolded in predetermined stages. These theoretical perspectives have been used as psychological underpinnings for many early childhood programs and popular texts in early childhood education throughout this century.

Examples of the Emotion-Focused Tradition

Largely because of these unique historical factors, an emphasis on children's emotional development has been a central feature of the "core tradition" in early childhood education. Numerous books, articles, and program models have reflected this tradition. Weber (1984) provides a thorough, scholarly overview of the effects of Freudian, neo-Freudian, and maturationist theories on teacher education and early childhood curriculum. Rather than attempting to summarize this and other accounts (Beane, 1990; Spodek, 1993), I will briefly illustrate the emotion-focused tradition with a few representative examples from the history of twentieth-century American early childhood education. In each of these examples, emotions take center stage as the central influence on children's development and learning.

Psychodynamic Influences. In the 1920s, many nursery school educators looked to Freud's theory to understand and guide the development of children under the age of 5. The City and Country School in New York City was established in 1913 by Caroline Pratt and was sponsored by the Bureau of Educational Experiments, later known as the Bank Street College of Education. Those involved in the Bureau also included Lucy Sprague Mitchell and Harriet Johnson. Johnson's (1928) book, *Children in the Nursery School,* reflects the viewpoint that children's development is strongly social and affective and that teachers should expect strong expressions of emotion in young children.

By the 1940s, neo-Freudian and maturationist theories converged to produce an unprecedented level of interest in children's emotional development (Weber, 1984). One outgrowth of this interest was the formation of the Teachers' Service Committee on the Emotional Needs of Children. Formed in the years immediately after World War II, the committee was chaired by Lawrence Frank, who had become a major influence on the field's attention to emotion issues.

One of the many publications from the committee was a down-to-earth pamphlet for teachers of young children, written by committee member James Hymes (1947). In this pamphlet and in many other writings, Hymes stressed the fundamental importance of the teacher's affective relationship with children. "Smile when your children come to school in the morning," he urged. "Put your arm around his shoulder or hold his hand. . . . Be just as generous as you know how with honest interest and appreciation" (p. 21).

Concerned especially with children damaged by the emotional stresses of the war years, Hymes (1947) used a psychodynamic metaphor to make his point that "everyone has angry feelings bottled up inside of him" (p. 27). Hymes recommended that teachers help children cope with their feelings by offering "safety valves" such as clay, punching bags, and pretend play, and that teachers talk openly with children about their feelings.

A second example from the post-World War II era was the appearance of *Understanding Children's Play* (Hartley, Frank, & Goldenson, 1952). This widely cited book, the result of another project guided by Lawrence Frank, compiled and interpreted play observations in scores of nursery schools and kindergartens, using a psychodynamic perspective. The authors used these observations to support the idea that play is both a window into children's emotional lives and an avenue by which children can express and master their feelings. The authors urged that negative emotions be recognized by teachers and allowed safe outlets: "Instead of making children feel guilty about destructive impulses, the teacher might do them a great service by arranging a 'throwing corner' [for blocks], with a piece of heavy wallboard to receive the blows" (p. 49).

The history of what is now the Bank Street College of Education reflects a unique attempt to integrate an explicitly psychoanalytic perspective with cognitive developmental theory. From its beginnings in 1916 as Lucy Sprague Mitchell's Bureau of Educational Experiments, Bank Street advocated early childhood programs that promoted the integration and interaction of "cognitive-intellectual and affective-social processes" (Biber, 1942/1984, p. 291). The following statement typifies this emphasis: "Affect, sensation, wonder, thinking—the child's experience is a rich composite of all of them, and his education should be a rich response to all of them" (Biber, 1942/1984, p. 16).

Biber described Bank Street's "developmental-interaction approach" as having been strongly influenced by psychoanalysis (particularly ego psychology), by the progressive education movement, and by the preventive mental health orientation promulgated by Lawrence

Frank and others, as well as by the cognitive theories of Jean Piaget. As seen through these lenses, emotion has a broad set of functions. Like other psychoanalytically oriented early childhood programs, the Bank Street model acknowledged that children need to express their negative feelings. However, Biber (1942/1984) also stressed the positive emotional bases of children's self-initiated learning: "satisfied curiosity, the pleasures and intrinsic rewards of mastery, identification with teacher figures, and the internalizations of the trusted adults' confidence in the child's competence" (p. 290). The cognitive-affective perspective embodied in Biber's words has been a major influence on early childhood teacher training and recommendations for classroom practices.

Open Education. The 1970s brought another upsurge of interest in the emotional aspects of young children's education. Influenced by British primary education, the "open education" movement fostered a renewed attention to emotions in American public and private schools (Nyquist & Hawes, 1972). From Isaacs (1930/1963) and other sources, educators constructed an approach that emphasized child-initiated projects using home and neighborhood experiences. Open educators used children's own experiences as the raw materials for the curriculum partly because they believed these events' emotional power would motivate learning and intellectual engagement. Open education also valued the emotional quality of classroom interactions. Children were expected to be direct and spontaneous. Both positive and negative feelings were valued and encouraged: "Since significant growth is expected to be accompanied by a wide range of emotions . . . at times children will become not only joyful but quite unsettled, doubtful, perhaps anxious" (Bussis & Chittenden, 1972, pp. 134–135).

Affective Education. A second widely influential movement in the 1970s was "affective education." Shaped by humanistic psychology, the affective education movement attempted to incorporate explicit emotion-related activities into the curriculum of elementary and secondary schools. Although less directly applied to prekindergarten programs, the movement's goals held wide appeal. Affective education aimed to encourage children to express their feelings in the classroom and to develop a curriculum that would help children to understand their own and others' feelings.

A number of writers offered teachers specific activities intended to stimulate children's empathy, their ability to label emotions, and their capacity to express emotions in a direct, authentic way. A book titled *Left-Handed Teaching: Lessons in Affective Education* (Castillo, 1974) exemplifies this approach. Castillo's introductory chapter acknowledges the influence of humanistic and Gestalt psychologists, including Maslow, Rogers, May, and Jourard. "Confluent education" is advocated as a way to permit the child "to develop his emotional abilities along with his intellectual abilities" (p. 13). As outlined by Castillo, the affective curriculum would consist of emotion-related lessons or activities organized around thematic units, including "Imagination," "Sensory Awareness," "Communication," "Aggression," and "Building Trust." The book's description of the unit on aggression shows that the direct expression of feelings is valued: One goal is "to be able to experience anger where and when it occurs." Like most other proponents of affective education, Castillo also emphasizes the appropriate socialization of emotions: "to know when and where anger can be expressed, and to express it at appropriate times and places" (p. 137).

Criticisms of the Tradition

These historical examples illustrate how emotion-related beliefs have influenced early childhood programs. However, this emphasis on the importance of emotions and emotional development did not go unchallenged. A focus on emotions often was regarded as dangerous to children's intellectual growth or as a fuzzily romantic residue of an earlier time.

Early Criticisms. Even in the earliest days of the Froebelian kindergarten movement in the United States, tension arose between those favoring a stronger emphasis on emotion and those with a more "rational" or academic bent. Shapiro's (1983) history of the American kindergarten movement described Elizabeth Peabody chiding public kindergarten founders William Harris and Susan Blow for overemphasizing rationality in kindergarten education, while Harris responded by warning that the "gushing hilarity" of children schooled in the practices of Romantic Froebelians would limit their intellectual development.

Criticisms from the Cognitive Revolution. The cognitive revolution of the 1960s brought strong criticisms of "traditional" early childhood educators' focus on emotional and social development. Deutsch (1967), for example, asserted that

> The overgeneralized influence on some sections of early childhood education of the emphasis in the child guidance movement upon protecting the child from stress, creating a supportive environment, and resolving emo-

tional conflicts has done more to misdirect and retard the fields of child care, guidance, and development than any other single influence. (pp. 73–74)

Evans' (1975) summary of the 1960s upsurge of interest in early childhood education labeled the renewed emphasis on cognition as the most significant trend of the decade. He emphasized the sharp disagreements between traditional adherents to social-emotional curricula and the "newer" proponents of a cognitive emphasis. Further, Evans characterized open education and informal education movements as having ill-formed goals and narrow perspectives. Evans argued that traditional early childhood educators cast cognitively focused programs in the worst possible light, assuming that their adherents must be "cold, authoritarian, rigid, and therefore 'bad'" while their own approach was "warm, open, flexible, and therefore 'good'" (p. 281).

This "mindless" characterization of emotion-focused early childhood education is implicit in Goodlad's *Early Schooling in the United States* (1973). This national survey of 201 nursery schools in nine cities concluded that most early childhood programs either ignored or trivialized cognitive content. Goodlad's description of a "traditional" program contains thinly veiled disdain for its socioemotional emphasis:

Let us open our exploration of the nursery school in the United States with a visit to what is perhaps a typical example of the species. The school, in the words of its principal, proudly bills itself as traditional. "Our children are here to play and enjoy themselves, to learn to get along well with others, and to be given the opportunity to develop into warm and happy little individuals," she tells us. (p. 21)

EMOTIONS TODAY

Whether attacked or advocated, emotions clearly provided a significant focus for many early childhood programs of the past. What is the status of emotions in today's early childhood programs? It is easier to look back systematically at the past than to get a handle on the complex, constantly shifting picture that early education presents today. Nevertheless, most professionals agree that the past 10 years have seen a decline in the field's traditional emphasis on emotional development. Several studies offer evidence of this affect-impoverished climate.

Evidence for Declining Emphasis

In an observational study of thousands of American elementary and secondary classrooms, Goodlad (1984) found a virtual absence of both negative and positive emotions. Joy, warmth, and harshness were rare; the pervasive "emotional tone . . . might be described most accurately as flat" (p. 108). This tendency to ignore or deny emotion extends to programs for even younger children (Leavitt & Power, 1989). In *The Erosion of Childhood,* Suransky (1982) described 2 years of participant observations in five nursery school and day care programs. Her book offers a detailed ethnographic portrait of teachers who created bland, affectively sanitized environments and who manipulated children's emotions to serve adult ends. Teachers often responded to children in what Suransky judged to be emotionally false ways, characterized by a "persistent denial of angry intentions" (p. 87). Suransky argued that these emotionally sterile programs are typical of broader trends in American child care.

Suransky may be right. A recent national study of child care quality (Whitebook, Howes, & Phillips, 1989) found widespread emotional insensitivity, detachment, and even harshness among early childhood teachers. In a study of early childhood classroom practices (Hyson, Hirsh-Pasek, & Rescorla, 1990), observers rated teachers on how often they talked about feelings with children. In one out of three classrooms visited, such emotion-talk was rated "not at all like" or "very unlike" the teacher's observed behavior.

Influences Upon the Decline

What accounts for these trends? First, widely publicized cases of sexual abuse in child care have made many professionals and parents cautious about expressions of affection. Second, the 1980s saw a heightened emphasis on formal academics in early childhood programs. Together, these concerns may have pushed emotions to the back burner of early education.

Sexual Abuse Concerns. Do concerns about sexual abuse actually influence emotion-related attitudes and behaviors of teachers of young children? Hyson, Whitehead, and Prudhoe (1988) tried to find out by showing people a videotape of scenes in which adults interacted with young children in a normal, friendly way. Some scenes included affectionate touches. Those who saw the tape were asked to indicate their approval of each scene. Before watching the tape, some viewers read a statement describing current concerns about sexual abuse, while others read about the benefits of physical affection. In addition, some viewers were led to believe that the adults in the videotape were parents, while others were told they were child care providers.

When approval scores were analyzed, it was clear that parent and college student viewers were more disapproving of adult-child physical affection (1) if they had read about sexual abuse, (2) if they thought the adults were child care providers rather than parents, and (3) if the physically affectionate adult was male. In fact, viewers were *most* disapproving of affectionate touch by male child care providers. The attitudes of early childhood educators did not follow this general pattern, however. They tended to be more approving of adult–child affection than were other viewers. However, in later discussions, many early childhood professionals told the researchers that while they believed that physical affection and touch were important, in their daily work they deliberately refrained from physically affectionate behavior out of fears of being falsely accused of sexual abuse.

Academic Curricula and Practices. Teachers who adopt formal academic curricula may be less emotionally responsive to young children. In classroom observation research, Hyson, Hirsh-Pasek, and Rescorla (1990) found that prekindergarten programs that emphasized teacher-directed formal academic instruction (using few concrete materials and offering children few choices of activities) were much more likely to receive low ratings on positive emotional climate. In contrast to teachers in more "developmentally appropriate" programs, academically oriented early childhood teachers talked little about feelings, were not physically affectionate, and tended to use competition and comparison rather than redirection as discipline strategies.

Similar results have been reported by Stipek (1992), who has conducted observations of the programs and emotional tone of 62 child care settings. Like the programs observed in the Hyson, Hirsh-Pasek, and Rescorla (1990) study, these classrooms varied greatly in their emphasis on formal academics. Stipek had reasoned that a high academic emphasis would not necessarily be associated with a negative emotional climate. However, her analyses showed that, in fact, a teacher-directed academic curriculum was almost invariably accompanied by lower amounts of teacher warmth and more negative approaches to dealing with misbehavior.

Effects of Decline in Emotional Emphasis

Children's emotional development can be significantly altered by the quality and emphasis of early childhood programs. Burts and colleagues (1992) have examined the effects of "developmentally inappropriate" kindergartens on children's development. Stress behaviors or signs of anxiety were observed more frequently in children attending narrowly academic, developmentally inappropriate programs, with the differences being more marked for boys than for girls, and with low-income African-American children being especially likely to exhibit stress behaviors during many of the "inappropriate" activities. In a follow-up study in first and second grade (Hart, Charlesworth, Burts, & DeWolf, 1993), those children who had attended the "inappropriate" kindergartens were rated as more distractable, less prosocial, and poorer in conduct and study habits. Similarly, in the academic environments study (Hirsh-Pasek, Hyson, & Rescorla, 1990), children from high-pressure, emotionally distant, or critical family and preschool environments developed more negative feelings about school, more test anxiety, and lower levels of creative behavior.

Longitudinal studies of early intervention programs have found that long-term curriculum effects are more likely to be found in the socioemotional or motivational domains than in narrowly academic performance (see Stipek, 1991, for a review). For example, Schweinhart, Weikart, and Larner (1986) found that low-income children who had participated in a didactic preschool program were, as adolescents and young adults, significantly more likely to report engaging in antisocial behavior than children who had attended preschools that allowed more autonomy and exploration.

It is not easy to identify what curriculum differences might have produced these emotional and motivational effects. As described above, research by Stipek (1992) and by Hyson, Hirsh-Pasek, and Rescorla (1990) showed that highly academic, teacher-directed curricula are typically accompanied by negative emotional climates. Thus, some of the child outcomes that have been attributed to "curriculum" in the narrow sense (i.e., the kinds of lessons taught, degree of structure, specific instructional techniques) may well be a result of variations in the emotional climate accompanying these instructional practices. Thus, research suggests three conclusions. First, there appears to be a reduced emphasis on emotion-related issues in today's early childhood programs. Second, a number of social factors have contributed to a less rich and less supportive emotional climate for many young children.

And finally, these variations in emotional climate may have significant developmental consequences.

Need for Renewed Attention to Emotions

Even with this evidence at hand, some might argue that it is no great loss if early childhood education moves away from its strongly emotion-focused past. Some may say that children's emotional development has such a strong biological basis that it will unfold without intervention. However, biology is not the whole story. Children learn about emotions from relationships and interactions with others. They learn by watching others express emotions; they learn by engaging in activities that elicit a range of emotion responses; they learn from having their own feelings and those of others labeled; and they learn from having opportunities to talk about feelings. These early experiences have far-reaching effects on children's affective, motivational, social, and intellectual development.

But why not rely on the family to provide the context for this early learning? This emphasis was appropriate at a time when children stayed home until they began kindergarten or first grade, and when "preschool" was viewed as a small, playful adjunct to family life. Things are different today. An unprecedented number of infants, toddlers, and preschool children now spend most of their time in out-of-home educational settings, including day care, early intervention programs, and private and public school prekindergarten programs.

Furthermore, many children today are growing up in environments that seriously compromise their emotional development. Many of them witness uncontrolled and even violent models of emotion expression at home and on city streets. Family disruption, unemployment, and work pressures create anxiety and stress in children's lives and may make it difficult for many parents to meet their children's emotional needs.

Thus, early childhood professionals are a potent, even essential influence on young children's emotional development. If this was true in the past, it is even more true today.

CONCLUSION

This chapter has shown that an interest in, and commitment to, emotional development in early childhood education has deep historical roots. Despite periodic challenges to this emphasis, the early childhood field has persistently believed in the importance of attending to children's emotional needs and using emotions as the underpinning of the early childhood curriculum. However, despite its long-standing interest in these issues, and despite its commitment to emotional development as the foundation of sound educational practice, early childhood education has lacked a comprehensive theoretical framework to support its convictions. Theoretical perspectives on emotion often have been limited in scope or have not been clearly articulated by early childhood educators. This problem has left the field defensive about its values and vulnerable to a recurring charge of fuzzy-minded adherence to social-emotional goals. In addition to the absence of a comprehensive, explicit theory of emotion in relation to early childhood education, practitioners have been unable to call upon sound empirical research to support their convictions about the importance of emotions in children's development.

It is ironic that the early childhood education field is being drawn further from its emotion-focused roots just when psychological theory and research have the most to offer the practitioner. The next three chapters will summarize the exciting new developments in the study of children's emotions and will show how they support early childhood educators' most valued goals.

Chapter 2

Anger, Interest, Fear, and Joy . . . What are Emotions For?

The four-year-olds in Ilene's Head Start class are winding up a long indoor free-play period. Soft music plays on the record player. Alone in the block area, Phillip lies on the floor, his body relaxed, slowly pushing a wooden crane back and forth on the rug. From time to time he stops, rolls onto his back, and gazes idly at the ceiling. Then he returns to manipulating the crane. Phillip's tongue sticks out to one side as he untangles the string that hooks objects to the crane. Will approaches from across the room. As he gets closer to Phillip, he peeks shyly at what Phillip is doing from under his lowered brows and then quickly looks away. Will picks up a bulldozer from the shelf and seats himself on the rug a few feet from Phillip. He begins to push his bulldozer back and forth, mirroring Phillip's actions but not looking at him.

Across the room four children sit on chairs, dangling fishing poles into a container of cut-out cardboard fish. Shrieks of delight are heard as they catch fish with the magnets on the end of their fishing poles. The children bounce up and down on their chairs in excitement and clap at their own success. As each fish is caught, the children quickly pull it off the magnet hook and toss it back in the "pond" for another try.

Hannah is exploring an indoor climbing apparatus set up in a secluded corner. With the children's help, the apparatus had been constructed to resemble a beehive (a class project about bees had been underway for a week, stimulated in part by the extraordinary yellow jacket population on the playground). Ilene, the head teacher, places a reassuring hand on Hannah's back as Hannah warily ascends the climber's ladder and emerges high atop the platform. Slowly, her fearful expression changes to a delighted smile as she surveys the room from her new vantage point. Min joins Hannah. The two girls, both wearing pipe cleaner antennae, play "bees," making the circuit of the beehive over and over, grinning at one another every time they reach the platform. Hannah buzzes loudly, grimaces, and jabs a pointed finger at a nearby adult as she rounds the corner for another trip to the hive. "Sting, sting, sting," she chants triumphantly.

The noise level in the room rises. Children's voices weave and overlap—loud, hesitant, whining, confident, amazed, outraged: "Ilene! Ilene! Look at mine!" "Look at this one!" "Wait a minute—I didn't get a turn." "You're pushing me off—stop it, Ben!" "Can I have a piece of that?" "Watch out! Here it comes!"

Tiny, intense Charlene begins to bustle from one group to another, shouting officiously, "It's clean-up time! Clean-up time!" as she glares at children who are still playing. Her message to the block builders is met with Daniel's even louder response: SHUT UP! I KNOW THAT! Charlene tosses her head, curls her lip disdainfully, and stomps away to another group.

As children finish cleaning up, they gather on the rug to look at books. Daniel scans the selections on the book display shelf. His eyes widen as he sees a book he especially likes. Pulling it off the shelf, Daniel holds his choice above his head, smiling joyously as he heads for his favorite parent helper's lap and snuggles close to her.

As these four-year-olds worked and played, there was never a moment when emotion was absent. Charlene, Daniel, Phillip, Will, Hannah, Min, and the other children in the group continually displayed a wide array of feelings. Their faces, voices, and actions conveyed pride, excitement, surprise, interest, shyness, anger, sadness, fear, and disgust.

Adults might respond in many different ways to these emotions. Some adults might actively create opportunities for children to express their feelings as openly and directly as possible. Some might favor certain emotions, or certain ways of expressing emotions. Still other adults might worry about emotions' disruptive effects and try to minimize emotional interference with children's work. And others might view emotions as unimportant aspects of classroom life, preferring to emphasize the development of reasoning ability and academic skills.

The fact that teachers can have such diverse reactions reminds us that there are wide differences in beliefs about how important emotions actually are and about the functions or purposes of emotions. In this chapter, we will examine some of the ways in which major theories of development and behavior have treated human emotions. I will argue that, despite their contributions, each of these approaches has had its own limitations as a guide for the emotion-centered early childhood practitioner. However, we also will see that new theoretical perspectives and research findings have emerged that emphasize emotions' adaptive, motivational, and communicative power.

EMOTIONS AND THEORIES OF CHILD DEVELOPMENT

Just as adults who work directly with young children have different perspectives on the importance, nature, and function of emotions, emotion-related differences also may be found in the major theoretical perspectives that have influenced early childhood education. The perspectives to be discussed are psychoanalytic theory (including Freudian and Eriksonian perspectives), Piagetian cognitive developmental theory, and traditional learning theory. This selection leaves out variations and recent modifications of these theories, including neo-Piagetian theories, the social constructivist perspective of Vygotsky, social learning theory, and information processing theory. A number of these approaches are relevant to specific aspects of emotions research and emotion-centered curriculum, and they will be referred to in later chapters. At present, the emphasis is on those approaches which have had the most direct influence on early childhood program development and on early childhood practitioners' belief systems.

Psychoanalytic Theory and Emotions

As pointed out in Chapter 1, psychoanalytic or psychodynamic theory has had a significant influence on early childhood programs for the past 75 years. Of all the major developmental theories, psychoanalytic theory has placed the greatest emphasis on emotions as contributors to development and has been most specific about how emotions influence children's lives.

Especially in his early work, Freud viewed emotion or affect as the root cause of all behavior (Rapaport, 1967). The "dark, inaccessible part of our personality," the id, is "a chaos, a cauldron full of seething excitations" (Freud, 1933/1964, p. 72). And the ego "is fighting on two fronts: it has to defend its existence against an external world which threatens it with annihilation as well as against an internal world that makes excessive demands" (Freud, 1940/1964, p. 200). Freud held that powerful, unexpressed and often unrecognized sexual and aggressive impulses frequently discharge themselves through indirect or symbolic pathways. According to Dodge and Garber (1991), Freud saw development as a continual "struggle between internal emotional impulses and attempts by the individual to control or regulate their expression" (p. 3), often through elaborate defense mechanisms. In one of Freud's (1909/1959) most famous case studies, he described five-year-old "Little Hans," who developed an intense fear of being bitten by horses. Freud's interpretation of Hans' behavior was that strong, guilt-ridden feelings of rivalry with his father caused Hans to symbolize his father in the person of powerful horses and contributed to the feelings that kept him from facing these creatures face-to-face.

It is easy to oversimplify and thus misrepresent Freudian theory. From a Freudian perspective, however, the behavior seen in Ilene's classroom of four-year-olds must be the product of strong, emotionally charged instinctual drives. Hannah's stinging the teacher is the most obvious example. Freudian theory would certainly emphasize the aggressive impulse behind Hannah's behavior. When Hannah pretended to be a bee stinging her teacher, she may have directed symbolic hostility toward her teacher and, indirectly, toward her parents. Similarly, Freudian theory might connect the children's fascination with the fishpond game to curiosity about all kinds of family secrets (including sexual secrets) that they could symbolically "capture" with their magnetized fishing poles.

As a follower of Freud, Erikson (1950) shared many of his views on emotion. There is no question that, like Freud, Erikson thought that affect was the basis for human activity and the primary impetus for growth. Like Freud, Erikson has emphasized that unconscious feelings may be expressed indirectly and symbolically, and his theory is in agreement about the harmful psychological consequences of denial or repression of "unacceptable" impulses.

There are differences between Freud's and Erikson's views of emotion, however. As compared with Freud, Erikson placed more emphasis on positive emotions and emotion-related tendencies. The well-known central conflicts of each psychosocial stage can be said to center around opposing emotion tendencies. Erikson (1959) describes these as "alternative basic attitudes . . . *a sense of*" trust versus mistrust, industry versus inferiority, and so on. These "senses" have three components or dimensions: "ways of conscious experience . . . ways of *behaving* . . . , and unconscious *inner states*" (p. 58). At each stage of development, the crisis through which children must inevitably pass is "beset by fears, or at least a general anxiousness or tension" (p. 78). As the child emerges from each crisis, more positive emotions appear to predominate: The healthy child now seems "more loving and relaxed and brighter in his judgment . . . in the free possession of a certain surplus of energy" (p. 78). In Erikson's theory, healthy development results from a resolution of each conflict, through which the child achieves a strong subjective sense of trust, autonomy, and other positive dispositions, in appropriate balance with the "dynamic counterpart" (p. 181) of basic mistrust, shame, and other negative senses. Most of the four-year-olds in Ilene's class would be at the stage of "initiative versus guilt" in Erikson's theory. Thus, much of their behavior could be viewed as an expression of this conflict, using the "intrusive mode" of curiosity, physical vigor, and social competition; for example, the pretend play with bees, or the fishing game, or the play with powerful construction machines.

In addition to working on emotional conflicts typical of their current psychosocial stage, some children may exhibit behavior motivated by issues from earlier periods of development. Daniel's exaggerated response to Charlene's bossiness might indicate that his sense of his own autonomy was still vulnerable to threats. Eriksonian theory might hold that Daniel is afraid he will be bossed by others, just as Charlene continually asserts her right to be a boss.

Erikson was much more specific than Freud in describing how children in every culture enact their deepest feelings through play and other symbolic activities. According to Erikson, children like Hannah not only use pretend play to "drain off" their aggressive feelings (Hannah stinging her teacher), but they also gain control over upsetting experiences through active, often repetitive, use of play materials. From an Eriksonian perspective, Hannah masters her feelings of fear by repeatedly climbing through the beehive climber, taking on the bee's role in a safe environment with adult support. But Erikson's theory is not entirely focused on negative emotions. Erikson also stressed the emotional satisfaction children obtain through challenging, mastery-oriented activities, such as the four-year-olds' fishing game.

Cognitive Theory and Emotions

Cognitive theories of development are seldom thought of as having an emotion component. To some students and practitioners, the label "cognitive" may suggest that the theory is specifically *not* relevant to emotions and may even be opposed to emotions.

Piaget's theory is, of course, the cognitive perspective that has had the most influence on early childhood education. Piagetian descriptions of development do seem focused more on the intellectual aspects of young children's activities than on their affective qualities. Watching Ilene's four-year-old group, a Piagetian might notice Phillip's use of spatial reasoning as he attempted to untangle the crane's string, or Will's accurate imitation of Phillip's actions with the wooden construction toys, or the fishing group's understanding of cause–effect relationships as they manipulated the magnetic "hooks." The Piagetian observer might pay relatively little attention to children's fear, anger, pride, glee, and other powerful feelings expressed during these "cognitive" activities.

Because of this selective focus, some writers have questioned the accuracy of Piaget's portrait of childhood. Cohen (1966) observed that the rational, problem-solving child described in Piaget's writings bears little resemblance to the vividly affective, social young children who are so familiar to parents and early childhood educators. Cohen also noted that Piaget's theory does not address an important fact: Not every child is equally eager to investigate and learn. Referring to the young children observed in Murphy's (1962) classic studies of early development, Cohen (1966) says, "Some of her children look very much like Piaget's happy explorers, [while] other children fear to experience and seem to suspect the worst in every new situation" (p. 217). Understanding these children is of crucial importance to early childhood practitioners, yet it is here that Piagetian theory seems to fall short of its potential.

However, some writers have noted that Piaget's theory may contain more feeling than it has been given credit for. Cowan's book, *Piaget With Feeling* (1978), underscores the implications of Piagetian theory for moral and social development. In an interesting analysis of Piaget's perspective on emotional development, Cicchetti and Hesse (1983) called attention to Piaget's often repeated—but often forgotten—claim that, although cognition supplies essential structures for development, affect or emotion provides the motivational energy. Piaget's writings frequently refer to the influence of emotions on children's tendency to explore their environment. Cicchetti and Hesse also pointed out that Piaget's central developmental process of "equilibration" is emotional as well as intellectual. Children's feelings of dissatisfaction with existing solutions to a problem, or their feeling of frustration when new situations cannot be dealt with by their present cognitive structures, may create a kind of emotional disequilibrium, pushing children toward higher levels of cognitive competence, and reorganizing old cognitive structures into a new equilibrium. Thus, Phillip feels frustration when he is unable to untangle the string on the construction crane. If it is not too intense, this feeling of frustration or anger may motivate Phillip to attempt a variety of solutions to the problem of the tangled string and may eventually lead to a cognitive reorganization of Phillip's understanding of spatial relationships into a more powerful cognitive scheme.

Despite these pertinent reminders about the relevance of Piaget's theory for emotional development, without question emotion has a less important role in Piaget's theory than in Freud's or Erikson's images of children's development and behavior. And even granting that Piaget does pay attention to emotions, the range and intensity of feelings is narrow. While psychoanalytic theory can be criticized for overemphasizing intense negative emotions and powerful sexual or aggressive drives, Piagetian theory does the opposite, emphasizing positive emotions and less intense emotion expressions. Even in Cicchetti and Hesse's (1983) thorough examination of Piaget's work, the full range of emotions is not really encompassed by Piagetian theory.

Learning Theories and Emotions

Learning theory has had only limited influence on "mainstream" early childhood programs, but it has had a significant impact on specific early intervention and early childhood special education programs. Many early childhood educators have been troubled by what they see as traditional learning theory's neglect of social and emotional development in favor of isolated skills and academic competencies.

Despite these concerns, it cannot be said that learning theories have ignored emotions entirely. Watson (1919), the "father of behaviorism," held that infants were endowed with innate emotions, including fear, rage, and love. Watson argued that these powerful feelings formed the basis for later personality development (shaped, of course, by environmental conditioning).

However, later versions of learning theory placed less emphasis on innate emotions. Typically, the theory has emphasized the outward manifestations of emotions, rather than unconscious or unobservable feelings. Unlike a psychoanalytic observer, a learning theorist watching Ilene's four-year-olds would be unconcerned with subconscious, inner feelings. Daniel's display of anger ("I KNOW THAT!") and Hannah's hesitation about climbing the "beehive" would be examined as behaviors in their own right, not as outward signs of underlying emotions. The learning theorist would be keenly attuned to possible environmental factors that support these behaviors: To what extent do Daniel's outbursts and Hannah's inhibitions gain attention from children and teachers? What models are children using to construct patterns of emotion-related behavior? Does Daniel have an aggressive older brother? Can Hannah's inhibition be lessened if she observes her bolder friend, Mary?

Early childhood programs that follow principles of traditional learning theory usually have not given priority to emotional development as a broad curriculum goal. However, these programs may strongly emphasize emotional control in the service of academic goals and may use rewards, time-out, and other behavioral techniques to shape desired patterns of emotion expression. In addition, the developers of didactic, behaviorally focused early childhood curriculum models have pointed to the emotional benefits of these programs. Bereiter and Englemann (1966) argue that contrary to detractors' assertions, children in these programs gain positive feelings and self-confidence from mastery of specific academic skills.

Limitations of Theories

With all of these well-known theories having something to say about emotions, why go beyond their bounds? Although the major theories differ in many respects, all are unsatisfactory as guides for the practitioner interested in young children's emotional development. Each of these theories has a narrow, incomplete view of the functions of emotions. Some regard children's emotions as disruptive or symptomatic, while others view emotions as servants of other, more developmentally important competencies. Furthermore, despite their aware-ness of emotional issues, these theories have produced little research to help the early childhood professional answer the guiding question of this chapter: What are emotions for?

This lack of a strong research base has historical roots. Psychoana-lytic theory, which has a clear emotional emphasis, has produced little empirical research, relying more on case studies and observational de-scription. Although many early childhood programs were psychoana-lytically oriented, the theory had only a limited influence on the wider field of child development, even in the earlier years of this century. And by the 1960s and 1970s, a cognitive revolution had taken place in child psychology. Child development researchers focused on the development of children's problem-solving and reasoning abilities and explored the effects of early experience on intellectual functioning. In the process, emotions were eclipsed by cognition. The 1970 edition of the compre-hensive two-volume *Handbook of Child Development* (Mussen, 1970) did not even contain a chapter on emotion, and the index contained only 23 references to the subject (Campos, Barrett, Lamb, Goldsmith, & Stenberg, 1983). If a typical 1960s-era developmental researcher had observed the children in Ilene's four-year-old class, he or she would have been primarily interested in children's *thinking* as it was revealed in their play. If emotions had been studied at all, it would have been because of what they revealed about children's reasoning.

NEW PERSPECTIVES ON EMOTIONS

By the late 1970s things had begun to change. Cognitive develop-mental research had illuminated many aspects of children's develop-ment. However, as developmental psychologists reviewed what they had learned from the "cognitive revolution," many of them began to recog-nize that young children's development could not be explained simply by reference to stages of logical thinking. A 1983 review of work in socioemotional development noted that "the neglect of emotion has be-gun to be replaced in recent years with a dramatic reevaluation of the importance of emotion, its consequences, and its development from in-fancy to old age" (Campos, Barrett, Lamb, Goldsmith, & Stenberg, 1983, p. 787). This trend has increased exponentially from 1983 to the present. In contrast to the cognitive domination of earlier decades, leading child development journals and professional conferences of the 1980s and early 1990s have prominently featured discussions of every aspect of emotion in early childhood.

These new theorists and researchers are certainly not in complete agreement about the precise function of emotions in children's development. However, they share three key ideas: Emotions help humans to survive and adapt to their environment; emotions serve to guide or motivate human behavior; and emotions support communication with others.

Helping Human Beings Survive and Adapt

In recent years, child development theorists and researchers have found that an evolutionary perspective is helpful in understanding many aspects of children's development and behavior. For example, Bowlby (1969) argued that children's attachment behavior evolved because it had survival value. Very young children cry, move closer to their adult caregiver, and cling tightly when threatened; these behaviors bring the young of the human species closer to their grown-up protectors, thus ensuring the species' welfare and long-term survival. Similarly, the play patterns of young children have been interpreted as part of our species' evolutionary history—a history that resulted in a long period of childhood and in behavior that invites experimentation and flexibility, characteristics that have strong adaptive or survival value for our species.

Like these universal patterns of human behavior, emotions are thought to have evolved and persisted because of their value in helping the human species adapt to its environment. In 1872, Darwin wrote *The Expression of the Emotions in Man and Animals,* in which he described the survival value of emotions such as fear and anger. This evolutionary perspective seems quite different from the position that emotions, especially "negative" emotions, are disturbing events that should be controlled or dismissed.

Today, many scholars share this evolutionary perspective on emotions (Campos et al., 1983; Izard, 1991; Plutchik, 1991). Emotions are a universal characteristic of the human species. Like Will, Hannah, Daniel, and the others in Ilene's class, children and adults in every culture and at every period of history have experienced and expressed emotions such as interest, joy, anger, fear, surprise, and sadness. Daniel's broad smile is a universal signal of joy, and Hannah's drawn back lips, furrowed brow, and widened eyes would signal fear in any setting, as they did to her teacher Ilene. People in widely different cultures and of every age experience the same basic emotions and display those feelings with similar facial expressions and bodily responses. When shown photographs of people posing various facial expressions, adults from 14 countries, including several isolated, preliterate cultures, labeled the emotions in the same way (Ekman, Friesen, & Ellsworth, 1972; Izard, 1991). Of course, each culture and historical period has its own unwritten rules governing when and how emotions are displayed. Daniel's loud response to Charlene's demands and Hannah's playful defiance of the teacher would not be tolerated in some times and places. Despite these variations, evidence strongly supports the idea that the fundamental human emotions are innate and neurologically based.

Guiding Human Behavior

As we have seen, emotions have often been regarded either as irrelevant to development or as disruptive influences. Anger kept people from thinking straight; fear prevented effective action; and even excitement could interfere with smooth classroom functioning. All of these outcomes are possible, of course, but a radical change in perspective has occurred. Most contemporary emotion researchers believe that the "emotion system" seems to guide or organize human thought and action (Bower, 1981; Campos, Barrett, Lamb, Goldsmith, & Stenberg, 1983; Emde, 1980; Izard, 1977, 1991). From this perspective, everything that is going on in Ilene's class is in some way directed by the children's—and adults'—emotions.

Many scholars assert that different emotions have distinctive motivational features. In the preceding section of this chapter, we saw that a basic set of emotions is recognized in widely different cultures around the world.

Izard (1977, 1991) holds that this set of distinct or "discrete" emotions includes feelings of interest, joy, sadness, fear, anger, and shame, and that each of these emotions has evolved to motivate certain types of behavior that are important for species and individual development. When Will saw Phillip playing with the crane on the rug, many different responses were possible. He might have ignored him, hugged him, or grabbed the toy. According to Izard and others, the particular pattern of response that Will *did* engage in was organized or structured by the particular *emotions* Will was experiencing. Feelings of *interest* drew him closer to Phillip, focused his attention, and motivated Will to copy Phillip's actions with the crane. Simultaneously, Will's inner feeling of *shyness* motivated a pattern of inhibited behavior that kept him from interacting directly with Phillip.

Anger, too, has organizational functions. Triggered by Charlene's bossiness, Daniel's angry feelings result in a patterned constellation of anger-related responses: His face takes on a fierce scowl, his voice is loud and harsh, his fists clench, his heart beats faster, and we may imagine that he is thinking dire thoughts about Charlene.

Seeing this display, we may not approve of Daniel's behavior. Nevertheless, we cannot help but recognize that there is adaptive value in being able to marshal one's resources to resist harm or to protest against oppression. Infants who are physically restrained will typically react with facial and vocal signs of anger. Even at four months, their anger seems to organize an active resistance—they arch their backs and pull away from the researcher's gently restraining hands (Stenberg & Campos, 1990). Similarly, most toddlers who are briefly separated from their mothers in a playroom will look and sound angry. This "negative" emotional response seems to lead to a series of patterned actions (shaking the barrier, pulling at the latch, swinging a leg up over the gate) that could reduce the distance between child and mother (Hyson, 1985). Thus, anger mobilizes an organized response, although Daniel's mode of expression may require some fine-tuning.

Research has uncovered many other examples of emotions' effects on the organization or patterning of behavior. Children's memory and learning can be enhanced when researchers create conditions that heighten their interest and happiness (Bartlett, Burleson, & Santrock, 1982; Renninger & Wozniak, 1985). Children are more likely to explore their environment if they are feeling positive emotions like interest and joy. When adults and children share these positive emotional states, the good feelings serve to organize and energize periods of "joint attention" to a book, a toy, or an interesting sight (Trevarthen, 1984). When Daniel takes his book to his favorite parent volunteer's lap, their shared feelings of interest and joy help them focus on the story and endow the entire episode with a positive glow that ultimately contributes to Daniel's cognitive as well as his emotional development.

Like the joyful, interested children at Ilene's "fish pond," when children are in a positive emotional state, they tolerate frustration better, are better able to wait to receive a reward, and are more inclined to be generous to others (Chapman, Zahn-Waxler, Cooperman, & Iannotti, 1987; Denham, 1986).

Supporting Communication

Finally, contemporary emotion researchers believe that emotions play a crucial part in signalling and communicating with others (Malatesta, Culver, Tesman, & Shepard, 1989). Because the basic emotion expressions appear to be universal, we quickly understand the meaning of a smile, a frown, a shyly lowered head, a clenched fist, or a delighted clap of the hands. A visitor to Ilene's classroom—even one from another culture—would find it easy to comprehend the children's reactions to one another and to their activities.

This "communicative function" of emotions is especially important in infancy. Without a well-understood repertoire of facial expressions and body movements, a baby would have few resources with which to convey her distress, excitement, or satisfaction. Because most caregivers pay attention to these vivid emotional signals, the infant's well-being is protected.

Even as children get older, their caregivers are guided by children's emotional reactions. Hannah never said, "I am scared to climb up there," but Ilene quickly noticed her fearful face and frozen posture and moved to reassure and support her. Similarly, adults' feelings are conveyed to young children through their expressions, gestures, and tone of voice; these signals, in turn, influence children's emotions and their behavior. Ilene's calm, friendly demeanor conveys confidence to Hannah, who scans her teacher's face to assess her response to the beehive play.

And children's communication with one another is saturated with emotional significance. The children in the fishing group bounce up and down with glee, not just to "drain off" their own excitement but to share their feelings with one another. Charlene deliberately signals her contempt for Daniel through her curled lip, her scornful expression, and her dismissive gesture. Even the quiet book-reading period is filled with emotion communication as children gaze at each other's selections, smile in recognition of favorite pictures, and move close to their friends with gestures of friendship and warmth.

CONCLUSION

These examples from research and classroom experience provide convincing evidence that emotions have important functions in human life. We have seen that each of the major theories of development and behavior has addressed this issue but that neither psychoanalytic, cognitive, nor learning theories have told a comprehensive story about emotions' significance in children's lives.

This story has gained in scope and power through the new emotion-related research of the 1980s and 1990s. Starting with an evolutionary perspective, these scholars remind us that emotions are universal. They offer convincing examples that both "positive" and "negative" emotions have helped human beings to survive, adapt, and learn.

They remind us that the language of feeling binds us together, transcending boundaries of culture and age.

Despite these common links, the expression of emotions does undergo changes as children grow. Chapter 3 will outline some of these changes over the first 8 years of life.

Chapter 3

Young Children's Emotional Development: What Can We Expect?

At ten o'clock on a cold February morning, Leslie, a family child care provider, has settled her children in her sunny living room. Most of the children are gathered around a table on which Leslie has set out a container of play dough with rollers and cutters. Several other children are examining colored paper and scissors, while eight-week-old Andy, the youngest member of the group, looks on from his infant swing. His eyes follow the older children's movements and his expression brightens as children stop to look him in the eye and show him their toys. "He's our baby," six-year-old Mary Anne tells the visitor with a proprietary air, reveling in her "special helper" status on a day off from school.

Three-and-a-half-year-old Zachary, three-year-old Denise, and two-year-old Caitlin work with the dough. Zachary sorts through the dough cutters looking for his favorite. "Another truck!" he exclaims, crinkling his nose in delight and waving the cutter above his head. He bends over his dough, placing his two truck cutters side by side and carefully pressing them into the play dough. Beside him, Caitlin plunges her fingers into her piece of dough, smiling with pleasure.

Abigail, who is 18 months old, approaches the play dough table. Abigail reaches across Zachary for a chunk of his dough. He sees her coming and protects his dough with his whole body. Abigail leans her sturdy shoulder against Zachary's and reaches under his arm. "Hey!" Zachary announces in a commanding tone. "No roughhousin' in here!"

Abigail whines and then squeals, looking appealingly at Leslie. She stomps her feet in a rhythmic dance of frustration as Zachary continues to protect his dough with righteous indignation. "Have something *else*," he declares, pressing his lips together. "I need my play dough." Abigail falls to the floor, sobbing and hiccuping. She stares straight ahead, lost in misery. Across the room, Mary Anne sizes up the situation and digs Abigail's blanket out of a basket. She approaches Abigail, handing her the blanket with a look of concern. Abigail stuffs her thumb in her mouth and caresses the blanket's satin binding.

During their play time in Leslie's living room, Andy, Caitlin, Zachary, Denise, Abigail, and Mary Anne displayed the full range of basic human emotions described in Chapter 2, including interest, joy, sadness, and anger. Every child smiled and laughed; every child expressed at least some anger or frustration during the morning; every child's interest was engaged by the people, materials, and activities in Leslie's program.

Despite these common characteristics, a visitor to Leslie's family child care home would be struck by age-related variations in the children's emotional responses. Like most groups of children in family child care, Leslie's group encompasses a wide age range, from eight-week-old Andy to six-year-old Mary Anne. Abigail and Zachary were both angry during their struggle over ownership of the play dough. However, eighteen-month-old Abigail expressed her anger by pushing, whining, and finally dissolving in a tantrum; her older playmate, Zachary, scowled, protected his possessions, and verbally reprimanded Abigail for her aggression. Andy's interest in his surroundings was expressed by intent gazing, smiling, and wriggling; Caitlin's interest in the play dough was seen in her explorations with her fingers, hands, and body; Zachary asked pointed questions about the dough cutters and excitedly compared one with another. All the children seemed attuned to one another's feelings. Even baby Andy stared soberly when Abigail dropped to the floor in frustration, but it was six-year-old Mary Anne who offered Abigail her blanket in consolation.

These examples illustrate some of the changes that occur in emotion expression and emotional regulation during early childhood. However, the process of emotional development is slow, uneven, and often frustrating to adult caregivers. To support children's growth, Leslie and other early childhood professionals need a sympathetic understanding of early emotional development. They need to know what emotional resources children typically possess at various points in their development and what emotional concerns may be especially important to children of different ages.

Early childhood educators lack consensus about these matters. In surveying hundreds of early childhood teachers, we (Hyson & Lee, 1992) have found great variations in teachers' ideas about the age at which children ought to be able to control certain emotion expressions or the age at which children ought to be exposed to various emotion-eliciting events. Some of these differences are the product of teachers' culture, personal values, belief systems (Sigel, McGillicuddy-Delisi, & Goodnow, 1992), and work settings. Many of these differences should be acknowledged and respected. However, some ideas about early emotional development are simply inaccurate and inconsistent with current knowledge. This chapter will attempt to fill in some of these gaps with research-based information about typical sequences in children's expression and understanding of emotions.

In this chapter we will take a closer look at typical trends and patterns in emotional development during the first 8 years of life. We will begin by describing age-related changes in five specific areas.

1. The way that children express their feelings through facial expressions, gestures and other body movements, sounds and words, and play and other symbolic activities;
2. Children's emotional control;
3. Children's understanding of emotions;
4. Children's reactions to others' feelings and to situations that arouse emotions;
5. Changes in children's emotional ties to adults and to other children.

In each of these areas, researchers have collected convincing data to document the timing and sequence of developmental changes.

In addition, some writers have also attempted to describe more general stages of emotional development, outlining key emotional issues and emotional "skills" that seem to dominate at different periods. In the last part of this chapter we will outline a few examples of these stage models of emotional development, emphasizing their strengths and their limitations.

Findings from the many recent studies of emotional development can help early childhood teachers to construct a more accurate base of professional knowledge. By integrating research with their own insights from practice, early childhood educators may expand their ability to understand typical emotion-related behavior and to create appropriate, supportive, and challenging expectations for children's emotional development.

CHANGES IN SPECIFIC ASPECTS OF EMOTIONAL DEVELOPMENT

Expression of Feelings

In Chapter 2 we saw that all human beings possess a basic set of emotions that help them survive and adapt to their environment. The fundamentals of this emotion system are present from birth. However, as children get older they have access to an increasingly wide repertoire of emotional resources. Those resources include children's facial expressions, their gestures and body language, their "vocabulary" of emotion-related sounds and words, and their use of play and creative materials to express emotions.

Facial Expressions. Smiles, frowns, and other facial expressions of emotion are present from early infancy, but their nature, frequency, and complexity change markedly over the first months and years of life.

One researcher was lucky enough to videotape her own newborn baby (Camras, 1988; cited in Malatesta et al., 1989). Over the first few weeks of life, Camras' infant daughter displayed facial expressions of happiness, sadness, distress, anger, and surprise. Many of these expressions appeared to be random movements, but others were clearly related to events in the baby's surroundings.

After the newborn period, babies add more facial expressions of emotion to their repertoire, and they display these expressions more consistently. Although newborns often smile in their sleep, babies' first "real" social smiles are usually seen around 3 weeks of age, in response to a high-pitched voice. A few weeks later, the human face (especially one that is close up and nodding) brings forth the same joyful expression. The children in Leslie's family child care home have learned that they can bring out Andy's brightest smiles when they approach him, lean over, and tip their heads back and forth. Both Andy and the older children love these encounters.

By 4 months of age, the infants in a longitudinal laboratory study were regularly expressing anger and surprise. Clearly identifiable expressions of fear and shyness were evident by the time infants were a year old (Izard & Malatesta, 1987; Malatesta, 1988). Other researchers have found evidence of these emotions at even earlier ages, especially if they asked parents about their perceptions (Klinnert, Sorce, Emde, Stenberg, & Gaensbauer, 1984) rather than trying to find examples of these expressions in a laboratory observation. This is more than parents' wishful thinking; parents and early childhood caregivers see children in a much wider array of situations and over much more extended periods of time than researchers typically do.

Some emotion expressions appear at an early age but are displayed more frequently as children get older. Anger is a good example. Although anger appears in early infancy, mothers have reported that anger expressions increase sharply between 9 and 14 months (Klinnert, Sorce, Emde, Stenberg, & Gaensbauer, 1984). Eighteen-month-old Abigail was far more placid 6 months ago; her full-blown anger displays are a fairly recent development.

Other facial expressions—those conveying pride, shame, shyness, embarrassment, contempt, and guilt—are simply not seen in very young infants. Some signs of these emotions appear after about 6 months, but they do not appear with any frequency until the toddler and preschool years. These later-appearing emotion expressions seem to require a certain level of cognitive ability and awareness of cultural values or standards. "I made *cookies!*" three-year-old Denise announced, her face beaming with pride as she displayed her play dough pieces. Abigail showed little evidence that she knew it was "wrong" to take Zachary's play dough, but her slightly older companion Caitlin hid under the table after doing the same thing.

Besides adding some new facial expressions of emotion, the older children in Leslie's family child care home also display more complex or "blended" facial expressions, which combine elements of several feelings at once. As he worked on his play dough creation while fending off Abigail, three-and-a-half-year-old Zachary's face reflected a complicated mix of emotions: interest in his work, subdued anger, and perhaps some guilt as he denied the younger Abigail access to the dough. When six-year-old Mary Anne produced Abigail's blanket, her expression conveyed empathic sadness, pride at her own competence, and even a bit of condescension at Abigail's "babyish" behavior. This increased complexity is possible not just because older children have better control over their facial muscles, but because they are able to experience more than one emotion at a time—for example, being happy at successfully acquiring someone else's play dough but also fearful of the other child's response and guilty about violating a social norm.

Gestures and Body Language. We have spent a good deal of time describing changes in how children use their faces to convey emotion, because most developmental research has focused on the face as a channel for expressing emotions. However, at every age, children use their whole bodies in expressing feelings. Good caregivers like Leslie are skilled "readers" of children's body language as it develops from infancy into the school-age years.

Even as infants, children convey their feelings in many ways. In fact, they seem more likely than older children to use their entire bodies to express emotion. Although Andy cannot yet move independently, his body is already an effective emotional instrument. Infants like Andy wriggle their bodies in happiness. When babies are distressed, they use their arms, legs, trunk, and fingers in varied ways, including turning away, kicking, and bringing their hands to their mouth (Fogel & Reimers, 1989). Babies of Andy's age express their sadness in a passive, slumped posture; anger may be accompanied by pushing away, kicking, or thrashing. Mothers recognize their infants' fear more through bodily tension and "freezing" than through any specific facial expression (Klinnert et al., 1984).

Thus, even infants have a wide repertoire of emotion-related bodily movements. As children get older, they use their increased large and fine muscle control to express their feelings in a more organized, deliberate fashion. For example, the emotion of joy can be accompanied by many gestures. Some of these are spontaneous, while others are deliberate and socially constructed. Leslie's juice-and-crackers snack was greeted with delight by all the children, but their joyful body movements and gestures differed in age-related ways. Seeing his bottle, Andy smiled, cooed, and wiggled his body. Caitlin smiled, too, but she also clapped her hands vigorously and bounced up and down in her chair—deliberate acts that used her greater physical control to communicate her happiness. And Mary Anne, the six-year-old, has mastered more subtle, culturally conventional expressions of emotion, using a "cool" thumbs-up sign when she spotted her favorite crackers on the tray.

The Use of Sounds and Words. Besides refining their facial and bodily display of feelings, children become increasingly able to express emotion in sounds and words—through what Malatesta (1981) called the *vocal affect lexicon:* a kind of nonverbal "dictionary" of emotion language.

Psychologists have found that certain voice qualities, including pitch, loudness, and tempo, clearly convey specific emotional messages, such as happiness, anger, sadness, and fear—even when the actual words have been filtered out of the recordings (Scherer, 1979). Thus, caregivers figure out infants' feelings from their voices, even before babies can speak and before they "intend" to communicate. Andy's pleased squeals and coos are unmistakable signs of happiness, and his fussy whimpers cause Denise to tug at Leslie's hand, saying "Andy needs you." Mothers in Klinnert and colleagues' (1984) study told researchers that they knew their children feared certain situations because of the characteristic sound of their cries. In another study, parents listened to tape recordings of eight- to twelve-month-old infants. Even when the babies were not their own, and even when the babies were from a different language background, adults were easily able to identify sounds that had been made in response to various situations; for example, a requesting sound, a sound of greeting, or a frustrated sound (Ricks, 1979; cited in Malatesta, 1981).

As children get older, sound or vocal quality continues to be an important tool for conveying feeling. Once children begin to use words, however, they have an even more powerful instrument to use in communicating their emotional state. Denise does not just scream, but yells "*My* seat!" as Zachary attempts to hold on to his chair at the play dough table. When Zachary passes out the snack, his happiness and generous mood are conveyed by both his tone of voice and his words ("Oh, boy! Three crackers for you!").

In recent years, many psychologists have studied the development of children's ability to talk about their own and others' feelings (Bloom & Beckwith, 1989; Bretherton, Fritz, Zahn-Waxler, & Ridgeway, 1986; Dunn, Bretherton, & Munn, 1987). As in other developmental domains, children begin with simple labels and move on to complex descriptions. Children often try to get their own needs met by talking about emotions ("I sad. Mommy kiss"). Two-year-olds already express cause–effect relations in describing emotion states (e.g., "I give a hug. Baby be happy" [Bretherton et al., 1986, p. 534]). Older children, like the six-year-old quoted by Bretherton, use language to express much more subtle and complex feelings: "Sometimes when I hit you and then I want to comfort you, you push me away because you're still angry." (p. 541).

Other Symbolic Activities. After they are about a year old, children begin to represent their feelings through pretend play and through the use of symbolic and manipulative materials. At first, these representations are simple, but after age 2, children begin to express a wide range of emotions during pretend play (Fischer, Shaver, & Carnochan, 1990). One-year-old Caitlin hugs and pats her doll lovingly, but six-year-old Mary Anne acts out a complex doll-play drama filled with sadness, jealousy, and an unexpected happy ending.

As children move through the toddler and preschool years, their ability to use play materials in the service of emotion communication expands. Because of its emotional power, both early childhood professionals and therapists have regarded play as a primary way for children to express and master troubling feelings (Erikson, 1977). Erikson also described the profound feeling of satisfaction that comes when children have the opportunity to experience play fully. Dramatic and symbolic play seems to help children to integrate all of their other emotional resources, including facial expressions, gestures, and verbal expression, and to use these to communicate their deepest feelings and to support other aspects of their development.

Emotional Control

The ability to control expressions of emotion is as important as the ability to use a variety of channels to express feelings. Children's self-regulation of their emotions develops gradually and unevenly. This is the area where many parents and caregivers are most likely to have inappropriate expectations. On one hand, some early childhood educators appear to believe that young children *always* need to "let their feelings out." On the other hand, some adults have the opposite view, expecting children to exercise total control of emotion expressions and of their underlying feelings. Certainly, some degree of self-control or management of the expression of feelings is important if children are to develop positive relationships with others and a good sense of their own competence. Children need to learn not to cry at minor disappointments, not to laugh when a classmate loses a contest, not to criticize a carefully chosen birthday gift. Thus, emotion regulation is a complex balancing act between the extremes of unbridled expressiveness and rigid repression of feelings.

A number of studies have recently focused on the development of emotion self-regulation (Eisenberg & Fabes, 1992; Garber & Dodge, 1991). As compared with older children and adults, infants show little sign that they are attempting to control or regulate their emotions (Malatesta et al., 1989). They express their inner states immediately, directly, and with their entire repertoire of facial, vocal, and bodily signals. These characteristics seem to be related to the way the young infant's brain and nervous system are organized; neural mechanisms have not yet matured sufficiently to inhibit or prevent certain kinds of behavioral expressions (Izard & Kobak, 1991). Eight-week-old Andy does not *decide* to cry when Denise pulls his bottle out of his mouth, and he does not attempt to hide his distress out of concern for what his friends may think.

Although they may not deliberately restrain their expressions of emotion, even very young infants have some surprisingly effective self-comforting resources. When Andy fusses and Leslie cannot come immediately, Andy brings his fist to his mouth, sucks vigorously, and gazes around the room. This spontaneous self-comforting may be the first sign of children's emotion regulation (Demos, 1986; Malatesta et al., 1989). By about 8 months or so, many children use their preferred "comfort strategies" in a more deliberate, intentional way (Fogel & Thelen, 1987).

One-year-olds are just beginning to exercise conscious, voluntary control over their own feelings. Kuczynski, Zahn-Waxler, and Radke-Yarrow (1987) found that children about 12 or 13 months old could pretend to be happy, angry, or sad. Demos (1986) closely observed two girls during their first 2 years of life. She found that, by the time they were a year old, they could intensify or reduce the intensity of their expressions of emotion in an apparently deliberate way. Abigail, at 18 months, seemed to exaggerate her unhappiness as she looked across the room toward Leslie, signaling her distress through outraged expressions and loud crying.

As children get older, they begin to be able to regulate or control a number of other aspects of their emotional lives. They become better able to inhibit certain emotion expressions—sometimes because they have learned that these outbursts will be disapproved of, or sometimes because they have seen other people refraining from showing their own feelings. Zachary's compressed lips seemed to be masking his anger when Abigail tried to take his play dough. However, *deliberate* masking of feelings (that is, pretending to be happy about a disliked gift) is extremely difficult for most children until after the age of 3, and even school-age children have a hard time pretending that they have positive feelings when they are actually experiencing negative ones (Saarni, 1979).

Finally, children gradually learn to conform to a set of cultural "display rules" for the expression of emotions. As Ekman (1972) found when comparing Japanese and American emotion expressions, every culture has certain unwritten guidelines concerning when and how feelings may be displayed, especially in public settings. Infants and toddlers are essentially unaware of these rules. Preschoolers and, especially, school-age children learn about these expectations through observation and through direct instruction. Most children increase their conformity with these cultural expectations over time. Leslie's children respond in varied ways when they do not like the food she has prepared. One-year-old Abigail is apt to spit out a disliked food with a frankly disgusted expression; two-year-old Caitlin may exclaim "Yuck!" Zachary, who is almost four, is more likely to push the disliked food aside without comment (or, occasionally, to hide it in his milk glass), while six-year-old Mary Anne, may claim that she really likes the lunch but "is just not hungry today."

Emotional Understanding

A great deal of research in the 1960s and 1970s was devoted to tracing the development of children's understanding of a wide variety of concepts, including time, space, number, and volume. However, only recently have researchers applied this knowledge to children's understanding of emotions (Harter & Whitesell, 1989; Kopp, 1989; Saarni & Harris, 1989). Because emotions are so deeply significant for young children, some have argued that children may actually understand emotions before they grasp other concepts. In any case, there are cer-

tainly many parallels between the development of emotional understanding and the development of children's understanding of other
kinds of events.

It is difficult to know exactly when children begin to understand
emotions. Some of the best research on infants' emotion recognition
abilities was done over 60 years ago by Buhler (1930/1974). As with
other aspects of development (for example, children's understanding of
number) recent research suggests that children's emotional understanding may begin at earlier ages than was formerly thought. This
does not mean that children's emotion recognition and emotion understanding abilities have improved over the past decades. Rather, new
research methods have made it possible to identify these abilities even
in very young infants, through careful analysis of videotapes, the use
of electronic monitoring of heart rate, and other innovations.

Some studies show that infants after 6 weeks of age can distinguish
between one facial expression and another (for example, baby Andy
notices the contrast between Abigail's smiles and her angry expression), but there is little evidence that the infant consciously "knows"
the difference between these two states. Other studies clearly show that
many two- and three-year-olds can associate pictures of various basic
facial expressions with simple emotion labels when they are asked. It
seems easier for toddlers to identify happiness than any other emotion,
and negative feelings such as anger and sadness are often confused.
However, as Bullock and Russell (1986) point out, even young children's mistakes in identifying emotions have a certain logic. And as
children get older, their selection of pictures to match emotion labels
more closely resembles adults' categorizations.

Children also become better able to identify *why* people feel the
way they do—angry, fearful, sad, happy, or surprised. Stein and Jewett
(1986) have asked young children to imagine how they would feel and
act in various hypothetical situations (e.g., "One day, you're sick in bed
with the flu and you can't get up and do things with your friends").
Using these and other methods, Stein and Jewett (1986) have found
that even three-year-olds have definite ideas about the causes of fear
(for example, anticipating that something bad will happen) and can
distinguish the causes of fear from the causes of anger and sadness.

Some studies show that preschoolers have great difficulty understanding that people can feel several emotions simultaneously ("I'm
angry with you, but I also love you") (Harter & Buddin, 1987). Harter's
research suggests that most children are 9 or 10 years old before they
have a firm understanding that people can feel two emotions simultaneously. However, others (including Stein and Jewett, 1986) believe

that these abilities develop earlier and can be detected with more age-appropriate research methods. This disagreement again underscores the advantage that caregivers have in understanding and tracking children's development, since their opportunities to observe and interact with children are far more extensive than those of researchers.

Responses to Others' Emotions

Certainly infants are aware of others' emotions. Babies who are only a few months old have clear emotional responses to changes in adults' expressions. When Leslie smiles warmly at Andy, he brightens up, looks at her, smiles, and wriggles playfully. But when an adult puts on a sad expression and speaks in a monotonous, depressed voice, infants typically look away, protest, and even begin to cry (Tronick, Ricks, & Cohn, 1982).

Older infants, toddlers, and preschoolers deliberately seek out information about others' emotional reactions, especially in new, ambiguous, or possibly threatening situations. When two-year-old Caitlin moved toward Zachary's temptingly ample pile of play dough, she glanced over at Leslie as if to check out her reactions to Caitlin's intended grab. This process of "social referencing" (Klinnert, Campos, Sorce, Emde, & Svedja, 1983) begins when babies are about 8 or 9 months and continues throughout the preschool years.

As toddlers, children appear fascinated by the emotions of other family members. Home observations and parents' reports offer many examples of how toddlers deliberately try to get their parents and siblings to show strong emotions—including expressions of anger (Dunn, Bretherton, & Munn, 1987). At one point during the morning, Caitlin deliberately pulled off a small piece of Abigail's play dough, even though she had a large amount of her own. As she did so, she looked intently at Abigail's expression. It almost seemed as if Caitlin wanted to instigate an intensely angry reaction (which she did, very effectively). This desire to get a rise out of others can irritate caregivers. Yet it gives toddlers the emotional raw materials to build a solid understanding of their own and others' feelings.

The gradual development of empathy (vicarious emotion, or feeling what another person feels) is especially interesting to follow (Hoffman, 1982). Eight-week-old Andy's happy mood changed to a serious one when Abigail began to wail. In hospital nurseries, staff notice that newborns begin to cry when other newborns are crying. Although few people would claim that this "emotion contagion" shows real empathy among newborns, these primitive responses to another's distress do set the stage for later development. These "pre-empathic" behaviors usually appear first during close interactions between infants and their caregivers. Before they are 4 months old, infants will match their caregivers' sad expressions (Izard & Malatesta, 1987). As time goes on, this emotional response to others' distress seems to motivate children to comfort and help their caregivers and peers (Radke-Yarrow & Zahn-Waxler, 1984), as Mary Anne did when she offered Abigail her security blanket.

As children get older, their basic emotions remain the same, but different situations may stimulate their emotional responses. Klinnert and colleagues (1984) asked parents what seemed to cause their children's displays of emotion. Generally, parents reported that the causes of emotional reactions became more complex and subtle as children got older. For example, parents of six-month-olds reported that a typical cause of their children's fear was loud noises; by their first birthday children were also frightened by strange people or changes in the appearance of familiar people.

Other studies of children's fears show the same developmental trend (Hyson, 1979). Fear begins in infancy with unfamiliar versions of concrete objects or persons (mother's new haircut; a doll with a missing nose). The later preschool years produce imaginary, symbolic fears—monsters, ghosts, bad dreams. In the school-age years children display more "realistic" fears of injury, illness, or natural disasters like tornadoes and fires.

Likewise, a situation that causes a negative emotional reaction at one age may be responded to with indifference or even pleasure at another age. Reactions to routine checkups are a good example. Six-month-old infants in a doctor's office showed very little negative emotion except during the actual physical examination; toddlers (around 18 months) showed considerable anger and distress; and preschoolers (ages 3 to 5) were the only group to show anticipatory fear, both in their facial expressions and in their language and behavior (Hyson, 1983). Early childhood professionals like Leslie cope with these age-related changes all the time: A bug crawling across the back porch may stimulate fascination from Andy, fear from Abigail, disgust from Zachary, and scientific interest from Mary Anne.

Emotional Ties to Others

The ability to form emotionally positive relationships with others is a key developmental task. Even young infants appear to have built-in tendencies to become attached to their caregivers, to seek them out for comfort, and to express affection to them in a variety of ways. The development of close attachments to parents and other caregivers provides children with a secure emotional base from which they can move outward, exploring their environment and extending their social relationships to others.

Bowlby (1969), Ainsworth, Blehar, Waters, and Wall (1978), and Bretherton and Waters (1985) have described age-related changes in young children's attachments to adults. Young infants like Andy are relatively undiscriminating in their attachments—they will accept cuddling from most adults and will express happiness in response to anyone's smile. But by the end of their first year most children develop close attachments to one or two adults. Although most research has emphasized parent–child attachments, close affectionate bonds may also be forged between young children and their caregivers in child care settings (Howes & Hamilton, 1992; Pianta, 1992). At every age, children express their desire for closeness through emotional signals, including smiling, crying, and clinging. Abigail, rejected by Zachary, buries her head in Leslie's lap as she sucks her thumb and cuddles with her blanket. As they get older, children are able to feel emotionally close without necessarily having physical contact. Kindergartner Mary Anne loves being Leslie's occasional senior helper, and she basks in Leslie's approving glances and smiles of encouragement when she "teaches" one of the younger children.

Children's emotional bonds include other children as well as adults. Sibling relationships are marked by strong emotions. Interactions among brothers and sisters provide many opportunities to learn about the expression and communication of emotion (Dunn & Munn, 1985). These feelings are often more positive than the stereotypes of sibling rivalry would suggest. Even infants show distress when their older siblings are away from home overnight, and these emotionally close relationships often persist into adulthood (Lewis, 1987). Beyond sibling relationships, children in child care settings develop emotionally close relationships with other children, at earlier ages than was thought possible in the past (Howes, 1988). The children in Leslie's group have truly become a family, quarreling with, supporting, and loving one another over the years that they spend together.

PUTTING THE CHANGES TOGETHER

Stage Models of Emotional Development

So far in this chapter, we have described a number of changes in six specific areas of children's emotional development. But can we step back from these details and come up with *general* age-related trends or stages? Like other contemporary developmental psychologists, those who write about emotions have generally avoided trying to capture a complex domain of development in a few all-encompassing stages. However, a few theorists have constructed models that are relevant and useful in pulling together some general patterns. With differing purposes and differing theoretical perspectives, Erik Erikson, Stanley Greenspan, and Kurt Fischer have each painted a picture of the broad sweep of early emotional development. Figure 3.1 shows the main features of each of these models.

Erikson: The Development of the Personality. Erikson's model stands apart from the others because it encompasses more than strictly "emotional" development. Rather, Erikson attempted to portray the sequence through which each component of the healthy personality emerges, "comes to its ascendance, meets its crisis, and finds its lasting solution" (Erikson, 1959, p. 56). The model is included here because, as I pointed out in Chapter 2, most of Erikson's "crises" or central conflicts are described in emotion language (e.g., "autonomy" versus "shame and doubt"). Furthermore, each developmental crisis is characterized by fluctuations of negative and positive feelings.

Figure 3.1 probably oversimplifies Erikson's complex theory. It does not display a feature of development that Erikson (1959) emphasized in his writing; namely, that each component of the healthy personality exists in some form at earlier developmental periods, well before the "crisis" unfolds. In Leslie's family child care home, infant Andy is already exercising autonomy, but autonomy issues achieve their full emotional resonance only in toddler Abigail. Similarly, Leslie's six-year-old "helper" Mary Anne may be seen to display signs of the emergence of a healthy sense of industry, while still dealing with emotion-related issues that dominated earlier periods of her life. Thus, every stage contains a rich kaleidoscope of emotional dynamics, but with certain feelings coloring some periods more intensely than others.

According to Erikson, at each stage many of the child's activities, perceptions, and relationships are organized around the central emotional issue of that stage. As children move through the four stages typical of the early childhood years, they widen their sphere of emotional attachments, and they express their conflicts not just through their bodies but through play and, later, culturally valued skills. Many practitioners have found Erikson's model helpful in identifying typical emotional issues and conflicts that children work on through play, peer relationships, and supportive interactions.

Figure 3.1 Some Models of Early Emotional Development

	Greenspan	Erikson	Fischer
Birth	Basic trust vs. mistrust (Favorable outcome: Hope and trust in environment. Unfavorable outcome: Suspicion and fear.)		Tier 1: Reflexes; components of basic emotional reactions
3 months		Self-regulation and interest in the world (0-3 months)	
6 months		"Falling in love" (2-7 months)	Tier 2: Sensorimotor action patterns for basic emotions (As development proceeds through Tier 2, various "action clusters" become better coordinated)
9 months		Developing intentional communications (3-10 months)	
1 year	Autonomy vs. shame and doubt (Favorable outcome: Ability to exercise choice and self-restraint; sense of self-esteem and pride. Unfavorable outcome: Propensity for shame and doubt about ability to control one's actions.)		
18 months		Emergence of an organized sense of self (9-18 months)	
2 years		Creating emotional ideas (18-36 months)	Tier 3: Representations of emotion situations through pretend play and spontaneous language
3 years	Initiative vs. guilt (Favorable outcome: Ability to initiate actions, enjoy accomplishments. Unfavorable outcome: Fear of punishment.)	Emotional thinking—the basis for fantasy, reality, and self-esteem (30-48 months)	
4 years			
5 years			(As development proceeds through Tier 3, emotion representations become more complex but continue to deal with concrete events and immediate experiences.)
6 years			
7 years	Industry vs. inferiority (Favorable outcome: Feeling of competence, ability to use skills to make things well. Unfavorable outcome: Feelings of inadequacy and inferiority.)		
8 years			

Greenspan: Overlapping Emotional Stages. More recently, Greenspan (Greenspan & Greenspan, 1985; Wieder & Greenspan, 1993) has built upon a neo-Freudian view of emotions to construct a description of six overlapping stages in the first 4 years of children's emotional development. Greenspan's (1989, 1991) approach can be characterized as a "developmental-structuralist theory" of ego development that includes consideration both of general developmental trends and of inborn, constitutional differences in children's affective, sensory, and behavioral responsiveness.

At every developmental stage, children are active constructors of their own emotional development. Even in infancy, children actively attempt to regulate their own emotions and to cope with feelings of anger, fear, and loss. Greenspan points out that, by the end of the first year of life, early attachment relationships lead to purposeful communication and to toddlers' creations of a coherent, positive sense of self, such as Caitlin shows in her pleased investigation of the play dough. These accomplishments then make it possible for the toddler and preschooler to use language, pretend play, and other tools to create "emotional ideas" and to engage in increasingly complex and differentiated "emotional thinking."

Not all children negotiate these stages with ease, however. Greenspan emphasizes that individual differences may create problems for some children (for example, if Abigail's auditory, visual, or tactile processing abilities lagged behind those of other children her age, she might have difficulty in creating symbolic representations of her own and others' feelings, which in turn could increase her frustration and anger when her desires were thwarted). In addition to these sensory and organizational difficulties, children's progress through these stages may be impeded because of adults' responses. Greenspan emphasizes that adults bring their own unresolved conflicts and emotional concerns to their relationships with their children, and that these may create miscommunication and ineffective patterns of interaction. Greenspan encourages adults to recognize their own affective biases and to take a positive, active role in helping young children to master the emotional tasks of early childhood.

Fischer: A Hierarchy of Emotional Skills. In contrast to these psychoanalytically oriented models, Fischer views emotional development as a hierarchy of skills related to the expression, representation, and understanding of emotions (Fischer, Shaver, & Carnochan, 1990). Fischer argues that, like other aspects of behavior, emotional development "involves the gradual and laborious construction of generalization of skills. . . . Virtually all components of emotional behaviors—the various appraisals, antecedents, responses, and self-control procedures—change with development" (p. 99). According to Fischer's framework, then, the basic elements of the emotion process are present in infancy, but in rudimentary form. "Skills at the later levels are built upon the more primitive skills from the earlier levels, which do not disappear but become components of the later skills" (p. 100).

Thus, as development proceeds, children use their emerging skills to control an increasingly complex set of "actions, perceptions, thoughts, and feelings" (p. 100). Through the years of infancy and early childhood, children gradually become more skilled at carrying out their emotional intentions and at integrating and combining emotion-related skills in complex patterns of responses. Mary Anne displays a sophisticated array of emotional skills when she observes Abigail's distress, thinks about its probable cause—and perhaps about her own distress at Abigail's continued screaming—and devises and acts upon a solution: bringing Abigail her blanket.

Common Themes and Trends

Looking across these models of early emotional development, and reviewing development in the six domains we examined earlier in this chapter, we can glimpse some common themes that thread their way through these diverse descriptions. Whatever labels are used, virtually everyone agrees that infants begin life possessing clear, powerful emotion signals. From a very early age, babies appear to feel some of the most fundamental human emotions, and they have a lively interest in their caregivers' emotions. These feelings help in the development of close, trusting ties with others and lead to confident exploration of the world.

As infants grow into toddlers and preschoolers, the scholars whose work I have summarized seem to agree on a number of major trends. Developmentally, children move toward

- Wider, more complex emotional relationships
- More varied, complex, and flexible ways of expressing emotions
- Better coordination and control of emotions and emotion-related skills
- More ability to reflect on their own feelings and those of others
- Representation of emotions through language, play, and fantasy
- Linking individual emotions to culturally valued skills and standards

- An integrated, positive, autonomous but emotionally connected sense of self

CONCLUSION

The picture that emerges from this summary description is a bit too tidy to satisfy the early childhood practitioner. Not all young children fit the stages outlined by Erikson, Greenspan, Fischer, and others; and many children do not develop according to the general emotion-related timetables identified by laboratory research. In addition, our discussion thus far has emphasized *what* develops but not *why* these developments occur as they do.

To supplement this normative picture, we need to focus our attention on the many factors that influence "typical" emotional development, and that create the many variations that early childhood professionals encounter in their work with young children.

Chapter 4

What Can Influence the Course of Early Emotional Development?

Ilene sits back in her chair, legs crossed, thinking about the year just past. Her 15 "fours" are close together in age: only 12 months separate the oldest from the youngest child. Yet as Ilene talks about the children in her Head Start class, their differences seem more striking than their developmental similarities.

"I had a few children this year who absolutely had to have whatever anyone else was using," Ilene recalled. "Charlene was like that. If another child took a book off the bookcase Charlene *had* to read it, and if she couldn't, it would cause a huge, dramatic crisis for her and everyone around her. She *would* not compromise about what she wanted. It's been interesting to see what has happened recently, though. Because Charlene wants so desperately to be Min's friend, she will give in and make some compromises if that's what it takes to play with her. But she still won't compromise with Kyle — she doesn't care enough about Kyle to make it worth her while."

Ilene's thoughts turn to Spencer, who worried incessantly about any changes in the class routine. "When we have a rainy day," Ilene explained, "we often change our schedule and set up climbers and tunnels inside. The prospect of these changes really bothered Spencer, and he sort of figured out how to deal with it by rehearsing what was going to happen, over and over again. If he even suspected that it might be rainy later on, he'd ask one of the helpers, 'Climbers today, right?' But one answer wasn't good enough for Spencer; he'd keep asking, over and over, as if he were trying to make sure that he had the order straight in his mind. Spencer was the only one who minded having a different schedule on rainy days; but some other children, like Rina, worried about other kinds of changes. The night before our first field trip, Rina told her mother she had a headache and couldn't go to school. Rina's also someone who has a lot of trouble initiating play when some new props have been put out in the classroom.

"That reminds me of something else about the class. There were such differences in the moods of different children. Oh, they all had their unhappy moments, but children like Min just seemed to bubble along, happy and cheerful despite almost anything. Then there was Elon. His face had a scowl a lot of the time. It didn't take much to set him off, yelling and punching. Quiana never got really angry the way Elon did, but more often than not, she's at least mildly unhappy. Other children's unhappiness really bothers Quiana, too — she has sometimes started crying if another child is crying, or she'll complain about a stomach ache if she hears someone else complaining. It's been a hard year for Quiana; her parents are splitting up and she has been shuttling back and forth between them, but even before that happened, she's just seemed like a child who doesn't have a very upbeat feeling about things. Darien also had kind of an unsettled family situation, but his reactions were different. He just pulled away from everyone for a while. Now he's his old perky self."

For Ilene and for other teachers of young children, it's helpful to know about the typical milestones of emotional development, as outlined in Chapter 3. But it is even more important for the effective practitioner to identify the *reasons* for those changes and to recognize the many, complex factors that create variations in the pathway of emotional development. Why is Spencer so worried about changes in the class routine? What keeps Min happy and even-tempered when her friends are fuming? Is Quiana's family responsible for her persistent sadness? Why does Elon fight and Darien withdraw?

Although there are no easy answers to these questions, by exploring them the practitioner can become more attuned to the roots of individual developmental patterns and can identify areas where a thoughtful, well-timed intervention may be helpful.

BEYOND "HEREDITY VERSUS ENVIRONMENT"

In emotional development as in other areas, it would be difficult to find anyone today who believes that development is caused entirely either by heredity or by environment—or even that development can be accounted for by assigning a certain percentage to heredity ("nature") and another percentage to environment ("nurture"). Both life and research are far more complex, and far more interesting, than that earlier debate would suggest. Like Quiana's persistent sadness, every aspect of children's development is shaped by a dynamic interaction of biological, environmental, individual, personal, and sociocultural factors.

The portrait of development is further complicated when we acknowledge that children are not just passive recipients of either hereditary or environmental influences. Children, it has been said, actually produce their own development. As in Charlene's relationship with the compliant, cheerful Min, children seek out friends, activities, and settings that provide a good fit with their own needs and behavioral style. Children's individual characteristics draw out certain responses from others, which then create further changes—including some long-lasting ones—in children's behavior. For example, Ilene noted that inexperienced volunteers in her class would sometimes overreact to Elon's behavior. By treating him as "rough," they seemed to produce even more anger, fighting, and arguing from Elon, confirming his image of himself as a tough customer.

For all these reasons, those who study children's development today paint a multifaceted picture in which almost no outcome can be ascribed to a single direct cause. Some might long for the simplicity of earlier developmental perspectives. However, the picture drawn by current writers is probably closer to what Ilene, and other early childhood professionals, know about young children's complex patterns of development.

KEY FACTORS IN EMOTIONAL DEVELOPMENT

In this chapter I will describe five factors that play a key role in emotional development in early childhood. By themselves and in dynamic interplay with one another, these factors account for the typical progression of emotional development described in Chapter 3. They also account for variations in that typical progression, including "normal" individual and group differences, and variations that may be of special concern to young children's parents and teachers.

The factors we will consider are children's

1. Biological and physical characteristics, including physiological processes
2. Individual differences in temperament
3. Skills and limitations in other developmental areas, including the cognitive, language, and social domains
4. Family environment and relationships
5. Cultural influences

In taking a closer look at each of these factors, I will briefly highlight recent research linking each of these factors to specific features of early emotional development. This discussion will set the stage for recommendations for an emotion-centered curriculum in later chapters of this book.

Biological and Physical Characteristics

Children's biological or physical characteristics may influence their emotional development in many complicated ways. These influences may occur as a result of: (1) the basic features of children's brains and nervous systems; (2) individual differences in children's physiological responses; (3) gender differences; and (4) atypical developmental patterns, such as autism, Down's syndrome, and visual impairment.

Features and Maturation of the Brain and Nervous System. As noted in Chapter 3, most contemporary writers emphasize that emotions have a biological basis. Feelings, emotion expressions, and emotional behaviors originate in the brain and nervous system (Fox & Davidson, 1986). Some writers believe that each basic emotion (such as fear, happiness, and anger) is associated with a specific set of circuits in the nervous system (Izard & Malatesta, 1987). If so, this would help explain why the expression of these emotions is so similar across individuals and cultures. There is good evidence that emotions such as anger, fear, and interest are associated with changes in children's heart rate, respiration, and brain activity. Researchers have also found actual variations in brain wave patterns, depending on whether children appear to be experiencing positive or negative emotions (Fox & Davidson, 1988).

The maturation of the brain and central nervous system helps children to develop better control over when and how they express emotions. In most normally developing children, this process occurs automatically and on a predictable schedule. Especially important is the maturation of the cerebral cortex, which plays an important role in inhibiting behavior. This allows children to stop themselves from expressing strong emotions and helps them to delay action instead of acting impulsively. Many of Ilene's four-year-olds have made considerable progress in their ability to stop themselves from grabbing what they want, and "cortical inhibition" may be one reason why this self-control is possible.

Individual Differences. However, children of the same age—like the four-year-olds in Ilene's Head Start class—also differ from one another in their physiological patterns of emotional response. For example, some infants and young children have more variable heart rate patterns than others. These normal, innate differences, which may be detected in newborns, can predict later differences in children's emotional responses, including their level of interest when interacting with a parent, their expressiveness, and their anxiety in new situations (Ekman, Levenson, & Friesen, 1983; Fox & Davidson, 1986; Kagan, Reznick, Clarke, Snidman, & Garcia-Coll, 1984). These kinds of differences may help to explain why certain children in Ilene's class, like Rina, worried more about new activities than did other children of the same age and family background.

Gender Differences. Gender is the most obvious biological characteristic that distinguishes children from one another. Like other factors discussed in this section, the influence of gender on emotional development is not at all simple and straightforward. It is true that many studies have found differences in boys' and girls' ways of expressing emotions (Haviland & Malatesta, 1981; Manstead, 1992). Newborn girls cry more in response to other babies' distress, and they spend more time oriented toward faces and voices (Haviland & Malatesta, 1981). In contrast, newborn boys startle more easily, cry more intensely, and tend to be more irritable and harder to soothe. In later years, girls smile more, are described by others as being more sociable than boys, and are better than boys at noticing, identifying, and interpreting others' feelings (Malatesta et al., 1989).

Although the fact that even newborns show gender differences in emotional responses suggests some biological basis, these boy/girl differences need not be entirely innate or "natural." Indeed, a number of researchers are investigating the ways in which adults influence boys and girls to adopt different styles of expressive behavior. Malatesta and colleagues (1989) reported that mothers smile more and are more expressive to infant and toddler girls than to boys. Adults also tend to read different messages into the nonverbal behavior of girls and boys. In talking about gender differences in her class of four-year-olds, Ilene described how some parent volunteers attributed angry or aggressive intent to boys' behavior, while interpreting the same kind of behavior quite differently in girls—"She must be upset today." Similarly, when Malatesta had adults judge the emotions expressed by children on videotapes, they attributed a greater amount of joy to the children who they were told were girls and a greater amount of anger to the children they thought were boys (actually, the children on the tapes were all of the same gender).

Atypical Developmental Patterns. So far, we have looked at normal variations in children's physiological characteristics. However, some children also have disabilities that may affect their emotional responses. In Ilene's class, Spencer has been diagnosed with attention deficit disorder. Ilene has noticed that Spencer often gets himself into social hot water because he has great difficulty "reading" other children's emotion signals. In addition, Spencer's incessant questions about the rainy day schedule, and his habit of policing all possible infractions of classroom rules, seem to be Spencer's way of creating some order in his often disordered perceptions of the world.

Autism is a major developmental disorder that is now thought to be caused by complex brain abnormalities. Children with autism have greatly impaired social and emotional functioning. Sigman, Kasari, Kwon, & Yirmiya (1992) observed how children with autism reacted when adults expressed distress or fear. Although most children are intensely interested in adults' emotional responses, autistic children paid little attention to adults' emotion expressions and thus had severely limited opportunities to learn about emotions by observing others.

Children with Down's syndrome have multiple physical and developmental disabilities caused by the presence of an extra chromosome. Although in many ways their development follows similar pathways, observations have shown some differences between the emotional responses of Down's syndrome children and those of children without mental retardation. As newborns, children with Down's syndrome usually appear less emotionally responsive. Their facial expressions of emotion are affected by their characteristically poor muscle tone. These expressions may be difficult for some parents and caregivers to interpret and respond to appropriately. When this happens, a negative cycle of interaction is created, one that makes it harder for these children to learn about emotion through adult–child interaction (Cicchetti, Ganiban, & Barnett, 1991).

The same negative cycle may affect the emotional development of children with visual impairments. Researchers have found that blind infants can produce all the basic facial expressions of emotion. As time goes on, however, they may do so less and less frequently, because they lack the visual feedback that nondisabled infants receive from their environment. Furthermore, adults caring for blind infants (like caregivers of babies with Down's syndrome) often misread their emotion expressions. Parents or other caregivers may think the visually handicapped child does not respond affectionately, since the usual cues of eye contact and responsive smiling may be absent. This misperception may cause a caregiver to withdraw from interaction or may result in inappropriate responses to children's emotion signals (Fraiberg, 1979).

Individual Differences in Temperament

Every early childhood teacher is struck by the sharp differences in children's emotion-related behavior. Stages of development and descriptions of developmental milestones do not begin to explain the huge differences between Charlene's typical style of behavior and Kyle's, when these children are exactly the same age, seem to have the same kind of family and cultural environment, and have had similar early experiences. Certainly both of these children experience and express the same basic emotions. However, temperamental differences influence *how* Charlene and Kyle express these emotions and how easily these emotions can be activated.

Recent research in developmental psychology supports the practitioner's awareness of individual differences in temperament or "behavioral style" (Bates, 1987). Some researchers have pointed out that temperament characteristics are closely related to children's styles of emotion expression and emotion-related behavior (Bornstein, Gaughran, & Homel, 1986; Goldsmith & Campos, 1982, 1990; Thompson & Lamb, 1983). Temperament studies, and the experiences of early childhood professionals like Ilene, clearly demonstrate that children have strong individual differences on a number of emotion-related dimensions. From an early age, children differ in how fussy they are, how easy they are to soothe, how irritable they become, how sociable they are, how fearful or inhibited in new situations. Children also differ in how intensely they express emotions, how quickly they become emotionally aroused, how well they can regulate their emotions and be comforted by others, and how they respond emotionally in stressful situations (Izard, Hembree, & Huebner, 1987; Lewis & Michalson, 1983; Sroufe, Schork, Motti, Lawroski, & LaFreniere, 1984).

Ilene vividly described her children's differing reactions to new student teachers from a nearby community college. "Some children deal with the change by acting mean," Ilene said. "They'll tell the student teacher to go away if she tries to play with them. Some of those children are actually shy, and they reject the student teachers' approaches so that they'll just be left alone. A couple of them would say to the student, 'You don't know the rules of our school'—that was the best put-down they could think of. Of course, then there are children who will instantly adopt *any* new adult who comes into the room."

Many of these differences appear to have underlying biological and genetic roots. For example, children observed to be temperamentally shy differ from other children in their heart rhythms (Kagan, Reznick, Clarke, Snidman, & Garcia-Coll, 1984). Children who are temperamentally prone to distress—"irritable" children, as Charlene was as an infant—may have levels of certain hormones that differ from those of more even-tempered children (Gunnar, Mangelsdorf, Larson, & Hertsgaard, 1989). Studies of adopted children and of twins who are reared apart offer evidence that tendencies toward characteristics such as "emotionality" or "sociability" may have a hereditary basis (Buss & Plomin, 1984).

In observing the same children over a number of years, researchers have found that differences in children's temperament and related emotion expression styles tend to persist over time. Individual children's characteristic facial expressions of emotion (how much anger or sadness they show in response to separation) tend to stay the same as they get older (Hyson & Izard, 1985; Izard, Hembree, & Huebner, 1987). Another research team followed the development of children who had been identified at an early age as having an "inhibited" style of behavior (being extremely shy and fearful of new situations). When observed at age 2, age 4, and then age 7, most of these very inhibited children maintained the same basic pattern of response in new situations (Kagan, Reznick, & Snidman, 1988). Similar consistencies are seen in several of Ilene's children. For example, Rina has had a hard time adjusting to new situations ever since she was a baby. Each transition, from weaning to starting Head Start to going on a field trip, has been difficult.

As seen with other biologically based differences, though, "innate" temperament patterns exert a complicated influence on development. Although children may seem to be born shy or irritable or sociable, as they get older these temperament/emotion characteristics may motivate them to seek out or avoid certain experiences. Then, those experiences as well as the temperament pattern itself may further shape children's social and emotional development. For example, if Rina's avoidance of new classroom activities continues, this pattern could possibly limit her knowledge base and restrict her cognitive development.

Individual differences in temperament also have powerful effects on parents and other caregivers. Min's joyful, sociable outlook creates warm responses from adults as well as from her peers. Furthermore, a caregiver's own emotional style may or may not provide a comfortable "fit" with that of a particular child. A talented but impulsive student teacher in Ilene's Head Start class found herself frustrated and ineffective in working with slow-paced Will. Interestingly, Ilene also observed that very shy student teachers were sometimes unable to draw out an equally shy four-year-old. "He just won't talk," they would complain, having little skill at making social connections themselves. In addition, adults regard some temperaments more favorably than others. Infants who have difficulty tolerating frustration may be harder to care for, and the kind of adult interaction they experience may differ considerably from that experienced by less "difficult" babies (Greenspan & Greenspan, 1985; Miyake, Chen, & Campos, 1985). Sroufe and colleagues (1984) found that preschool children who clearly displayed their emotions, particularly positive emotions, tended to be highly regarded by teachers and peers.

Does this mean that children with different temperaments will deviate from the basic developmental pathways outlined in Chapter 3? Descriptions of milestones in emotional development are composites or averages of studies that include large numbers of children. An individual child may differ greatly from the "typical" or "average" patterns described in Chapter 3. Most of those differences are normal, and they are also what makes life with children so interesting.

Development in Other Domains

The course of early emotional development is also influenced by children's advances or limitations in other developmental areas. For example, physical skills appear to influence the development of fear. Bertenthal and Campos (1990) found that once babies could crawl, they reacted to the "visual cliff" experiment with obvious fear, whereas non-crawling infants of the same age were less perturbed when faced with an apparent drop-off. On the more positive side, Mahler (Mahler, Pine, & Bergman, 1975) vividly described the increased joy and excitement that most children display in the months after they learn to walk, calling it a "love affair with the world".

Cognitive skills also exert a clear influence on emotional development. When children become able to symbolize or mentally represent experiences, they can use pretend play to act out emotional issues or conflicts. When children begin to understand general cause–effect relationships, their awareness of the causes of emotion is enhanced.

Children's limited understanding of certain concepts and processes sometimes results in fear, sadness, or distress. For example, a toddler may fear a caregiver with a new, short haircut because he fails to comprehend that the teacher is still the same person although her physical appearance has changed. In Ilene's class, Hannah at first refused to participate in group activities that required her to pretend she was someone or something different, such as a butterfly or a plant or a cat. Her feelings about this were so negative that Ilene finally decided Hannah really believed she might turn into these fantasy creations (as the "beehive" example in Chapter 2 showed, Hannah gradually overcame this reluctance and in fact used pretend play to master her fears).

Children's emotional development is also influenced by their developing language skills. Two-year-olds' crying bouts decrease as they become able to describe and negotiate about their "self needs": "No gonna do it!" "I want these" (Kopp, 1992). Toddlers' new ability to use language allows them to label their own feelings and those of others; indeed, "feeling talk" often forms the content of toddlers' earliest attempts at language. Within the family, they use language to express affection, to comfort others, and even to tease or joke about emotional states (Mother: "Do you like your mommy, Ned?" Child, smiling teasingly: "No yes!") (Dunn & Brown, 1991). Later increases in vocabulary give school-age children a much wider repertoire of language tools to express both positive and negative feelings. But language also can pose emotional barriers: Last year, Ilene had several children in her class who spoke little English early in the year. Ilene believed that their intense distress at separation was partly caused by their lack of language outlets.

Finally, the domains of social and emotional development are closely related; thus, it is not surprising that children's emerging social skills help them with their emotional development. The peer group often becomes the place where children unambiguously find out what happens when they inappropriately express or regulate their emotions. In Ilene's class, Spencer gradually realized that other children would simply avoid him if he screamed for them to do his bidding. A close relationship with another child (like Charlene's friendship with Min), or with a special caregiver, may enrich children's emotional lives, stretching their capacity to feel deeply and to reciprocate another's affection.

Family Environment and Relationships

Many of the individual differences observed by Ilene and other teachers of young children may be connected with the child's family environment and parent–child relationships. As with other influences on emotional development, though, the direction of these effects is complex. Children influence their parents at least as much as parents influence their children. Different children in the same family are treated differently. Parents' own temperament characteristics and styles of emotion expression may affect children through parents' interactions with them; but these same parental characteristics may also be transmitted to children through genetic inheritance.

For all these reasons, children's family environments have a strong impact on the course of their emotional development. From early infancy, children are predisposed to attend to their parents' emotion-related behavior (Kagan, 1970). As we have seen, toddlers are intensely interested in the emotions of other family members (Dunn, 1988; Dunn & Munn, 1985). Older children continue to be tuned in to adults' facial and vocal expressions of emotion. Children are especially likely to look to adults for emotional information in new, uncertain situations (Klinnert, Campos, Sorce, Emde, & Svejda, 1983).

As Dix (1991) has observed, "parenting is an emotional experience. Raising children involves more joy, affection, anger, and worry than do most other endeavors" (p. 3). Parents' expressions of emotion influence children's immediate behavior as well as their long-term development. Both beneficial and harmful effects of adult emotion have been identified. On the beneficial side, parents' positive emotions capture and hold babies' interest in toys, books, and interesting sights. These episodes of affectively positive "shared focus" are essential for early cognitive development (Trevarthen, 1984). Children whose parents converse with them about feelings, especially when conflicts occur, develop a better understanding of emotion (Bretherton, Fritz, Zahn-Waxler, & Ridgeway, 1986; Dunn, Bretherton, & Munn, 1987; Dunn &

Munn, 1985). More competent preschool children often have parents who are emotionally expressive (Denham, 1989). And children whose parents warmly encourage them to express their sadness and distress—but who also help them cope effectively with negative emotions—are likely to develop more sympathetic, adaptive, competent patterns of social behavior (Eisenberg, Fabes, Carlo, & Karbon, 1992; Roberts & Strayer, 1987).

Unfortunately, parents' patterns of emotion may also produce less beneficial influences. Even very young infants show marked negative reactions to mothers who are unresponsive and detached when the infants try to engage them in play. In the face of this adult detachment, children who began by displaying persistence and distress often lapse into passivity or avoidance of their parents (Stoller & Field, 1982; Tronick, Ricks, & Cohn, 1982). Children whose mothers express a great deal of negative emotion are often sadder and less mature in their peer relationships. Depressed mothers are more likely to have insecurely attached children who show early social withdrawal and a greater risk of behavioral problems in later years (Cicchetti, Ganiban, & Barnett, 1991; Zahn-Waxler, Cummings, Iannotti, & Radke-Yarrow, 1984). Darien, one of Ilene's four-year-olds, appeared to be affected by these kinds of family influences. Earlier in the year, his mother left for weeks at a time to work in another city. Overwhelmed by caring for Darien's baby brother and two other children under 6, Darien's grandmother became exhausted and emotionally distant. Darien's response at Head Start was to withdraw: When he was even mildly rejected, he would give up and walk away, refusing to stand up for his needs or to say what was bothering him. By spring, a more settled family situation helped Darien to sustain positive feelings about himself.

Anger within the family can have profound effects on young children. Children who are exposed to high levels of adult anger play in a more disorganized fashion (Cummings, 1987; Cummings, Iannotti, & Zahn-Waxler, 1985). Laboratory studies are beginning to show that unhappily married couples tend to pull young children into their conflict, resulting in high levels of frustration, anger, tension, and anxiety as noted by observers of the children's behavior (Lindahl & Markman, 1993). In Ilene's class, Quiana's low threshold for sadness and distress, although temperamentally based, seems to have been heightened by her parents' conflicts and separation. Researchers have also found that children of abusive parents have major deficiencies in their ability to express emotions and to understand other people's feelings, as well as difficulties in controlling their own aggression (Camras, 1985; Cicchetti, Ganiban, & Barnett, 1991; Dix, 1991). These few examples suggest the many ways in which early experiences within the family shape children's emotional development.

Cultural Influences

Over the past few years, Ilene's class has included children from China, Korea, and India, as well as from diverse American ethnic groups. What difference do culture and ethnicity make in children's emotional development?

Although the basic emotions may be universal, many researchers have begun to investigate the influence of culture on how children express emotions and how they think and talk about their feelings. Those who have traveled in, lived in, and worked with children and families from different cultures cannot help but notice that cultures differ greatly in how openly people express emotions and in how acceptable it is to talk about emotional experiences within and outside the family (Harkness & Super, 1985; Lutz, 1985). Every culture has unwritten rules about how feelings should be displayed. For example, the Javanese culture strongly prohibits intense expressions of feelings and encourages reserved, distant emotional relationships, even between parents and children. Children are not considered truly Javanese until age 5, when they begin to be able to adhere to these rules for emotional displays. The Korean culture discourages open displays of emotion and has an approving phrase ("myu-po-jung") for a lack of facial expression. In Korea, casual smiling to strangers may be viewed as inappropriate (Lynch & Hansen, 1992). Ilene's Asian four-year-olds tend to be more compliant and less aggressive than their Anglo-European peers (although Ilene noticed that this year two otherwise peace-loving Asian children fought continually with one another).

Every culture holds beliefs about which emotions are natural or appropriate for children to express at different ages, and which emotions should be targeted for socialization (Gordon, 1989; Harkness & Kilbride, 1983; Lutz, 1983). Lewis (1988) conducted observations in 15 Japanese nursery schools. In contrast to typical practices of American early childhood programs, the Japanese teachers in Lewis' study routinely allowed children to express anger through physical aggression, as long as other children were not badly hurt. Teachers believed that these quarrels reflected a growing interest in others and that eventually children would learn better ways to resolve problems. Especially in the development of more complex "social" emotions (such as pride, shame, and guilt), cultural values play a very important role. In fact, some emotions are so specifically tied to cultural values that it is almost impossible to translate the words for these emotions into other languages.

How do children learn the rules specific to their culture, when it comes to understanding, expressing, and controlling emotion? As we have noted, young children are intensely interested in adults' feelings and will closely observe their responses, especially in uncertain situations. This observational learning, as well as adults' selective reinforcement of children's emotion expressions, will lead to cultural variations in emotion expression patterns even at relatively early ages. In turn, these emotional reactions will influence adults' willingness to expose children to certain experiences. For example, Japanese babies are almost never separated from their mothers. As a result, they express what American observers might mistakenly call "abnormally" intense levels of distress during routine separations. In Ilene's experience, two- and three-year-old Asian children often have particular difficulties with separation, even when their language skills are adequate.

Like the Asian children in Ilene's Head Start program, increasing numbers of young children in the United States grow up in several cultures. By the year 2000, it is estimated that 38% of all U.S. children under 18 will be nonwhite and non-Anglo (Lynch & Hansen, 1992). Yet many public and private early childhood programs remain staffed by predominantly Anglo-European professionals. When cultural or ethnic environments are different at home and at school, children and their caregivers face considerable difficulties. Patterns of emotion expression or talk about emotion that is appropriate and encouraged in one setting may be inappropriate and discouraged in another. Adults in different cultures or different ethnic groups may have very different ideas about what kind of social or emotional behavior is desirable in children. Harwood (1992) found that Puerto Rican parents placed a high value on toddlers' close emotional bonds with their mothers, while Anglo mothers were more concerned with children's development of independence. At home, some African-American children may be taught to refrain from direct eye contact with adults, only to have Anglo-European teachers regard them as shy or evasive.

These examples underscore how important it is for caregivers to be sensitive to culturally prescribed expressive styles. This sensitivity will allow early childhood professionals to understand, respect, and support each child's unique pattern of emotional development.

CONCLUSION

In this chapter we have reviewed many factors that affect early emotional development. Children's biological characteristics, temperament, skills in other developmental areas, cultural settings, and family environments all work together in complex ways to produce the kinds of emotion-related patterns that Ilene saw among her four-year-olds. Some of these patterns seem to persist over time: according to her mother, Rina's reluctance to try new things changed very little since she was a baby. In other situations, major emotional changes are created by one or more of those factors, as when the increased stability in Darien's family resulted in greater self-confidence and positive mood.

In addition to these powerful influences, children's out-of-home environments also shape the course of emotional development. As we saw in Chapter 1, early childhood programs have been found to differ enormously in their emotional climate. Teachers range from warm, affectionate, and sensitive to harsh and detached. Like parenting, teaching young children is, by nature, a highly emotional process. In child care settings, children develop ties with their caregivers that are similar to the kinds of "attachment relationships" children have with their parents. And as in parent–child attachments, these relationships may be secure or insecure, avoidant or anxious (Howes & Hamilton, 1992; Pianta, 1992).

Along with the quality of teacher–child interactions, the planned curriculum, materials, and activities may help or hinder early emotional development. Thus, early childhood programs have the opportunity to build upon and integrate the many factors discussed in this chapter, creating an emotion-centered curriculum that supports the full development and learning potential of every child. Chapter 5 will outline the key features of such a program.

PART II

Constructing
an Emotion-Centered
Curriculum

Chapter 5

The Emotion-Centered Curriculum: An Overview

The two-year-olds have been playing together for about an hour. On this day, many children cluster around a table where they can use foam rubber shapes to make collages. The children seem fascinated with peeling off the paper to expose the sticky backing of the foam circles and squares. Natalie, the teacher, sits on a low chair near the table. Several children lean comfortably against her as they examine the collage materials.

A few other children are over at the bulletin board, which today has been covered with a sheet of contact paper, sticky side out. Children are choosing pieces of yarn, colored paper, and cloth from a box on the floor and sticking the materials to the bulletin board. Other children work at spreading peanut butter on miniature bagels that will be served at snack time.

These young two-year-olds are not big talkers, but Natalie keeps up a flow of conversation and commentary on the children's doings. "Carl, can you help Erin turn the water on?" "Here's the orange paper you wanted, Mandy. Did you want to finish your picture now or later?" "Do you hear what Aaron is saying to you? He's saying no." "Krystal, are you happy today?" Natalie asks as Krystal walks by with her arms over her head. "Aaron, did you go in the tunnel? Is it dark in there? Aaron's going in again. I won't see him now. Oh, there he is back again!"

Besides participating in the activities that have been set out, some children work intently on self-chosen "projects." Paulina spends several minutes struggling to get some play dough out of a plastic bag set into a large container. When she gets her piece she smiles with satisfaction. Next, she works at opening the latch on a lunch box that she found in a cupboard. Once she manages to open the lunch box, she pulls small pieces off her lump of play dough and carefully places them inside. Carrying her lunch box, Paulina crosses the room to a wooden riding bench placed in the block area. She sits contentedly on the riding bench, turning the steering wheel. "There goes Paulina on her trip," says Natalie to several children at the collage table. "Send us a postcard, Paulina. Bye, bye!" Paulina gives a small wave and a pleased smile from her perch across the room. The whole enterprise has taken more than 10 minutes.

Loud growling comes from inside a plastic tunnel. Carl peers out with a fierce expression, growls even more loudly, and retreats into the tunnel. Several children look a little alarmed. After a few minutes, Natalie walks over to the tunnel, sits down, talks quietly to Carl, and returns to the collage table. Softer growls come from the tunnel.

Several puzzles and small-shape sorting toys have been put out on the rug. Krystal and Aaron lie flat on the floor, working on opening a plastic house. Using a color-matched key, Aaron opens one of the doors and pulls out two miniature people. "My daddy!" Aaron exclaims. And "My mommy!" as he finds another figure. He extends them toward Natalie as he scrambles up from the floor and approaches her. "Oh, Aaron, look at the mommy and daddy," says Natalie as Aaron presses them together. "Are they hugging each other?" Aaron nods with conviction.

Even a short visit to Natalie's two-year-old program shows that the curriculum is truly emotion-centered. Of course, if we acknowledge that children's behavior and learning are always motivated by emotions (as the theory and research discussed in previous chapters show), then *every* early childhood program is emotion-centered. In this book, however, the term "emotion-centered curriculum" is reserved for programs that *deliberately, positively,* and *reflectively* use emotions as a starting point in designing experiences to support every aspect of young children's development.

An emotion-centered early childhood curriculum explicitly recognizes the central importance of emotions in young children's development. The development of emotional competence is seen as an essential foundation for effective academic and social functioning. Curriculum planners use current knowledge about emotions to make informed decisions about curriculum goals, selection of activities, teacher–child interactions, and assessment of children's progress. This chapter will describe the basic ingredients of an emotion-centered curriculum, recognizing that each teacher mixes these ingredients with a personal style. In presenting these ingredients, I also will address some real-world concerns expressed by practitioners who are considering a more emotion-focused approach to early childhood education. I will try to show that this approach is consistent with recent developments in curriculum and teaching practices, enhancing rather than undermining the development of academic skills. Finally, the chapter will recommend some steps practitioners might take in "refocusing" on emotions.

INGREDIENTS OF AN EMOTION-CENTERED CURRICULUM

Every early childhood program is different. Differences in children, staff, and settings combine to create unique ecologies for programs for young children. Nevertheless, emotion-centered programs will have certain distinctive ingredients. Visiting a classroom like Natalie's, a perceptive observer will notice certain hallmarks or clues that this is indeed an emotion-centered program.

Emotional Engagement

In an emotion-centered program, children are emotionally engaged in their life at school. This does not mean that every child displays a big smile throughout the day; constant "fun" is not the goal of an emotion-centered curriculum. But most of the time, children's faces, voices, and bodies indicate a high level of absorption and emotional involvement. Whether peeling the backing off a foam rubber disk, spreading peanut butter on bagels, crawling through a tunnel, or trying out different ways to unlock the doors of the plastic dollhouse, the children in Natalie's class (like other children in emotion-centered programs) display curiosity and interest. As they go about the activities of the day, their faces reflect concentration and involvement: Their brows often furrow in concentration and their lips press together as they focus intensely on the work they have chosen to tackle. Their jaws may drop open and eyes widen in surprise when they experience a new sound or scent, solve a new problem, or produce an unexpected result. From time to time, sounds of glee may punctuate the hum of busy activity. Whether the child is an infant fitting a block into a container or a first grader printing a note to her teacher, an observer will notice focused attention, concentration, and personal satisfaction at the successful completion of tasks.

In programs that use an emotion-centered curriculum, children approach new materials and activities with relish. Children appear optimistic about their ability to figure things out and to get help from adults and other children when they need it.

Warm Adult–Child Relationships

In these kinds of classrooms, children's relationships with their teachers are strikingly warm and mutually engaged. Like Mandy, Ellie, Carl, and others in Natalie's class, children approach adults with confidence. They smile at, touch, show things to, and seek assistance, collaboration, and comfort from adults. In turn, teachers appear genuinely delighted by the children, showing spontaneous interest in their activities and sharing their problems and triumphs. The flavor of this relationship certainly varies with the children's ages and with the program's cultural context. Natalie is gentler and more physically comforting with her two-year-olds than is the kindergarten teacher next door. But whatever the specific situation, adult–child relationships are always characterized by genuine mutual liking and emotional connectedness.

Emotion-centered teachers create relationships that support children's emotional development. They accept children's feelings and respond to their needs for recognition, comfort, and inclusion. "Mandy has a little skiing person on her shirt," Natalie says affectionately, stroking Mandy's sweatshirt and gently turning Mandy so the other children at the table can see. "What happened to your fingers, Helen?" says Natalie, touching Helen's three bandaged fingertips, and adds, "Hi,

Kimberly," to a small girl standing diffidently outside a group of children near the table. Natalie's welcoming tone and warm smile included Kimberly in the group without pressuring her to assume center stage.

Direct Expression of Feelings

A visitor to an emotion-centered program sees children express their feelings openly. "I *want* to make this for my mommy," Carl demanded, as he barged into the collage group clutching paper and scissors. Krystal joyously flung her arms over her head in spontaneous pleasure as she walked toward her teacher. Mandy bounced across the room on tiptoes to put her carefully torn pieces of orange paper in her cubby. Individual temperament and cultural standards may influence how intensely children display their emotions, but an emotion-centered curriculum always has room for feelings.

Individuality

Children in emotion-centered programs may strike the observer as being highly individual in their interests and expressive styles. Programs lacking a strong emotional focus often subdue individuality because children can perform activities in only one stereotyped way. In contrast, after only a short time in Natalie's class, a visitor has a clear sense of Ellie's tentativeness, Carl's boisterously expressive manner, and Mandy's warm responsiveness. In an emotion-centered program, teachers value and encourage individuality. Natalie frequently refers to children's personal desires and interests, showing those children and others in the group that these individual qualities are to be respected and enjoyed. "Ellie, did you want to feed the fish?" "I think Erin wanted to make a reindeer with the play dough cutter. Is that right, Erin?" "Aaron, do you want Sarah to put on two pairs of sunglasses? What do you think, Sarah? Would that be fun to do?" Natalie and other emotion-focused teachers allow children to place their own stamp on activities while remaining sensitive to cultural differences in expressions of individuality.

Attunement to Others

Despite this encouragement of individuality, children in an emotion-centered program may seem especially attuned to others' interests, feelings, and needs, because adults encourage this affective awareness. Natalie's toddlers are at an age that many teachers regard as hopelessly egocentric. Nevertheless, Natalie supports their growing awareness of others' feelings: "Thanks, Mandy, for passing that to Aaron. He really needed it." "Krystal, she might not want to put that in your lunch box," as Krystal attempts to get Becky to relinquish a piece of paper. "Oh, she *does* want to!" says Natalie warmly and delightedly, as both girls beam with satisfaction over the transaction.

Emotionally Relevant Activities

Teachers using an emotion-centered curriculum select activities that have *emotional relevance* for children. Planned and impromptu activities encourage children to talk about, write about, and play about emotionally important issues. Teachers like Natalie know that emotionally relevant activities will build strong links between affective and cognitive development and will result in more persistent, engaged, and enthusiastic learning.

What is emotionally relevant will vary with children's age, culture, and individual needs. Many of Natalie's two-year-olds are intensely interested in issues of separation and reunion, disappearance and reappearance. In Natalie's classroom, children love the plastic tunnel. Besides its benefits for physical development, it allows children to control their appearances and disappearances and to playfully experience positive and negative feelings. The small dollhouse with its doors, keys, and small people inside engages the two-year-olds' curiosity and interest not just because of the fine motor skills involved, but because of their fascination with retrieving the little human figures hidden inside the house—and then making them disappear again.

Many of the activities in Natalie's room gain their emotional power because they let children have an immediate, personal effect on their environment. Pressing objects into play dough to leave marks, sticking yarn onto the contact paper wall, hammering golf tees into a large block of styrofoam—these and many other activities allow the children to experience what Piaget has called "pleasure at being a cause."

It would certainly be possible to find other activities that emphasized the same concepts and skills. However, by selecting emotionally relevant activities, the emotion-centered teacher ensures that children will engage in sustained, purposeful exploration, resulting in both intellectual and emotional benefits.

"YES, BUT . . . ": SOME REAL-WORLD CONCERNS

After reading this description of the core characteristics of an emotion-centered curriculum, some early childhood teachers may still have concerns.

Denial of Teachers' Individual Styles

"I'm not one of those touchy-feely types—I've never been comfortable telling children how I feel about everything or fawning all over them whenever they have a problem."

Being an emotion-centered teacher does not mean adopting a new or artificial style. Just as children have distinctive "emotion biases" and styles of expressing their feelings, and just as they have different thresholds for experiencing different emotions, so too do teachers. One teacher may have a lively, open expressive style, displaying positive and negative feelings directly. Another teacher has a lower-key style, with muted, subtle expressions. Still another teacher may be open in expressing some emotions—joy, for example, but not anger or sadness; or she may express emotions only in the context of program activities and not reveal her personal feelings to the children. Culture, family environment, temperament, and personal belief systems (Hyson & Lee, 1992) all may influence the early childhood teacher's personal emotion style.

Are all of these variations acceptable and helpful in teaching young children? Some variations are unlikely to support healthy emotional and intellectual development. For example, children's play become disorganized when they are exposed to extreme displays of adult anger (Cummings, Zahn-Waxler, & Radke-Yarrow, 1981), and the children of chronically sad or depressed parents have a variety of difficulties in expressing emotion (Cicchetti, Ganiban, & Barnett, 1991). Barring these extremes, though, children can probably benefit from varied models of emotion expression style.

Furthermore, being emotion-centered does not mean overwhelming children with solicitude and misplaced "love." Natalie and other emotion-centered teachers are careful to give children room to struggle with problems on their own, while being ready to "scaffold" children's efforts. "This is hard for you, huh, Thomas?" Natalie says with warm concern, as Thomas struggles to push up his sleeves. Later, as Aaron walks out of the bathroom with his striped shirt just covering his bare bottom, Natalie casually comments, "Did you need some new pants,

Aaron? Did you have a little bit of an accident? Do you need some help with the pants or are you all right?" This sensitive balance of autonomy and support creates conditions for the development of both intellectual and emotional competence.

Neglect of Academic Content

"Doesn't this emotional emphasis neglect academics and cognitive development? My children have so much catching up to do to get them ready for later success in school. My top priority has to be their academic skills and concepts."

Centering the curriculum on emotions does not require that the entire curriculum must be *about* emotions. Just as "child-centered" does not mean "child-dominated" (Bredekamp & Rosegrant, 1992), "emotion-centered" does not mean "emotion-only." As we have seen, many researchers now believe that emotions are the primary motivators and organizers of all development and learning. These writers also emphasize that emotion and cognition are closely linked throughout development, but especially in the early childhood years. Thus, the program planner who starts with a concern for emotions will actually increase the likelihood that children will benefit intellectually and academically. A focus on emotions will help early childhood educators to make their entire program more effective.

Overemphasis on Self-Expression

"Doesn't this emphasis on emotions encourage children to express their feelings without any restrictions? My children need to learn to *control* their feelings, not to let them out."

It is easy to see why teachers might worry about this. Those who lived through misinterpretations of progressive education, open classrooms, or "free schools" may be especially hesitant to endorse a renewed emphasis on emotions. However, adopting an emotion-centered curriculum in no way requires teachers to allow unbridled expressions of feeling. In fact, the previous two chapters should have made it clear that culturally and developmentally appropriate self-regulation of emotion, and learning to understand and respond to others' feelings, are important goals in young children's development. Children do not gain these abilities automatically. To achieve appropriate emotional control and emotional awareness, young children require many opportunities to observe adult models, a secure base of relationships with others, and loving guidance as they try out their emerging skills in many contexts. Like Natalie, other emotion-centered teachers let children know that their feelings are accepted. At the same time, these teachers continually guide children toward age-appropriate, culturally valued ways of expressing those feelings.

Fitting in Another "Curriculum"

"Our early childhood curriculum already has so many components—we have an ecology curriculum, a new math curriculum, and an anti-bias curriculum. When would I have time to teach a curriculum on emotions?"

This, too, is an understandable concern. Many teachers are required to implement special subject-area curricula. However, the description of Natalie's program should reassure teachers that the emotion-centered curriculum is not a burdensome addition to existing programs. Some affective education curricula center around teacher-planned units on feelings, or they schedule 20 minutes a day to address emotional issues in classroom meetings. The approach proposed in this book is different. Rather than creating a separate curriculum about emotions, a concern for emotional issues permeates and supports every aspect of the program. As we will see, an emotion-centered perspective can inform and enhance existing curricula in mathematics, social studies, literacy, and the arts. This perspective will assist the teacher in deciding whether existing curriculum guidelines are appropriate and effective. An emotion-centered perspective may also suggest ideas for modifying these guidelines to increase children's engagement in the curriculum content and to enhance their acquisition of important concepts and skills.

PROFESSIONAL GUIDELINES AND EMOTION-CENTERED PROGRAMS

An emotion-centered curriculum is very consistent with a number of recent developments in early childhood curriculum and teaching practices, including curriculum in several specific content areas.

Developmentally Appropriate Practices

The National Association for the Education of Young Children (NAEYC) guidelines for developmentally appropriate practices in programs for young children (Bredekamp, 1987) emphasize that adults should respond to children's interests and emotional needs in a warm, sensitive manner. In addition, the guidelines call for a teaching style that supports children's self-esteem and builds confidence, security, and positive feelings about learning. The NAEYC guidelines also emphasize the importance of attending to all areas of young children's development, including emotional development.

The recently published NAEYC volume *Reaching Potentials: Appropriate Curriculum and Assessment for Young Children* (Bredekamp & Rosegrant, 1992) extends NAEYC's earlier focus on developmentally appropriate practices to a more specific discussion of appropriate curriculum content for young children. A theme of this volume is that curriculum content must be *meaningful* in order to be both developmentally appropriate and educationally worthwhile. Inevitably, curriculum that is meaningful to young children is linked to emotionally significant people and events. When curriculum is meaningful, children set their own goals and feel the satisfaction of exploring problems and discovering solutions. Eleanor Duckworth's phrase (1987) "the having of wonderful ideas" captures the affective-cognitive integration of a meaningful, emotion-centered curriculum. Ideas are wonderful to children when they "have" the ideas through repeated learning cycles of *awareness, exploration, inquiry,* and *application* (Bredekamp & Rosegrant, 1992). Curiosity, focused attention, surprise, and joy accompany this learning process; children may also experience sadness, anger, and even fear as they tackle problems alone or with others. Encountering and coping with *all* of these feelings provides a rich context for early learning.

Emotions and the "Project Approach"

A number of recent publications recommend that the early childhood curriculum should be centered around projects or themes (e.g., Bredekamp & Rosegrant, 1992; Katz & Chard, 1989; Krogh, 1990). These writers stress that a thematically organized curriculum should be more than a superficial collection of topics plucked out of a resource book. Rather, project work is an intellectually challenging activity that allows children to gain insight into important concepts through personally constructed knowledge. Anyone who has done this kind of project work knows that children can become deeply engaged in investigations of many facets of their world. This emotional engagement sustains a remarkable level of attention and effort. Two persuasive examples are the year-long "penguin project" described in Ayers's book, *The Good*

Preschool Teacher (1989), and the descriptions of project work in the Italian preschools of Reggio Emilia (New, 1992). For this level of involvement to occur, teachers must invest the topic—whatever it is—with emotional significance, and they must be able to stimulate and sustain children's deep interest in the project or theme.

Whole Language and Emotional Development

The "whole language" and "emergent literacy" curricula that have recently appeared in such profusion (e.g., Clay, 1982; Kamii, Manning, & Manning, 1991; Strickland & Morrow, 1989) also rely on emotions, by linking reading and writing to personally meaningful, emotionally powerful experiences. Successful whole language programs encourage children to write about personally relevant matters. In these programs, children create their own books—encouraging pride and joy—and children read and are told stories that address emotionally significant matters.

Most of these programs are "literature-based" (Hancock & Hill, 1988). Good children's literature does more than tell stories. It engages children's laughter, astonishment, empathy, and every other emotion. Because of this, children who are "real readers" (and their adult counterparts) become emotionally attached to language and to books.

Whole language programs for young children also stress the warm interpersonal context of early literacy experiences. When children cuddle on soft pillows as they read with their friends or their teachers, or when caregivers hold toddlers as they look at and talk about books, children receive far more than physical comfort. The emotional power of these warm settings can strengthen children's disposition to use language and to love books and reading. Thus, the teacher using a whole language or "emergent literacy" curriculum in her classroom already has constructed a secure emotional foundation for learning. A more explicit focus on emotions should strengthen literacy learning, rather than detracting from it.

Math, Science, and Emotions

Similarly, several professional groups have published recommendations to improve mathematics and science curriculum (American Association for the Advancement of Science, 1989; National Council of Teachers of Mathematics, 1989). These recommendations strongly emphasize that math and science must be personally and socially meaningful to children. The title of one of the most popular early childhood math curriculum guides, *Mathematics Their Way* (Baratta-Lorton, 1976), reflects a belief that math will be understood and used by children when it builds on their enthusiasms, interests, and natural curiosity. Baratta-Lorton's book and other recent guides emphasize the use of familiar, personally relevant materials and situations, and they encourage children to experience the excitement of discovery and the emotional satisfaction of meeting self-selected challenges. Like emergent literacy proponents, recent curriculum developers in early childhood science and mathematics also recommend embedding mathematical and scientific learning within a social context. Children are encouraged to work in cooperative groups, sharing ideas and expertise. This social context also includes the family; in many math programs, children are encouraged to do "homework" that brings parents and children together to count, classify, or identify patterns in home and neighborhood events.

Emotions and the Anti-Bias Curriculum

Many early childhood educators have recently adopted a multicultural or "anti-bias" curriculum, most coherently presented through publications and workshops of the Anti-Bias Curriculum Task Force (Derman-Sparks & the A.B.C. Task Force, 1989). This group and others (e.g., Ramsey, 1987) urge early childhood educators to take an active role in countering discriminatory attitudes, including biases based on gender, ethnicity, religious affiliation, and disability. The anti-bias approach explicitly rejects the "tourist curriculum" of traditional approaches to multicultural education (a week in Japan, a Hanukkah party, and so on). Instead, the developers of the anti-bias curriculum favor an integrated approach that challenges young children's stereotypes and addresses issues of exclusion and inclusion in age-appropriate contexts. The anti-bias classroom is rich in environmental stimuli (analogous to the "print-rich environment" of the whole language classroom), including pictures, toys, art materials, and books that embody diversity. These informal approaches are combined with suggestions for more focused teacher-designed activities such as mini-skits with character dolls representing a variety of ethnicities, disabilities, and other individual differences.

This brief description should show that, as with other early childhood curricula described above, an anti-bias approach is fully compatible with an emotion-centered curriculum. Awareness of children's emotional responses to exclusion, bias, and difference helps early childhood practitioners to select appropriate classroom strategies, monitor their impact, and adapt curriculum to individual needs. The anti-bias curriculum advocates an affectively based approach to issues of fairness and equity, stressing empathy and emotional as well as intellectual identification.

Thus, anti-bias goals and an emotion-centered curriculum can be mutually supportive. When children read, play, and talk about bias-related issues, they have rich opportunities to experience, attend to, and express emotions. And children's feelings of curiosity, anger, and sadness can be used to consolidate their understanding of the anti-bias curriculum's content.

Many recent innovations in early childhood curriculum can be enhanced if they are integrated into an emotion-centered framework. Rather than taking time away from these subjects, the emotion-centered curriculum can unify and integrate them. Each of the new curriculum approaches that we have discussed has certain features in common: a strong foundation in personally relevant content, a belief that children's feelings and their learning are essentially *one,* and an emphasis on adult–child relationships as scaffolds of children's early learning and development.

REFOCUSING ON EMOTIONS

Because it fits so well with these widely adopted innovations, and because of its heritage in the core traditions of early childhood education, an emotion-centered curriculum should be neither strange nor threatening. For most early childhood professionals, building an emotion-centered curriculum will not mean starting from scratch. Rather, it will involve *refocusing,* to place greater, more thoughtful emphasis on emotions; to integrate emotional concerns more fully across the curriculum; and to thoughtfully consider emotion-related criteria in selecting curriculum goals, content, teaching strategies, and assessment practices.

The process of curriculum development is—or should be—highly individual. Every practitioner has different personal, emotional, and professional reasons for undertaking an emotional refocusing. Whatever the reasons for undertaking the refocusing process, it requires reflection upon, and decisions about, three topics.

Selecting Goals

This book will not provide a handy list of preselected goals. The refocusing practitioner needs to begin by reviewing the program's existing or proposed goals, asking three questions: Are the program's goals fundamentally compatible with an emotion-centered approach? Do these goals adequately support children's emotional development? Do those program goals that are "non-emotional" (such as goals in academic skill areas) provide room for emotions to be integrated with other goals?

A number of existing, widely respected goal statements are consistent with an emotion-focused approach. For example, the Head Start goals make specific reference to emotion-related areas such as "self-confidence, spontaneity, curiosity, and self-discipline . . . a climate of confidence . . . the enhancement of the sense of dignity and self-worth within the child and his family" (U.S. Department of Health, Education, and Welfare, 1973, p. 7). While NAEYC has refrained from prescribing a narrow set of goals, the sample list in NAEYC's *Reaching Potentials* volume also may be a good reference point, since it includes many emotionally relevant areas: for example, "responsible adults want children to develop a positive self-concept . . . develop curiosity about the world . . . develop relationships of mutual trust and respect" (Bredekamp & Rosegrant, 1992, p. 18). If an existing set of goals (either a comprehensive set for a whole early childhood program or goals for a specific content area) shows that emotions are not adequately represented, Saarni's (1990) description of the ingredients of "emotional competence" may offer additional assistance to the program planner. Figure 5.1 presents a summary of these ingredients, simplified and targeted to the early childhood years.

Re-examining Content and Teaching Practices

Refocusing on emotions also requires the practitioner to examine existing curriculum content and teaching practices to ensure that they contain rich opportunities for children to develop emotional competence and to link emotions to learning. The chapters to follow will provide many examples. This process will vary depending on the professional setting in which teachers work and the program's current state of curriculum development.

For example, perhaps a team of primary grade teachers is reviewing an already adopted math curriculum. Focusing on the content and recommended implementation strategies from an emotion-centered perspective, they might decide that children would benefit from sharing their work with their families as a way of building pride and confidence. Therefore, the teachers might decide to add a "family night" to a planned unit on measurement, and they might plan to build

Figure 5.1 Components of Emotional Competence

The "Emotionally Competent Person . . . "

1. Is aware of his or her own emotional state, including the possibility of experiencing multiple emotions, and at even more mature levels is aware that one also might not be consciously aware of one's own feelings.

2. Is able to discern others' emotions, based on culturally meaningful cues in the situation and in people's expressive behavior.

3. Is able to use the kind of language about emotions and emotion expressions that is commonly available in his or her culture or subculture.

4. Is capable of being empathically involved in others' emotional experiences.

5. Is able to realize that an inner emotional state is not necessarily matched by outer expression of feelings—either in oneself or in others.

6. Is aware of culturally accepted rules for the display of feeling.

7. Is able to take into account unique personal information about individuals and to apply that information when drawing conclusions about a person's emotional state.

8. Is able to understand that his or her way of expressing emotions may affect other people and to take this into account in choosing strategies for presenting oneself to others.

The "Emotionally Competent Person . . . "

9. Is capable of coping adaptively with unpleasant or distressing emotions by using strategies that alleviate the intensity or duration of such emotional states.

10. Is aware that close personal relationships are in part defined by emotional immediacy or genuineness and by equality of emotional sharing within the relationship, and that these may differ depending on the exact nature of the relationship.

11. Is capable of emotional self-efficacy: Emotionally competent people view themselves as feeling, overall, the way they would prefer to feel.

   Note. This list includes some competencies that require a high level of cognitive and inter-personal maturity. Nevertheless, these competencies are often present in earlier forms among young children and may form appropriate long-term goals for an emotion-focused program.

From "Emotional Competence" by C. Saarni in *Socioemotional Development* (Nebraska Symposium on Motivation, Vol. 36; pp. 117–118) by R. A. Thompson (Ed.) and R. A. Dienstbier (Series Ed.), 1990. Lincoln: University of Nebraska Press. Copyright 1990. Adapted by permission.

several activities around measuring objects at home, enlisting the help of family members. The team might also find that creating a cozy math corner with pillows, math-related books and puzzles, and other problem-solving materials could foster a sense of comfort and security and a more sociable environment than if children are seated at formica-topped tables. They might consider increasing the laughter quotient in the math program by posting a "math joke" or "math riddle of the day." The teaching team might also consider strategies to deal with the inevitable frustration some children may experience as they tackle the new math materials, with the goal both of maximizing children's success and of using the math curriculum to build children's capacity to deal with their own negative emotional states.

Using vignettes from a number of high quality early childhood programs, the chapters to follow will offer many more examples of how emotional refocusing can help teachers and children get the most out of the early childhood curriculum.

Analyzing Assessment Practices

For many reasons assessment practices in early childhood programs have been closely scrutinized in recent years (NAECS/SDE, 1987; NAEYC, 1988; National Commission on Testing and Public Policy, 1990; U.S. Congress, Office of Technology Assessment, 1992). Hills (1992) summarizes these concerns: In addition to their failure to validly document children's progress, current assessment practices have been accused of undermining children's self-confidence and creating negative feelings about learning.

However, assessment of children's progress need not have harmful emotional consequences. Recent recommendations and descriptions of innovative approaches to assessment (Genishi, 1992; Grace & Shores, 1991; Hills, 1992; Mitchell, 1992) appear well suited to an emotion-centered curriculum. In such a program, teachers need to be sure assessments are conducted in a positive emotional climate, minimizing children's fear, distress, and sadness. Collecting work samples, developing portfolios, and conferencing with children about their activities are all strategies that can support rather than undermine young children's emotional development and that can create a richly textured portrait of children's developmental progress. The results of assessment should lead to emotional as well as academic benefits for children, increasing children's feelings of pride, competence, and self-efficacy.

In addition to ensuring that all assessments take place in a supportive emotional climate, teachers also need to adopt specific strategies to assess the emotion-related aspects of children's progress. To do this, teachers must assess children's *feelings* about curriculum content and their *dispositions* related to learning (e.g., curiosity, initiative, and tolerance for frustration) as well as their mastery of skills and concepts.

Teachers in an emotion-centered program will implement procedures for assessing children's emotional competence, using knowledge about expectable developmental characteristics as well as information about individual children's culture, temperament, and family context. Unfortunately for the practitioner wishing a quick-and-easy emotional "check-up," no simple list is available for these tasks, and perhaps that is just as well. The emotion-focused teacher can look at a number of sources of criteria and even specific items to use in developing such an assessment. For example, the measures described in Chapter 9 (La-Freniere, Dumas, Capuano, & Dubeau, 1992; Lewis & Michalson, 1983) may be helpful, as well as the emotional competence domains outlined by Saarni (1990) and referred to earlier in this chapter.

CONCLUSION

Beginning with a description of Natalie's program for two-year-olds, this chapter has outlined the central features of an emotion-centered early childhood curriculum. It also addressed some concerns practitioners may have about this approach to early childhood education. Countering these concerns, I have emphasized that a focus on emotions can support every curriculum area and every area of development. The chapter has offered suggestions on how to begin the process of "emotional refocusing," suggesting careful attention to program goals, curriculum content, and assessment practices.

Now this broad overview needs more specific embodiment in practice. Therefore, the remaining six chapters in this book will present strategies needed to reach the goals of an emotion-focused program. These include (1) creating a secure emotional environment, (2) helping children to understand emotions, (3) modeling genuine, appropriate emotional responses, (4) supporting children's regulation of emotions, (5) recognizing and honoring children's expressive styles, and (6) uniting children's learning with positive emotions. Four of the early childhood practitioners who were introduced earlier—Hope, Terry, Christine, and Denise—will be featured in these chapters.

In Chapter 6, we will focus on what may be the most basic goal of an emotion-focused program: creating a secure emotional environment. We will begin by looking at how Hope approaches this task with her group of primary grade children.

Chapter 6

Creating a Secure Emotional Environment

The children in Hope's multi-age primary class are huddled in small groups, working intently at deciphering some printed "job application" forms. The class is preparing for an open house to be held that evening. Today they will make sandwiches and Jello treats in an assembly-line food factory and make signs advertising their café. Tonight, parents and other family members can buy snacks at the café.

Hope has created forms on which are listed various jobs and their requirements: "Sandwich maker: Must be clean, know how to use a plastic knife, know how to make sandwiches." "Label maker: Must have neat printing, be careful worker, like to write." Under each job, there is space for children to write their name, age, and qualifications for the job.

Earlier, Hope had assigned the children to small groups, mixing ages and reading skills. Before the children began the task,

Hope told them to think about the things they know how to do, and like to do, and see which jobs have requirements that fit their skills. Now each group has found a comfortable spot to meet. One group is in the book area, furnished with soft cushions and large stuffed animals. Another group settled in behind the easels, pulling chairs into a circle. They work together to read the job descriptions and to decide which jobs they would like to apply for.

"I can carry and add," Serena announces to her group, looking at the requirements for "Banker." "I make sandwiches real good at home," Xavier declares. Mario comes up to a visitor, holding out the form. "I can't read that word," he says matter-of-factly, pointing at *organized.* Having figured it out with help, he rejoins the group and tells them what it is.

Each group approaches the task in its own way. In some groups, one child is clearly in charge. Seven-year-old Eileen directs each child in her group to take turns reading. In another group, Serena reads to the rest of the children, holding up the application as she points to the words. While the children work, Hope walks around, reminding them to "think about what things you are good at," helping with hard words, and listening with interest to children's descriptions of their experiences in sandwich making, money handling, and writing.

"You have to be *very delicate* when you cut Jello Jigglers," Amanda patiently explains to one of the younger children. "If you mess up with the cutter, the Jello gets all smooshed. Do you think you can be very delicate?" Corey nods solemnly. "Then you could apply for that," Amanda pronounces.

The classroom community experienced by Hope's children embodies all the characteristics of a *secure emotional environment.* The emotion-centered teacher's first responsibility is to establish a setting that creates emotional security for young children. Without this foundation, an emotion-focused curriculum will be impossible to achieve. In this chapter, we will examine evidence that emotional security is the foundation of healthy personalities, and we will remind ourselves that social and economic disintegration is placing young children's feelings of security at ever increasing risk. I will point out some specific ways that early childhood teachers can build an environment of predictability, acceptance, and responsiveness. The chapter will recommend a variety of security-building affective communication processes, including smiles, gazes, touches, and words, while emphasizing the need for cultural, developmental, and individual sensitivity. Finally, we will reflect upon how transitions and new challenges may influence children's security needs as the year progresses and how emotion-centered teachers can meet those needs in flexible, appropriate ways.

EMOTIONAL SECURITY AND THE HEALTHY PERSONALITY

The Importance of Security

Feelings of security are the basic ingredients of a healthy personality. Many clinicians, researchers, and developmental theorists have attested to the importance of emotional security.

Erik Erikson (1950, 1959) described a sense of *trust* as the first accomplishment of infancy. Through repeated experiences, most babies learn that adults can generally be relied on to meet their needs and to provide love and admiration. If this healthy balance of "trust versus mistrust" is not achieved during the first year of life, later development will be difficult. However, Erikson also pointed out that issues of trust recur at each period of development. These later experiences (including those provided by high quality early childhood programs) can offer new opportunities to strengthen a child's sense of trust.

Mahler (Mahler, Pine, & Bergman, 1975) and Ainsworth (Ainsworth, Blehar, Waters, & Wall, 1978) both emphasize the importance of a "secure base" in early childhood. When children feel they can count on important, loved people to provide comfort, they have a strong foundation of confidence that allows them to explore their surroundings. This exploration may take many forms, including the first tentative steps of the toddler (who then staggers back to her caregiver's embrace), the three-year-old's friendship overtures with unfamiliar children, and the first grader's struggle with a new book.

Risks to Security

Early childhood classrooms have always included a certain number of children whose emotional security was fragile. However, in years past, early childhood teachers assumed that most children entered their care with a well-established sense of trust, emotional security, and psychological safety. For these children, the teacher's task seemed relatively simple. The teacher needed to help the child to extend her existing "secure base," transferring feelings of affection and trust from parents to other caregivers and, in time, to peers.

In the 1990s this task is no longer so simple—if it ever really was. Teachers routinely encounter young children whose early environments have given them little opportunity to develop feelings of security. Many children arrive at day care, Head Start, or kindergarten with a history of inconsistent, shifting care arrangements, which may have included multiple foster placements or rapid turnover of caregivers. Parents whose own early environments were insecure may have treated their children in unresponsive, neglectful, and even abusive ways. Seeing rage and violence at home or in their neighborhoods, children come to the early childhood program with no confidence that their world is safe, predictable, or helpful. Even children from stable families sometimes feel that they stand on emotionally shaky ground, because their parents may seem to value them only for their academic performances and their adherence to adult standards.

Many studies have shown that "insecurely attached" children are at risk for developmental problems as they grow up. When they are 2 years old, they may be less enthusiastic about tackling difficult tasks, becoming either clinging or angry when they are not successful (Matas, Arend, & Sroufe, 1978). During preschool, children with insecure attachment histories may show lower self-esteem. When observed in day care settings, these children are often extremely dependent or extremely disruptive (Sroufe & Fleeson, 1986). In a longitudinal study, friendship patterns of ten- and eleven-year-old children at summer camp could be predicted from their earlier attachment security, with securely attached children spending more time with other children and less time being ridiculed and excluded by others (Elicker, Englund, & Sroufe, 1992). These patterns may even continue into adulthood. Insecurely attached individuals may be more anxious and hostile in making the transition from home to college (Kobak & Sceery, 1988). At all ages, people whose early relationships have left them with insecure attachments seem to have a hard time finding a healthy balance of emotional self-regulation. Many either avoid negative emotions or express anger in uncontrolled, inappropriate ways.

For all these reasons, the task of creating a secure emotional environment within the early childhood program is more important than ever. It is also more difficult. The same children who lack a foundation of emotional security are often the targets of further criticism and harsh treatment in early childhood programs, because teachers and peers react negatively to their inappropriate behavior. This cycle further undermines their feelings of security and decreases their ability to benefit from intellectual and social opportunities. Yet emotionally positive relationships with teachers can go a long way toward compensating for insecure family environments, even those experienced by maltreated children (Pianta, 1992).

BUILDING SECURITY THROUGH PROGRAM ENVIRONMENTS

Young children have several basic needs that must be met if they are to develop or reconstruct a feeling of emotional security. First, they require an environment that is *predictable*. A predictable environment builds security by letting children know how people are likely to behave and how events are likely to unfold. Second, children will feel emotionally secure in an environment that is warmly *accepting* of who they are and what they think and feel. Third, children require an environment that is *responsive*. A responsive environment shows children that they matter, that their actions have consequences and can make a difference in what happens in their world.

An emotion-centered early childhood program deliberately sets out to meet these needs.

Predictability

Hope's multi-age classroom is much more flexible in its schedule and style than many other first- or second-grade programs in public schools. The foundation of *predictability* that Hope has built allows the children to function comfortably in this seemingly "unstructured" setting. Arriving on a Monday morning, a visitor would see the group deciding who will take responsibility for various classroom jobs, including "General Inspector," "Library Helper," "Table Washers," and "Writing Inspectors." Different children volunteer for these jobs each week, but the structure of this routine provides a secure base. For a program like Hope's, which includes a wide age range and is organized differently from what children experienced in other classrooms, well-defined routines are an especially important source of security.

Other routines may not last the whole year, as the "jobs" routine does, but they provide a shorter-term framework of security. For the past few weeks, Hope's class has been learning how to skip-count by fives. Every morning, Hope has led the class in the same practice exercise. She gives them a number to start with (e.g., 25) and the children silently count forward by fives as she beats slowly on a tambourine. When she stops, the children compare their ending points. Hope knows that many of the children have a hard time representing numbers this way. She helps children feel secure through a predictable daily counting routine that scaffolds success and minimizes failures.

Other aspects of Hope's program are predictable also. The routine of breaking into small groups to work together on a task, and then returning to the rug area to report on findings, is a recurring pattern. Although the content of these small-group collaborations may vary from one day to the next, the format is familiar and, therefore, security-enhancing.

"Whisper to your neighbor" is another familiar pattern in Hope's class. In group meetings, Hope often poses a problem or challenge to the group and asks the children to think of a solution and whisper it to their neighbor. Individual children then report what their partner said and alternatives are discussed. Again, the content of these discussions varies from day to day, but the children feel freer to tackle new challenges within a familiar framework of routines.

A predictable physical environment also provides emotional security to children. Good early childhood teachers know that children derive pleasure and comfort from knowing where things are and from having personal space for loved possessions. There are important reasons to have cubbies for children, to have a special shelf for in-progress art projects, or to have a "treasure basket" where personal items can be deposited until it is time to go home. These reasons go beyond classroom order and cleanliness. They speak powerfully to children, letting them know that this environment is one they can depend on.

Acceptance

Hope has also created a program permeated with *acceptance*. Part of the climate of acceptance comes simply from Hope's attitude. As she greets children and as she talks with them about their lives, her manner conveys sincere enjoyment. Children clearly feel that their ideas and personal stories will be appreciatively welcomed. "Mrs. Connor," Maria shyly injected during a group discussion about parents' night, "My aunt saw my picture in the post office" (a local newspaper had carried a story about Hope's class). "Was she excited to see it?" Hope responded, leaning forward with interest. Maria nodded vigorously, and the discussion turned back to jobs for the food factory.

Acceptance is also reflected in the early childhood program's physical environment. Hope's classroom, like that of other emotion-centered programs, celebrates children's out-of-school experiences. Photographs and drawings of the children's families, homes, and pets; stories about familiar events and people; familiar, culturally valued objects — all of these surround children with a comfortable blanket of security as they tackle the new challenges of child care, Head Start, or first grade.

In the accepting early childhood program, children's mistakes are treated matter-of-factly. Mistakes are not signs of inadequacy. "Did you find the mistake you made? Good!" Hope commented to Rachel. Because of this attitude, children readily admit their mistakes to Hope and to other children. "I lost count because of the door closing," Carlo admitted after the tambourine exercise. Later on, Nicholas stated, "I don't know what to do," pointing at the job application form. "I can help Nicholas, Mrs. Connor," said Eric, moving his chair closer to his friend.

Mistakes can also be fixed. Serena worked diligently to create a sign for the café. First she lettered SUPER GOOD FAST FOOD on a large sheet of paper, using large block letters. Then she began to paint the letters "in a pattern," as she said, with three different colors. She lost control of the brush and made a small green streak in the wrong place. "I messed up," she confessed to Hope. "You know what grown-ups do when they make a mistake?" Hope said. "They use white-out to fix it. I have some right here, and you can use it after the painting dries."

Hope's multi-age primary class includes typical variations in temperament and learning style, together with an unusually wide range of ages and skill levels. As the earlier examples show, Hope's program is organized so that these variations become strengths, not problems. While conveying confidence that children will develop additional competencies over time and with practice, Hope also helps children feel accepted right now, with the skills they have. The weekly job lists and projects like the food factory show children that many skills and interests are needed for big jobs to get done. "Serena, you know a lot about that. You will be a very important person in the food factory. When we have a problem with making the signs, we can go to Serena."

Responsiveness

Hope's program illustrates the value of *responsiveness* in establishing emotional security. A visitor to Hope's classroom has no doubt that children feel they can have an effect on their environment. The walls of the room are covered with signs and pictures that the children have made; the shelves contain class-made books. Many decisions in the café project have been made by the children, including what to sell, where to post signs, and what the signs should say.

After the morning's work, Hope gathered the group on the rug again. "I'd like to talk about our food factory experience," she explained. "We've never had a food factory before. How did you feel about it? Did you feel a sense of accomplishment?" (It is hard to convey the sincere tone of these questions, which differs in important ways from the artificial whipping up of enthusiasm that typifies some early childhood programs.)

Heads nodded and children beamed as they looked at the cartons of sticky baggies filled with peanut butter and fluff sandwiches, crackers, and Jello Jigglers, each labeled with the name of the snack and the price. "Did it seem like you were working in a factory?" asked Hope. "I think I should be *paid* for something like that!" Molly vehemently declared. This opinion led to an extended discussion of how the children might "pay" themselves, with ideas ranging from eating all the food to giving everyone some money afterward.

BUILDING SECURITY THROUGH AFFECTIVE COMMUNICATION

Early childhood teachers can help build a climate of emotional security with their faces, bodies, and voices. Smiles, warm gazes, physical closeness, affectionate touches, and supportive words all help children feel comfortable and accepted. However, to be most effective these avenues of communication must fit children's developmental, personal, and cultural characteristics.

Smiling and Gazing

Adults' facial expressions contribute to emotional security. Children feel emotionally secure when their teacher smiles warmly at them. There is a big difference, however, between smiles that are impersonally and even falsely distributed and the personal, private smile that says to a child, "I see you and you are important to me."

When a teacher looks directly into a child's eyes, this usually conveys the message that the adult is deeply interested in the child's thoughts and feelings. Nevertheless, cultural standards differ concerning eye contact between adults and children. Some children, especially those from Asian, African-American, or Native American cultures, may have been brought up to regard mutual gazing as disrespectful and inappropriate in certain contexts. Emotion-centered teachers need to be sensitive to these cultural norms, because children will feel *less* secure if teachers violate the customs of family and community.

Although the specific style of interaction may vary by culture, very young children respond best to immediate, contingent facial reactions.

Parents naturally engage in playful turn-taking interactions with infants, reacting to the babies' expressions, sounds, and actions with immediate, spontaneous expression changes. When adults do not respond in this "contingent" kind of way, many infants are visibly disturbed: They may become physically agitated, fuss, cry, and eventually turn away helplessly.

Proximity

Simply sitting close to a child can also build security. Natalie, the teacher in Chapter 5, is constantly surrounded by children. The twos have a direct physical need for her as their secure base in a way that Hope's older children do not. Natalie's twos are continually "refueling" at her side, spending most of their time in close proximity to her, and then moving off for brief forays to other parts of the room. Natalie often positions herself near an activity that she wants the children to try, knowing that the two-year-olds will be more likely to explore a new art material, for example, if they can do so in their teacher's comforting presence. Looking at the older children in Hope's class, one still sees evidence of this emotional "refueling" process as children touch base with their teacher to show her their work or whisper a confidence.

Affectionate Touch

Smiling, looking, and sitting nearby are not enough. At every age, children gain emotional security from affectionate touch. The need for contact comfort is so fundamental that even baby monkeys have rejected milk artificially dispensed by a "surrogate mother" made of stiff wire in order to cling to a surrogate mother that dispenses no milk but is wrapped in soft cloth (Harlow, 1958).

The need for touch is most apparent in caring for the very young. Guidelines for sensitive, developmentally appropriate infant-toddler caregiving emphasize the importance of gentle handling, carrying, and stroking (Bredekamp, 1987; Caring for our children, 1992). Besides its physical benefits, the caregiver's gentle touch conveys admiration of the child's body and creates affectionate bonds between caregiver and child (Honig, 1981).

Culture may also determine children's expectations about being held and cuddled. In many Korean and Chinese families, children are "babied" beyond the age that many Anglo-European teachers would feel is appropriate. Toddlers and even older, preschool children from Asian cultures have generally come to expect that adults will respond to their distress by immediately picking them up, holding them, and carrying them around for long periods. Although teachers need not adopt every practice of the child's culture in order for the child to develop emotional security, the emotion-centered teacher will work closely with families to become aware of these differences, modifying interactions to provide the child with a predictable, culturally safe environment (Lynch & Hansen, 1992).

What is sometimes forgotten is that, in any culture, the need for affectionate touch does not stop with infancy. However, the climate of concern over sexual abuse accusations has dampened adults' willingness to offer children security through physical affection. Some teachers (espeically male teachers) fear that their hug or affectionate back rub may be misinterpreted by supervisors, parents, or even children (Hyson, Whitehead, & Prudhoe, 1988). There is no easy answer to this dilemma. However, the emotion-centered teacher recognizes touch as a foundation of young children's emotional security and will attempt, through open discussion with parents and staff, to ensure that these fundamental needs are met in appropriate ways.

Differences in Preferences for Hugs. Not every child desires an equal dose of physical affection. Some children seem to be less "huggy" than others, even as newborns. They prefer to be held upright, viewing their surroundings, rather than being snuggled close to their caregiver's body. As they get older, these children may pull away when hugged or touched affectionately. The sensitive teacher respects these individual differences and finds other ways to build emotional security with the noncuddlers.

A few children may have had frightening experiences that color their responses to physical contact in the early childhood program. Physically abused children may shrink from any touch, fearing that it is a sign of danger, not affection. Sexually abused children may place erotic interpretations on adult touch, creating complex problems that require professional consultation (Cicchetti & Carlson, 1989).

Some periods of development may bring wide fluctuations in children's need for affectionate touch. Mahler (Mahler, Pine, & Bergman, 1975) describes how, within just a few minutes, the newly walking toddler may oscillate between two extremes: clinging to the caregiver and angrily pushing the caregiver away, wanting to "do it myself!"

Affection and Older Children: Making Adjustments. Despite these fluctuations, most preschool children welcome physical affection. Some experienced preschool teachers find it difficult to make the transition to teaching older children, because primary grade children may actively reject hugs from grown-ups. These teachers may run the risk of overwhelming children with unwanted displays of affection, reminding children of their dependency on adults—a dependency that many of them are actively trying to move away from. Sometimes teachers deal with children's rejection of their affectionate touches by abandoning all physical contact. Teachers who are experienced with older children find that the children do need and want physical affection, but they may prefer it with—literally—a light touch. Hope does not overwhelm her children with physical affection. Instead, she will touch a child in passing, give a casual rub on the head, a quick squeeze around the shoulders, or a hand on a seven-year-old's back as he struggles with a writing task. These contacts may meet the older child's need for physical nurturance without arousing his fears of sliding into a dependent, babyish relationship with adults.

The Contribution of Words

"Do you know how to spell FAST FOOD? Then I think you're the woman for this job." Words can build emotional security, and Lauren's happy grin when Hope expressed confidence in her skills showed that she treasured her teacher's words.

Words are important at all ages. Children blossom when adults talk to them. Even before they can carry on a conversation, infants and toddlers revel in the sound of parents' or beloved caregivers' voices. Natalie, a teacher of two-year-olds, keeps up a running commentary on the children's activities. Her warm, reassuring, interested tone of voice conveys security; with these very young children, the words may be less important than the sound.

In using words to build security, the emotion-centered teacher again needs to be aware of cultural variations. Not every culture emphasizes intensive, face-to-face conversations with infants and toddlers. For example, Heath (1983) described rural African-American communities in which toddlers spend a great deal of time observing adults talking with each other about family and community events. The adults do not seem to consider that their conversation should be directed at the children, and yet the children's language skills—and their sense of emotional security—are strong.

With older children, teachers can use words to recognize children's accomplishments. Young readers welcome little notes from their teacher ("Hi, Rachel! I am glad you are back with us today"). Words can help children feel more secure when they have to wait for something ("I just have to finish up this job, and then I will sit and look at your book with you, Andrew.")

Security grows when teachers' words help children to link past and present experiences: "Remember when Jason brought the snake to school, Tad? That was like when you brought your guinea pig, wasn't it?" or "I remember that long walk we took up the hill in the snow. I wonder what the hill looks like now that the snow is all gone?" or "Here is a new book that just came in the mail. It's sort of like the one we read last week, about the very hungry caterpillar. Let's take a look at it." These and other simple strategies build children's confidence that their secure foundation of past experiences will serve them well as they explore new activities and materials.

SECURITY THROUGHOUT THE YEAR: CRITICAL TIMES AND CHANGING NEEDS

Children's emotional security needs may change at different points in the year in response to transitions and developmental challenges. The emotion-centered teacher is aware of these ups and downs and ensures that children's needs are appropriately met.

Entering a New Program

A critical point in children's emotional security is, of course, the beginning of the year, or whenever the child enters the early childhood program. At any age (including adulthood), entry into a new setting brings uncertainty, anxiety, and a search for familiarity and stability. Depending on children's ages and previous experiences, they may cope with this transition through tears, tantrums, withdrawn or "babyish" behavior, quiet observation, frantic activity, and other strategies of varying effectiveness.

This is a time at which familiarity is especially helpful in building emotional security. Experienced teachers employ a number of techniques to help children feel secure in their new setting (Griffin, 1982; Hendrick, 1992). Some visit the child at home; others ask each child to bring a family picture to school. When possible, many teachers have each child visit the program when other children are not present, to explore materials and check out the environment. Most high quality programs encourage parents—usually the original "secure base"—to stay with their child for a time. Early in the year, teachers try to be prompt and explicit in orienting children to the new setting and meeting children's basic needs. "Here is a tissue for you, Robert," Natalie says warmly. "Now your nose will feel better." "Let's look at our chart to see what we will be doing right after lunch," says primary grade teacher Hope, helping new children visualize the predictable sequence of the day.

In the first weeks, new children feel more secure with familiar activities that guarantee success. For example, kindergarten teacher Christine usually puts out play dough and simple construction materials early in the year, and she sets up the dramatic play area with basic household props. Books are selected to represent themes of family and home, with pictures reflecting the children's cultures and household compositions.

Emotion-centered teachers plan beginning-of-the-year activities to allow insecure children to watch from a distance or to participate in a low-key way. Edward preferred to sit in his cubby during music time for the first month, watching intently but never participating—until the day when his kindergarten teacher got stuck on a verse of "Over in the Meadow" and Edward confidently filled in the missing words. In another class, three-year-old Megan refused to participate in any indoor activities for the first few weeks, sitting forlornly near the door despite the staff's efforts. Only when she was outside on her favorite red tricycle (which, incidentally, was just like her trike at home) did she appear secure. The teacher moved some indoor equipment outside, and Megan triked over to the easel, where she painted picture after picture perched safely on her three-wheeled secure base.

Most children are more confident in a new setting if they are encouraged to bring special objects from home. For very young children, security blankets or beloved stuffed animals build bridges over the emotional gap between home and the child care setting. New children often will clutch the familiar object all day, but as time goes on they may need it only when they are sleepy or distressed.

Some teachers wonder if allowing children to have these attachment objects makes them more insecure and dependent. Research indicates that that is not the case. Furthermore, home observations of toddlers and preschoolers have shown that children typically do not spend all their spare time clutching their security blankets. Rather, they use their loved objects during brief "refueling stops" before setting them aside to take on new challenges (Gay & Hyson, 1976). Thus, blankets, bears, and bunnies give many young children an even firmer "secure base" to support exploration and learning in a new environment.

Older children rely less on concrete representations of security. However, they gain pride and confidence from sharing pictures and objects from home, especially at the beginning of the year. Some teachers have a special display table for children's prized objects; others create a bulletin board collage of photographs. One teacher creates a class book every fall, with a page for each child; another has each of her kindergartners create a "book about me," with drawings and dictated descriptions of family, favorite foods and activities, and so on. The laminated books become part of the class library and can be borrowed overnight.

Finally, emotion-centered teachers provide beginning-of-year security by establishing and maintaining clear limits for children's behavior. Just as children feel better in a new situation when they know where the bathroom is and what happens after juice time, they also need to know what behavior is expected and what is not allowed. They need to know that teachers will protect them and other children from their own actions and will help them to figure out how to deal with arguments and fights. Despite the security that these limits provide, young children also need to be sure that teachers will not reject or abandon them if they violate classroom rules.

Losing a Special Caregiver

Typically, children's emotional security develops strong roots after the first weeks in a new program. However, children's security may be shaken when teachers leave during the year. With turnover averaging 40% annually, staff changes have become a common occurrence in many child care centers (Whitebook, Howes, & Phillips, 1989). Children develop close relationships with early childhood teachers, relationships that can be very similar to the kinds of attachments that children develop with their parents (Howes & Hamilton, 1992). Infants and toddlers in full-time child care often develop an especially close attachment to one caregiver. If that caregiver leaves, sadness and distress may result.

Does this mean that such close attachments should be discouraged? Not at all. Close, loving relationships with parents and teachers allow children to explore, learn, and develop social and academic competence. Nevertheless, the loss of a special caregiver is distressing and temporarily disruptive for a child. If the departure can be anticipated, it is important to talk with the child about the separation. Many people are reluctant to do this, knowing that children will be upset. Some teachers may think it's better to just disappear. This is never a good idea, as it undermines children's confidence that adults are trustworthy people. Instead, children can talk about the change, channel their feelings into creating mementos or planning a party for the teacher who is leaving, and begin to develop new relationships. Overlap between caregivers is advisable to provide continuity and to allow children to begin to see the new caregiver as a dependable source of support and comfort.

Working on Difficult Skills

As the year goes on, difficult new activities may shake children's emotional security. Brazelton (1992) emphasizes that children often experience a period of emotional disorganization when working on a new developmental achievement, even if the task has been self-initiated rather than required by adults. This disequilibrium requires a large dose of adult support. Even emotionally secure children may worry about failure or (especially if they are a bit older) looking "dumb" in their friends' eyes. But children do not need to be protected from every possible failure. A certain amount of challenge and even frustration helps children feel secure about their own ability to cope with difficulties. In a program that emphasizes child choice and cooperative learning, children feel more secure in trying new things. Like Hope's primary graders, children can help one another, learning that some people are great at cutting out Jello shapes while others are good at printing, spreading peanut butter, or counting play money.

Emotion-centered teachers are also aware that the intensity with which young children work on new skills often results in frustration, exhaustion, and stress for children and for their adult caregivers. Teachers need to respect the child's drive toward mastery while also ensuring a healthy balance between intense bursts of work on new skills and relaxed times to settle into old, familiar activities.

CONCLUSION

Hope and other emotion-centered teachers begin the job of building an emotion-centered program by establishing a foundation of emotional security. This chapter has shown how important this task is, whether the goal is to strengthen and consolidate children's early, positive experiences or to compensate for insecure or even abusive family relationships. Although the physical environment and program organization contribute to emotional security, the teacher is the most crucial component of the secure environment.

It is not easy to be a child in an early childhood program. Imagine experiencing it for the first time. You come into a strange building full of other children and adults who are strangers, full of enticing toys that are not your own. Mysterious rituals are to be followed, for washing hands, for lining up, for waiting for turns at circle time. There are many things to learn about—but in order to learn you have to wade in and try things. Learning is hard work and it involves taking risks. You have to pick up the guinea pig in order to find out what he looks like underneath. You have to make marks on the paper in order to print your name. You have to walk over to the blocks and start building in order to get some classmates to play with you. You have to pick up the red and green cubes if you want to try to make a pattern. All along the way, there are risks—risks of being laughed at, of being wrong, of being ignored or rejected. Yet this desire for mastery is what leads to social and intellectual competence. It is almost impossible for children to have the courage to start on this journey without a foundation of emotional security.

In Chapter 7 we will examine another strategy for implementing an emotion-centered curriculum. Focusing on Terry, a family child care provider, we will see how a skilled practitioner can help children understand their own and others' feelings.

Chapter 7

Helping Children to Understand Emotions

"Oh, Mister Impatient!" Terry says with an affectionate laugh to baby Warren, who is wriggling and fussing in his infant seat on the kitchen counter. "Your breakfast is coming right up. Take a chill pill, sweetie." The toddlers in Terry's family child care home are finishing their toast and banana slices. Three of Terry's children are triplets. One of them, Barry, has had continuing respiratory problems related to the triplets' premature birth and must use an inhaler twice a day. "I know, Barry," says Terry calmly when Barry twists away from the mask. "It'll just take a couple of minutes and then we'll be all done for now." The other children look on from their high chairs as Barry breathes in the mist.

Music comes from the sunny family room, where Terry's sister-in-law, who helps with the children, has turned on the tape player. Doreen and Nina, the "big girls" at ages 3 and 4, are danc-ing on the carpet, twirling and grinning at each other. "Are you ready?" Terry asks the younger children as several of them pro-test and reach out to her from their seats in the kitchen. "Want to sing and dance now? Get down?" She sets each toddler on the floor with a hug and a friendly smile, and carries the youngest into the family room.

Nina solemnly shows Terry a "booboo" on her knee, the scab barely visible. She tells Terry and her friend Doreen how she was riding her bike at her grandma's and "I fell off my bike. It was bleeding and I cried and cried." Several other children join in showing their scrapes and bruises as Terry listens and inspects the damage. Kisses and several colorful bandaids are applied.

Brenda, another of the triplets, has been having a hard time getting involved this morning. Sadly she wanders from group to group. "Brenda, what is it?" asks Terry. "Do you want your woober [Brenda's name for her blanket]?" Brenda nods. "How's that, Brenda?" asks Terry, giving Brenda her blanket and settling her into the big armchair. "Maybe you got up too early. Let's see if you feel better in a little bit." Thumb in her mouth, Brenda con-tentedly watches the others from the chair.

Rachel has been walking for just 2 weeks. She staggers around the room, intent on her new independence. She moves toward a long chain of large beads that hangs from the ceiling. Three-year-old Doreen has been playing with the beads, sliding them up and down. Rachel squeals and grabs at the chain, yank-ing it away from Doreen and starting to cry as Doreen holds on grimly. Terry gently detaches Rachel's fingers from the chain. "Rachel says, 'I wanted that,'" Terry explains to Doreen as she hands Rachel another toy. "Maybe you can let her play with it in a few minutes."

In her family child care home, Terry provides many ingredients of a high quality early childhood environment. Indoors and outdoors, the environment is child-centered, colorful, and inviting. Riding toys, puzzles, dramatic play props, a rabbit and guinea pigs, bird feeders, soft cushions, a playhouse in the yard—every feature of Terry's home reflects her understanding of young children's interests and needs. Each child, from five-month-old Warren to four-year-old Nina, is treated with personal, respectful, delighted attention. Ethnic and cultural diversity is welcomed, with Asian, African-American, and Anglo-European families represented among those served in Terry's rural program. Terry's husband, teenage children, and sister-in-law provide a warm extended family for the children in her care. Within this setting, Terry places an especially high priority on fostering children's understanding of their own feelings and the feelings of others.

Terry's priorities are consistent with much developmental research. Typically, children do become better at understanding emotions as they get older, but this does not happen automatically. And at any age, some children are more emotionally attuned than others.

Understanding emotions has many benefits. Children who understand how others may be feeling are more likely to behave sympathetically, to help those in distress, and to share resources with others (Eisenberg, 1992). Furthermore, children who have a better understanding of emotions are more socially competent. As Cassidy, Parke, Butkovsky, and Braungart (1992) noted, "emotions are central to social interaction . . . and it is easy to conceive that understanding of emotion-related experiences, of the meaning of emotions, of the causes of emotions, and of the responses appropriate to others' emotions would both influence and be influenced by social relations with peers" (p. 614). Indeed, as children get older, failure to understand their own feelings and those of others is seen as an indication of serious developmental problems. Abused children, for example, are notably poor at identifying emotions accurately. Children with autism can certainly feel and express emotion, but they have extremely limited ability to understand why other people feel the way they do (Harris, 1989). Successful adaptation requires that children develop competence in emotional understanding.

This chapter will begin by listing the basic elements of emotional understanding. We will see that developmental, individual, and sociocultural obstacles may stand in the way of children's achievement of this understanding. The chapter will present examples of how early childhood professionals set the stage for understanding emotions through an emphasis on conceptual development and on emotionally rich adult-child and peer interactions. We will then examine care-givers' use of specific strategies to encourage children's insights into their own and others' feelings. Despite this emphasis on active adult involvement, the chapter will end with some cautions about excessive, intrusive, and inappropriate labeling of children's emotions, emphasizing sensitive individual responses to young children's growing understanding of self and others.

"BASICS" OF EMOTIONAL UNDERSTANDING

What do children need to understand about emotions? Saarni's (1990) discussion of the ingredients of emotional competence, summarized in Chapter 5, includes many abilities related to emotional understanding. The concepts that Terry's children and other young children are developing in early childhood probably include the following "basics":

1. *Everyone has emotions.* I feel happy this morning. So does Brandon, and so does Barry. Terry, my caregiver, has feelings, too. She is excited and surprised sometimes, and sometimes she is serious or unhappy.
2. *Emotions arise because of different situations.* Lots of things make me happy: my toast on my high chair tray, a hug from Terry, the click of beads on the chain when I tug it. When someone takes my toy, or when I fall off my bike, or when I just get tired after lunch, I get angry or sad.
3. *Emotions can be used to communicate how I feel and how others feel.* I know that Terry is happy when she laughs and smiles and hugs me. If I hang my head and stick my lip out, I show how bad I feel. When baby Warren fusses, I know he is upset about something.
4. *There are different ways of showing feelings.* Warren fusses a lot when he doesn't have something he really wants, like his bottle. Doreen just comes right over and grabs things. Nina tries to talk me into giving her my toys or gives something in trade. And sometimes I whine and pout.
5. *Other people may not feel the same way I do about everything.* When I am tired, I want my woober, but Barry just sucks his thumb when he's tired. I like to ride around the patio on my trike very, very slowly, but Nina wants to go fast and get ahead of me.
6. *I can do things to change how I feel and how others feel.* When I'm sad, I can go sit in Terry's lap or in the big chair and after a while I feel

better. Sometimes when baby Warren is fussing, I make funny faces at him and he starts to laugh.

OBSTACLES TO UNDERSTANDING ABOUT FEELINGS

Important as these basic concepts are, children do not arrive at emotional understanding quickly or automatically. As seen in earlier chapters, developmental limitations, family and community environments, and cultural differences may create obstacles along the way. Infants and very young children, although attuned to others' expressions of emotion, have only limited ability to infer the reasons for others' happiness, sadness, or anger. And even somewhat older children have a hard time drawing conclusions about the causes of emotion when the situation is unfamiliar, or when the other person's feelings are different from those the child would have. Similarly, young children may have trouble understanding the cause–effect connections between an event and an emotional response, and they have particular difficulty understanding complex emotional experiences or mixed emotions (Harris, 1989).

Family experiences, too, may make emotional understanding more difficult to acquire. Differences in family expressiveness (Cassidy, Parke, Butkovsky, & Braungart, 1992; Halberstadt, 1991) influence children's ability to understand various emotional situations. Generally, more expressive families provide richer opportunities to develop emotion understanding. However, there are clearly limits to the benefits of expressiveness. Conflict-ridden families and violent communities offer many emotionally intense experiences, but these environments leave young children frightened, confused, and frequently unable to process emotion signals in accurate, adaptive ways (Camras, Grow, & Ribordy, 1983).

Finally, cultural contexts may sometimes get in the way of children's development of emotional understanding. Emotional "display rules" and emotion expressions that are easy for children to understand in the familiar culture of home and community may be puzzling in a culturally different child care or school setting.

This list of obstacles to emotional understanding should not lead early childhood professionals to sit back and await the results of maturation or to throw up their hands in despair. Rather, the emotion-centered teacher will develop a rich array of strategies to help children of every age, family history, and cultural environment to move toward better understanding of their own and others' feelings.

SETTING THE STAGE

Before turning to specific strategies, we might examine how early childhood professionals can "set the stage" for learning about emotions. Much positive learning about emotions occurs without direct adult instruction. Terry supports children's emotional understanding by establishing an environment that enhances concept development, by allowing children opportunities to experience, observe, and express feelings during "unprogrammed" peer play, and by being attuned to teachable moments throughout the day.

Supporting General Concept Development

Although emotions have their own unique features, in many ways the understanding of emotions parallels and is a product of children's understanding of many other concepts, such as time, space, number, and causality (Carey & Gelman, 1991). Conceptual development *is* different in different domains of knowledge, but it is supported by similar factors. Thus, by creating a climate that broadly enhances cognitive or conceptual development, early childhood professionals will simultaneously enhance children's understanding of concepts of emotion.

As happens in Terry's family child care home, children gain conceptual understanding when their learning is embedded in many real-world exemplars of a particular concept. Many psychologists believe that young children use these exemplars to construct models or prototypes of particular concepts, including concepts about emotions (Gordon, 1989; Shaver, Schwartz, Kirson, & O'Conner, 1987). A child's mental representation of "sad," for example, comes to include not just the vocabulary term but associated causes, frequently observed sad situations, and behaviors commonly observed by the child. Thus, the more children are able to observe peers and adults expressing emotions in a variety of ways—and having those emotions responded to in a variety of ways—the better able children may be to construct emotion concepts. We also know that cognitive development is supported when children see others using thinking skills effectively, and when children get many opportunities to practice their emerging skills in a social context with concrete materials and personally relevant situations (Bredekamp & Rosegrant, 1992; Seifert, 1993). Programs like Terry's ensure that these opportunities are available to children.

Allowing Emotion-Rich Peer Interactions

Children cannot understand emotions unless they have had many opportunities to experience, observe, and express them. Terry sets the stage for learning about feelings by allowing the children to interact with one another in spontaneous, unhurried blocks of time. Children are not hustled from one preplanned activity to the next, nor does Terry's homelike playroom even contain formally designated "learning centers." Rather, for much of the day children invent interesting things to do with the many appropriate materials available in the house and yard. Terry supports these activities but knows when to step back and let the children play and learn together.

Close friendships have developed among Terry's children. Spending all day together 5 days a week, this small group has become extremely cohesive. In contrast to some large classes in which children may select a clique of close friends and ignore or reject others, in family child care there are few friendship options. Spending so much time together, children develop an intimacy much like that seen in sibling relationships. These peer relationships are important in developing an understanding of emotions. Children express more of both positive and negative emotions when they are with friends than when they are with nonfriends—friendship seems to open the door to displays of all sorts of feelings (Hartup, Laursen, Stewart, & Eastenson, 1988). And these kinds of emotion-laden interactions, although often wearing on caregivers, provide young children with essential raw materials for the development of concepts about emotions.

Terry's program also incorporates personalized, unhurried routines that contain colorful emotional exchanges among children. Meals, naps, and toileting bring out children's joy, anger, disgust, surprise, pride, and virtually every other emotion. Because Terry's children are at such different developmental points, and because of their ethnic diversity, the affective style of their responses differs in always interesting ways. Terry vividly described the other children's fascination with the triplets' toilet training adventures. Children spontaneously imitate one another's facial and vocal expressions of emotion; waiting for Terry to dish up their spaghetti lunch, one child playfully called out "Mommy!" and immediately every child in the kitchen mock-plaintively chorused "Mommy, mommy, mommy, mommy!" as Terry laughed and distributed their plates. At breakfast every day, Barry's protests and eventual acceptance of his inhaler treatments—as well as Terry's calm handling of the procedure—are closely observed by the group.

Identifying Prime Times for Understanding Feelings

Besides laying the groundwork for learning about emotions through general cognitive development, Terry is also on the alert for certain "prime times" when she can heighten children's emotional understanding. Her affectionate one-on-one interactions offer an especially rich context. Whether cuddling, talking intimately, or sharing focused interest in a toy, a bird at the feeder, or a scraped knee, at these moments children seem especially receptive to learning about emotions. Conflict situations offer equally promising avenues for the children to learn about feelings. With infants, toddlers, and preschool children who know one another almost like siblings, Terry's group has inevitable clashes over possessions, turn-taking, and status. Terry knows that these situations can help her to foster insight into the causes and consequences of emotion expression. Terry's awareness of the possibilities embedded in these and other day-to-day events allows her to build a sound foundation for the development of emotional understanding.

STRATEGIES TO ENCOURAGE EMOTIONAL UNDERSTANDING

But setting the stage is not enough. In her family child care home, Terry uses many strategies to enhance her children's understanding of their own and others' feelings. Like other emotion-centered teachers, she relies more on informal, on-the-fly techniques than on formal "lessons" about emotions.

Emphasizing Activities That Support Understanding

In a corner of Terry's playroom, a cozy area has soft carpeting, doll beds, blankets, baby dolls, and toy telephones. Doreen and Nina have lifted several dolls out of a doll bed and are huddled in the corner with their "babies." Doreen holds some band-aids that Terry had dispensed earlier, when the children were showing her their scrapes and cuts. Doreen and Nina solemnly examine their babies for "booboos." "She gots one right here," Doreen says, showing Nina a spot on her doll's leg. "Kiss it,"

Nina recommends. "Oh, no!" exclaims Doreen dramatically. "My baby's hurt! She's hurt bad!" "Get the phone!" says Nina. Dropping the babies, they race to get the play telephone. "Mommy, mommy, help! Help!" shrieks Doreen into the mouthpiece. "Come help the baby!" Terry, smiling, moves closer. "Do you need a mommy to help?"

Dunn and Brown's research (1991) indicates that pretend play is critically important for learning about emotions. Their home observations of toddlers showed that pretend play situations were among the most frequent occasions for children to use emotion language and to act out emotionally vivid scenes. Terry actively encourages similar opportunities by providing materials, support, and well-timed collaboration. Doreen and Nina's doll play includes moments of tenderness, pride, intense fear, and joy. No soap opera can match the high drama of a typical scene of spontaneous pretend play. The feelings that are enacted and re-enacted provide rich material for emotional understanding.

For this to happen, though, adults need to balance the benefits of support against the risks of overinvolvement and overstructuring. Some early childhood professionals are so eager for children to "learn" from dramatic play that they impose a high degree of adult structure on play content and interactions. Their programs may channel all pretend play into preplanned themes that tie in with curriculum units and specific academic goals: "Today, boys and girls, the dramatic play area is set up as an art museum. You can pay admission, look at paintings, and give me a tour. . . ." These efforts often result in play that, while pleasing to adults and easy to "manage," is emotionally flat, allowing few opportunities for children to express, experience, and construct a genuine understanding of the rich tapestry of human emotion. In contrast, emotional understanding is especially enhanced by the kind of free-form personalized fantasies woven by Terry's children, who have been given time, space, and raw materials with which to pretend, and whose affective liveliness is respected and gently guided by responsive adults. (It is also heartening to see how children will subvert adult-dominated play to their own ends; "robbers" invariably show up to steal the art exhibit's paintings, or a frisky "dog" disrupts a dull, teacher-planned museum tour.)

In addition to pretend play, many other activities and materials in the emotion-centered program will support the development of emotion understanding. Well-chosen books, songs, and videotapes can help children understand their own feelings and those of other people. Creative arts activities allow children to portray emotions in a variety of media and to compare their portrayals with those of other children. For older children, writing offers yet another tool to explore the meaning of emotion-related experiences. Later chapters will elaborate on teachers' use of these activities not only to assist in understanding emotion, but also to extend children's repertoire for expressing and regulating their feelings.

This chapter deliberately de-emphasizes the use of formal activities and lessons to help children understand emotions. For the early childhood professional who needs suggestions, numerous resources are available. Books about feelings—either those explicitly "about" certain feelings or those portraying relevant, emotionally rich situations—can be valuable additions to the early childhood program. Games about emotions, such as matching faces to pictured situations, can also be interesting for children and are readily available.

However, there is a risk in relying on these kinds of strategies to build children's understanding of emotions. Developmental research has shown that concepts are constructed out of many interrelated experiences, not in a one-shot lesson. Having closets full of emotion-related books and activities at their disposal, some teachers may neglect the developmentally more important learning that can be embedded in spontaneous play, daily interactions, and routines. Worse yet, they may offer children contradictory messages about emotions. It is not unusual to observe a program that boasts of its "affective education" component (a scripted group lesson twice a week, with puppets demonstrating warmth and consideration) and spends the rest of the time ignoring emotions or humiliating children for showing their feelings. With these cautions in mind, though, teacher-planned activities can be an appropriate part of a more comprehensive approach to enhancing emotional understanding.

Mirroring Children's Emotion Expressions

> Terry sits on a low armchair holding baby Warren. He gazes intently into her face and begins to smile. Looking down,
> Terry smiles back, raising her brows in spontaneous imitation of Warren's expression and tipping her head back and forth.
> Warren squeals in pleasure and smiles even more broadly.

Emotions develop within a social context. Expressions like Warren's smile are indeed universal and innate, but Warren's understanding of his own and others' feelings depends on having those emotions reflected, imitated, and amplified. As laboratory observations show (Malatesta et al., 1989), most parents intuitively copy many of their infants' emotion expressions, shifting from interest to joy to surprise to distress as their babies' faces display each of these feelings. Malatesta and others have argued that these face-to-face "imitation games" have clear developmental benefits. Through them, children are exposed to many thousands of examples of a wide variety of emotion expressions that reflect and implicitly comment on children's own feelings. At the same time, Warren and other babies are beginning to learn that their emotions can influence other people (Dunn, Brown, & Beardsall, 1991) and can communicate a "feeling state" that others share, too.

Responding to Children's Feelings

> Brenda has been kneeling on the patio looking into the guinea pigs' cage, an expression of interest and longing on her face. Terry comes over and unlatches the cage. She lifts one of the guinea pigs out and places it on Brenda's lap. Brenda shrinks back a little as the guinea pig wiggles around. Terry smiles re-assuringly and keeps one hand on Brenda's leg while touching the guinea pig with her other hand. "Oooh," says Brenda, giggling nervously. "Silky's scratching me." "Here," responds Terry, "Let's give Silky some nice touches." Terry strokes the guinea pig gently as Brenda watches. Tentatively, Brenda extends her hand and pats Silky on the back. As Terry and Brenda look at Silky, Doreen walks by them several times, alone amidst the children riding trikes on the patio. Terry looks up. "Are you lost, little girl?" she asks warmly. "Come sit by us for a while."

Emotions can be powerful avenues for communication. Terry is sensitively attuned to her children's emotional states. Out on the patio, she noticed Brenda's interest in the guinea pigs and followed up on it by taking Silky out of his cage. When Brenda shrank back and appeared fearful, Terry acted calmly and reassuringly. And Doreen's nonverbal expressions of sadness and aimlessness were also noted and responded to with an invitation for Doreen to join Terry and Brenda. "Contingent responses" like these are valuable both to the children directly involved in these interactions and to other children who may observe Terry's words and actions.

These kinds of interactions help children realize that their emotions can have consequences. Children find out that other people understand something about their inner states if they show their feelings in verbal or nonverbal ways. If they are fortunate enough to have a sensitive parent or caregiver like Terry, children also learn that adult responses can be relied on to help them feel better when they are sad, to share their joy when they are happy, or to place supportive limits around them when they lose control.

Labeling Children's Emotions

> Warren has been sitting in his bouncing chair for some time now, watching the older children drawing with chalk on the cement patio. He begins to whimper and then to wail, twisting
> his body as if to get out of the chair. "Well, well," says Terry to Warren. "Is he mad? Do you want to draw too, buddy?" She lifts him out of the chair and hugs him. "Are you happy now that you got up here?"

Young children have a wide range of feelings but do not come equipped with language to talk about these feelings. Terry often provides emotion labels to describe what the children in her group may be feeling. The terms "mad," "happy," and "sad" are frequently heard, along with other affective language like "wants to," "likes it," and "what's the matter?" Besides validating children's emotion expressions, Terry's simple words and phrases begin to provide children with emotion categories that enhance their understanding of their own and others' feelings.

These emotion labels also introduce children to the ways in which their particular culture, or that of the caregiver, categorizes emotion states. Terry's labels of "happy" and "mad" are typical of Western definitions. Some African languages use the same label for anger and sorrow; one Alaskan Inuit group has separate labels for fear of physical harm (*iqhi*) and fear of being treated unkindly (*ilira*) (Russell, 1989).

Talking About Causes of Feelings

> Terry's children are in the playroom cleaning up before lunch. Rachel stoops down and stands up again quickly, whining and pouting. "Rachel, what is it?" Terry asks with concern. "Did you hit your head under the table?" As the children finish cleaning up, Terry wipes their faces, saying to several protesters, "I know, I know; no one likes to have their faces washed." As Terry walks past him, Warren again begins to fuss, holding out his arms. "Did you think I was going to pick you up, Warren?" Terry asks.

"I will in just a minute." Nina tries to help Abel button his pants, but four-year-old Abel pushes her hands away angrily, as Nina looks pleadingly at Terry. "Nina, he doesn't want you to do that," explains Terry. "He wants to do it himself today."

With these and other comments, Terry frequently and informally talks with her children about the causes for their feelings. As we have seen, emotion-related conversations help young children understand their own emotions and those of others. These kinds of conversations go beyond simply providing labels for feelings; rather, Terry and other emotion-focused early childhood professionals talk about *why* children may feel the way they do. Through many such experiences, children begin to understand that different emotions may have different causes, and that different people may feel angry or happy for different reasons. Such conversations, embedded in daily routines, highlight these concepts for children and lead to better abilities to take the perspective of others (Dunn, Brown, & Beardsall, 1991).

OVERLABELING: SOME CAUTIONS

In encouraging early childhood professionals to mirror, label, and interpret feelings for children, we need to emphasize that this approach can be—and often is—carried to extremes. There is a big difference between Terry's informal, lighthearted approach and a heavy-handed overinvolvement in children's every emotional nuance. Although adults' "contingent responding" to changes in children's emotion expressions generally shows sensitivity and warmth, Malatesta (Malatesta et al., 1989) has found that some mothers have inappropriately high levels of contingency. Their inclination to react to the child's *every* emotion expression actually predicted less secure parent-child attachment; and, as these children got older, they showed less and less enjoyment during interactions with their mothers.

Many early childhood educators agree that "some teachers spend too much time talking with children about their feelings" (Hyson & Lee, 1992). Like nonverbal contingent responses to children's emotions, feeling-talk is essential if children are to develop an understanding of emotion, but it can also become intrusive and inappropriate. Several guidelines may help in this delicate balancing act.

Concepts of "developmental appropriateness" (Bredekamp, 1987) can be very helpful in deciding when and how to use the strategies outlined above. At different ages, children may benefit from different approaches to emotion understanding. Mirroring or copying children's nonverbal emotion expressions is especially appropriate and important in face-to-face exchanges with infants. Providing emotion labels is probably most important when children are just developing language skills. And interpreting the underlying reasons for others' emotional reactions becomes increasingly important as children develop friendships and broader social interests, from age 2 onward. But as children move toward the school-age years, they often resent adults telling them what they are feeling inside, or coming up with pat explanations for their unhappiness or worries. Just as they are developing a greater desire for privacy in their personal habits and friendships, they may seek emotional privacy as well. Sensitive adults allow children this privacy while remaining attuned to their needs.

Beyond these age-related considerations, children's individual characteristics must also be taken into account. Children whose family life has provided few opportunities to learn about emotions may need more frequent and more explicit labeling and interpretation of feelings and more focused, formal interventions to increase emotional understanding. And early childhood professionals whose groups include children with disabilities often find that extra effort is needed to help everyone to understand the many ways that people express emotions.

CONCLUSION

In this chapter we have seen that early childhood professionals can take advantage of countless ways to develop emotional understanding in children. By laying a foundation of emotionally vivid interactions, and by mirroring, labeling, and conversing about feelings, teachers enhance children's ability to comprehend their own emotional responses and those of others. In turn, this ability fosters children's social competence, empathy, and perspective-taking ability.

But understanding emotions is not enough. Terry and others who work with young children also want children to *behave* in ways that are emotionally genuine, direct, and appropriate within a particular setting and cultural context. In Chapter 8, we will turn to kindergarten teacher Christine's active use of *modeling* as a powerful strategy in emotion socialization.

Chapter 8

Modeling Genuine, Appropriate Emotional Responses

The kindergarten children were sitting in a circle on the rug. Christine, their teacher, had just finished explaining that they would be doing the "weekend news" a different way today (every Monday morning the class has been dictating news of their weekend doings, as a language development activity). Today, Christine explained, the children would pair up and tell their weekend news to each other. After they finished, they would return to the circle, where each person would then tell the partner's news to the rest of the group. Christine finished her explanation and paused for effect. "Kids, look at me. *This is hard*," she said emphatically, with a serious tone of voice and a sad facial expression. "You might forget your partner's news, or you might leave something out. That's okay, because you've never done this before." Her tone and facial expression began to brighten at this point, and she looked intently at each child in the group. "But we'll be doing this today, and next week, and the week after that. And you know what?" Christine asked, still brighter and more confident sounding, and continuing to look at each child in the group. "You'll get better and better at remembering, because you'll be getting so much practice!" She ended with a firm nod and a wide grin.

Practitioners who adopt an emotion-centered curriculum have clear developmental goals. Among other things, the emotion-centered teacher wants children to associate positive emotions with problem solving and effortful intellectual activities, to begin to control their emotion expressions when they might be hurtful to others, and to use language to talk about their own and others' emotions. This chapter will focus on an especially potent strategy in helping children reach these goals: the teacher's *modeling* of genuine, appropriate emotional responses.

Children learn from observing other people. Bandura (1977a) and other social learning theorists have described this process in detail. They note that children are capable of remembering and reproducing even complex behaviors after watching others' actions. Their research indicates that modeling can occur even when the model is not aware of being observed, and when the child is not explicitly rewarded for noticing and remembering the model's behavior. Bandura has argued that modeling is one of the most powerful mechanisms of social learning.

Parents are the child's first models and remain the most significant influences for the majority of children. However, early childhood teachers are also important models. In child care programs children may spend as much as 10 hours a day in their caregivers' company. As children get older they increasingly look for models beyond the family. Teachers, coaches, club leaders, adult friends, TV characters—all may be observed and imitated. The child's repertoire of behavior, personality characteristics, and values become colored by the behavior, characteristics, and values modeled by a significant adult.

In this chapter, we will describe how adults model emotions for children, and how these encounters influence children's emotional development. Then we will see how these processes are actually used in early childhood programs. We will examine effective strategies that practitioners can use to increase the likelihood that children will imitate desired patterns of emotion expression. Finally, we will consider some of the complexities and difficulties in adults' decisions about when and how to present children with models for imitation.

MODELING EMOTIONS

Adults As "Emotion Models"

In the example at the beginning of this chapter, Christine was doing much more than simply describing a new variation on a language development activity. As Christine previewed the activity during group time, her face, voice, and language presented children with a mixture of emotions. Through emotions, Christine showed that she thought of the "partner news" as a serious, difficult task, that difficult tasks require effort, and that they may initially cause some frustration. When she talked about the possibility that children might forget their partners' information, her tone and language acknowledged the reality of disappointment and failure. But she also described with interest and joy the gradual improvement she expected to see and implicitly allied herself with the children in working toward that long-term goal.

In many ways, Christine was serving as an "emotion model" for her kindergarten children. Her actions during the group time were typical of what adults frequently, yet often unconsciously, do in the course of children's development. Parents, teachers, and others provide children with models of how to express emotions, when to express emotions, how emotions are managed or regulated, how emotions are labeled, and how emotions can be interpreted and understood (Lewis & Michalson, 1982).

Fortunately, children are predisposed to tune in to adults' expressions of emotion, watching their faces and listening carefully to their tone of voice. Children are especially likely to look to adults for "emotional information" in new, uncertain situations, a process that has been called "social referencing" (Klinnert, Campos, Sorce, Emde, & Svejda, 1983).

Effects of Adult Emotion Modeling

Children's observation of adults' emotion-related behavior influences many aspects of their behavior and development. Even in early infancy, children imitate adults' expressions of emotion. When facial expressions of mothers and infants are videotaped and coded, it is easy to see how mothers' emotions influence their babies. Changes in infants' emotion expressions usually follow closely after changes in their mothers' expressions, and they are usually (but not always) close matches (Malatesta & Haviland, 1982). It almost seems as if the babies watch for changes in their mothers' expressions and are primed to respond with their own expression changes. Among the participants in Malatesta and Haviland's study, certain mother–infant pairs had very similar expressive styles. A mother who frequently raised her eyebrows was likely to have a baby who did the same thing, and a mother who smiled a great deal often had a smiley child. Over several months, babies' expressive styles tended to become even more like their mothers'.

Researchers have also found that adult modeling of emotion expressions communicates messages about new and possibly risky situations. For example, when a stranger approaches, infants typically turn and look at mother—if mother smiles and looks friendly, the baby is much more likely to behave in a friendly way herself. Similarly, when a crawling infant gets near an area that might be hazardous, the child will search the mother's face, apparently looking for information about her emotional response. If mother appears positive and encouraging, the infant will be more likely to attempt to crawl across the space; if mother's face shows a frown or a worried look, the infant is likely to hesitate, turn back, or begin to fuss (Klinnert et al., 1983).

Older children's observation of adults continues to provide important information about emotions and about how to cope with emotion-laden situations. For example, children who observe many instances of adults modeling empathy, generosity, and frustration tolerance are more likely to develop these qualities themselves (Maccoby, 1980).

EMOTION MODELING IN EARLY CHILDHOOD PROGRAMS

Because emotions are present in every aspect of life, and because emotions are important motivators of human behavior, virtually every adult expression, comment, and action provides a potential emotion model for the young child. Early childhood educators should not be content to leave this process entirely to chance. Competent, thoughtful professionals consciously decide what emotions and emotion-related behavior to model. They identify opportunities for emotion modeling in the daily program, and they take steps to increase the effectiveness of modeling on children's development and behavior.

Selecting Emotion-Related Targets for Modeling

Deciding which specific emotions or emotion-related behaviors to model is, to some extent, a question of values and personal philosophy. It depends on the developmental level of the children in a particular class and on the teacher's knowledge of their earlier experiences, strengths, and needs. The examples below reflect Christine's priorities, her individual personality, and the characteristics of the children in her class, and the list is far from exhaustive.

Joy and Pleasure in Personal Relationships. Christine considers it important for children to find pleasure in working and playing with others. She finds many opportunities to model this in her own relationships with children and adults in the classroom.

> Christine was seated at a table, engrossed in conversation with the father of one of the kindergarten children. A child who had been out of school for the past week came into the room. Immediately Christine interrupted her chat and exclaimed in a delighted tone, "*Here* she is! Hi, Patricia, I *missed* you!" which she accompanied by a hug and a pat on the back. "If you stay away this long, you get to do the calendar when you come back."

Interest and Curiosity. According to Izard (1991) and others, interest is a fundamental human emotion that motivates exploration and learning. One of the most important things teachers can do for young children is to serve as a model of interest and fascination in finding out more about the world.

> As a way of assigning partners for "weekend news," Christine had given each child one half of a picture to match with another child's half. After the children found their partners by matching puzzle pieces, they were asked to come up in pairs and show the pictures to Christine. As each pair came up, Christine sincerely displayed curiosity about who got paired with whom and about their completed puzzle. "Who's your partner, Tim? Ricardo's your

partner. Hi, Ricardo; you're Tim's partner for the news, huh? What did you and Ricardo get? Oh, a camel! Isn't that great?"

Listening to this exchange repeated for each of 10 pairs of children, one was impressed by the real curiosity and warmth behind Christine's comments. Her interest demonstrated to the children that working with new people and solving puzzles together were activities worthy of emotional involvement.

Tolerance for Frustration. As a kindergarten teacher, Christine knows her children are beginning to encounter learning tasks that they will find both challenging and frustrating. As Katz (1977) has emphasized, not all learning is fun, and not all learning is easy. Feelings of disappointment, annoyance, and even anger may interfere with the acquisition of important academic skills. Christine tries to help children cope with these feelings by letting them observe her own emotional responses to frustration and failure.

Early one morning Christine was putting up a bulletin board. As she tried to staple a sheet of paper, the stapler kept jamming. Almost talking to herself, she muttered, "I am *so* annoyed with this stapler. It is *not* working right. I really want to get this bulletin board finished, and I can't if this stapler is broken." As Christine opened the stapler, she said, "Let me see, now. Ah-ha! There's a staple stuck in it. Let me see if I can poke it out. Yes!! *Now* maybe I can get this bulletin board up."

To the few children who happened to be watching, this informal running commentary (done in Christine's typical, slightly exaggerated style, with much gesturing) showed that even grown-ups encounter frustrating situations. Christine also demonstrated that frustration and anger can be expressed in words. And finally, Christine modeled a constructive response that was motivated by her feelings of frustration: She worked hard to fix the annoying stapler.

Pride in Hard Work. As seen in this example and in the anecdote at the beginning of this chapter, Christine deliberately points out to children that learning is hard at times. She emphasizes, however, that accomplishing difficult tasks makes you feel great, and that the harder the task, the greater the feelings of pride, joy, and satisfaction when the task is finally completed.

Christine described to the class an art project they could do, in which they could make "stained glass windows" with colored tissue paper and starch. She seriously and carefully described the process that would have to be followed by the children who chose this activity. It involved a number of steps (selecting colors, cutting the tissue, placing it between sheets of black paper, letting the starch dry) spread out over several days. Christine then turned to the windows in the classroom, pointed to them, and said with great feeling, "Then, when the stained glass windows are all done, I'm going to climb up on a stepladder and hang every one of them right there. The sun will shine right through the colors in the tissue paper. Every one will be different, and they will look *so beautiful*."

Finding Opportunities for Emotion Modeling

Once teachers have selected priorities for emotion modeling, they need to let children observe these target emotions and behaviors. Emotion modeling should permeate all aspects of classroom life. Too often, though, deliberate emotion modeling occurs only in response to children's misbehavior, or during formal periods devoted to "affective education," using a canned script and lesson plans unrelated to other aspects of the program. In an emotion-centered program, teacher modeling of genuine, appropriate emotion expression is deliberately integrated into every kind of activity and every kind of adult–child interaction. Some modeling may take place as the teacher goes about her own routine activities. It may also happen in one-to-one or small group interactions with children, by simply adding an emotion modeling component to activities the children have chosen. Finally, teachers can deliberately model emotion responses in activities specifically planned or adapted for that purpose.

Teachers' Routine Activities. First, teachers may look at their own daily activities as opportunities for informal emotion modeling. Like Christine with the recalcitrant stapler, all early childhood teachers are constantly engaged in routine "housekeeping" tasks that call forth varied emotions and emotion-related behavior: finding materials, cleaning up spills, dealing with visitors, losing a form to be sent to the principal's office, setting up a learning center. Teachers also share their emotional responses to events in their out-of-school lives: their own children's successes, vacation planning, car trouble. Children watch, remember, and learn from their teachers' emotional reactions in these day-to-day contexts.

Joint Activity with Children. In a developmentally appropriate early childhood program, teachers are often involved in children's activities. As they sit at a table or on the floor together, teacher and child may focus their attention on a set of blocks, a puzzle, a lump of clay, or a tray of collage materials. Teachers can take advantage of these times of "shared focus" (Trevarthen, 1984) to model a variety of desirable emotional responses. Working collaboratively or in parallel with the child, the teacher can let the child see her handle the materials and link her activity to her feelings. With facial expressions, words, and actions, teachers are able to demonstrate interested engagement in challenging tasks, surprise at unexpected outcomes, and pleasure at success. Children are especially susceptible to this kind of modeling when they are in new, uncertain situations. In deciding how to feel, they rely heavily on their teacher's emotional response to the new challenge they are facing together.

Responses to Children's Behavior. The observant early childhood teacher finds that children's spontaneous behavior provides an open door for emotion-related modeling. One brief example will illustrate the possibilities.

> Christine was on the playground. She saw a group of boys building with some large wooden crates. They had made a high, teetering structure, higher than was allowed by the rules of the class. Christine walked over to the group. With widened eyes she commented on the high building they had made and said that it looked like they had worked really hard on it. Then her facial expression changed from surprise and pride to sadness. In a sincerely regretful tone of voice, Christine told them that the building had to be taken down. Looking carefully at each child, and with a slightly fearful expression, she explained, "This is so high. I'm worried that it could fall and hurt you guys."

In this example, Christine demonstrated how emotions may be connected with specific events or situations (pride at their skill in building; sadness when she had to request the structure's demolition; fear at the thought of injury to the children). Her facial expressions, voice, and language modeled concern and empathy at the same time that she matter-of-factly enforced a standing rule of the school. The impact of this emotion modeling was evident when one boy who was talking with Christine unconsciously echoed her facial expressions as he listened to her explanation.

Teacher-Planned Opportunities. In addition to all of these informal settings for emotion modeling, teachers may create more formal, planned opportunities to model emotion-related behavior.

Christine, for example, often uses skits in her class. Sometimes the children produce their own skits, but she also uses skits acted by herself and her student teachers for a variety of purposes. Sometimes the skits are intended to introduce the children to a new activity or to highlight a class problem that will be discussed at a later group time. One morning, she and her student teacher acted out the roles of a customer and a cleaning company employee, to demonstrate the procedures the children were to use when they later played "spring cleaning." Besides going over the rules for use of the equipment and showing how the children might write down orders and record payments, Christine and the student teacher modeled great interest in and enjoyment of the challenging tasks of taking orders and systematically cleaning the classroom.

Similarly, teachers have used puppets and dolls to demonstrate emotion-related behavior. Although the teacher is not actually the model in these kinds of activities, she controls the "script" and the sets the conditions for modeling to take place. Especially when dealing with emotions that may be difficult for the teacher to express directly, or that may not occur frequently in the classroom, these tools are very helpful. For example, puppets may model the expression of emotions at the loss of a friend. Puppets may cry, express sadness and anxiety verbally, and comfort each other. Dolls could model ways of coping with fear after a violent incident or could be used to demonstrate empathic responses to others' distress.

Increasing the Characteristics of Effective Emotion Models

Christine is a very effective model. A visitor to her class is struck by how much children want to be like Christine, even in small behaviors. One sees children unconsciously copying Christine's mannerisms and some of her typically exuberant outbursts ("Get outta *town!*" is one of her favorites, often used in mock incredulity when a child tells her about some particularly exciting accomplishment). But beyond this superficial imitation, children are also reproducing Christine's attitudes toward work, her ways of using materials, and her ways of acting toward others.

Not all teachers are as successful as Christine in having children notice, remember, and reproduce their emotion-related modeling. Christine has developed many characteristics that have been associated with effective modeling (Bandura, 1977a).

Nurturance. Christine is highly nurturant, and social learning research emphasizes that children model themselves on nurturant adults.

> The children were taking attendance one morning. Sean had just come back from a 3-day absence. "Sean, what was wrong with you?" Christine asked in a concerned tone of voice, leaning forward from her low chair in the circle. "I missed you." "Sean wasn't sick!" one of the other children called out. "I know it, because he was at Amber's birthday party." "Well, you weren't here anyway, were you, Sean?" Christine continued. "You were out of school Wednesday, Thursday, and Friday. I really missed you."

As discussed in Chapter 6, there are many ways to be nurturant. Christine is not a quietly serene teacher who exudes calm acceptance and gentle warmth. Christine's style of nurturance is more exuberant and direct. She is affectionate with children, but her affection is expressed in a "buddy" pattern rather than in a more maternal style. Christine is a dominant physical presence in the room. She spontaneously finds opportunities to touch, nudge, drape an arm around, and share a laugh with the children in her kindergarten class. This nurturant quality "primes the pump" for children to attend to and respond to an adult model's behavior.

Power. Christine is powerful. It is obvious to the children that she is in charge of the classroom, and that she holds the key to resources they desire and value.

> Just before free-choice time, Christine was describing how the children could use various kinds of equipment to clean up the room (the class was exploring a project theme of "spring cleaning" that week). She gave them explicit guidelines for how to take things off the shelves, how to wash and dry the shelves, and how to replace the materials where they found them. "If I notice that things are getting messier and not cleaner, I'll have to say, 'Sorry, kids, you can't use the cleaning equipment.'"

Another time, Christine had been telling a small group of children about a new game in the math area. In a confident tone, she told the children, "This game is harder than the other ones — but you are such smart kindergarten children. I'm the teacher, and I'm supposed to keep making things harder for you, so you'll keep learning new things. That's my job."

Although Christine uses her power sparingly (having an "open" classroom with much free choice and very few rules), the children are very aware of it. Christine is an enormously important figure to the children, and as a result children pay attention to everything she says and does.

Similarity. Similarity is another factor that influences whether children imitate models. The more similarities the child perceives between him- or herself and the model, the more likely it is that the child will respond to the model.

As Martina hung up her jacket, she told Christine that she had gone to the ballet over the weekend. "Oh, great!" Christine exclaimed with enormous delight and enthusiasm. "I wish I could have gone with you. I love the ballet." The other children snickered. "No, I really do," Christine insisted. "But it was *little* kids' ballet," Martina explained. "I love little kids' ballet, too," Christine responded.

As the children took their places in the circle after exchanging weekend news with their partners, Bruce leaned over and said to Christine, "I think it's nice to sit next to your partner." "It *is* nice," answered Christine, rubbing Bruce's head. "I like it, too, Bruce."

Christine's personality and her interactions with the children serve to highlight similarities. She knows and shares many of the children's interests, and she makes a point of noting the things they have in common. Although children are more apt to model themselves on adults of the same gender, Christine is able to overcome this. She has a style of interaction that seems appealing both to girls and boys. She genuinely enjoys a bit of rough and tumble play on the playground, she likes sports, and she sometimes adopts a joking, almost teasing style of conversation that strikes an especially responsive chord with some of the kindergarten boys.

Enhancing Children's Imitation of Adult Emotion Models

Even if children perceive that an adult is nurturant, powerful, and similar to them in some ways, they may not model themselves on the adult. By attending to several critical factors, early childhood professionals can further raise the likelihood that children will imitate desired patterns of emotion.

Child Focus. In order for modeling to take place, children must focus on the model's behavior. Children do spontaneously attend to adults who have warm, powerful qualities. However, adults can further increase the chances of imitation if they deliberately focus the child's attention on the behaviors to be modeled. Christine does this frequently and naturally. She will often preface a statement with, "Children, watch me" or "Listen to this," and then will wait until she has the children's attention. As in the example at the beginning of the chapter, her deliberate pauses, voice inflections, and eye contact all emphasize the attitudes and behaviors she wants the children to observe and follow. Attention is enhanced when adults not only express emotions nonverbally, but simultaneously talk about their feelings and the situation that caused the feelings to come about.

Developmental Appropriateness. No matter how potent adults are as models, they cannot expect children to model behavior or attitudes that are beyond their developmental capacities. In Christine's kindergarten classroom, she is constantly stretching children's skills but is also sensitive to their limitations. Verbally and in her nonverbal behavior, she acknowledges that the children may not be able to do something the way she demonstrated the first time or that they may make mistakes. As these examples have shown, one of the things Christine models is how to deal with mistakes and frustration.

Praise and Attention. Finally, praise and attention are helpful in encouraging children to reproduce adult behavior. Researchers have found that children usually remember adult behavior even when they are not rewarded for remembering. However, rewards increase the likelihood that children will actually copy the behavior. For example, after Christine and her student teacher had demonstrated the "spring cleaning" procedures, many of the children chose that activity during free-choice time. Christine made sure to comment specifically and warmly on the careful way in which children followed the procedures she had modeled.

COMPLEXITIES AND DIFFICULTIES IN EMOTION MODELING

In some ways, the preceding suggestions sound simple. This may be deceptive. Actually, the desire to provide young children with models of emotional expression raises a number of complex, difficult issues for early childhood professionals.

"Genuineness"

The ability to experience and express honest, genuine emotion is usually considered a mark of the mentally healthy person. In order for children to develop this ability, it is important for their adult caregivers to model honest, genuine expression of emotion. However, when teachers try to apply the principle of genuineness in early education settings, they discover many complexities.

In order to be emotionally genuine, do teachers have to express their feelings exactly the same way with children as with adults? Watching Christine, one sees that she tends to be more exaggerated in her style of emotion expression when she is talking to the children than when she turns to talk to a student teacher or a parent. This phenomenon of exaggeration and "peaking" of expressive behavior is typical of how adults spontaneously talk with and communicate with young children (Malatesta & Haviland, 1982). Most adults do this without even thinking about it. This does not mean the feelings are false; rather, adults seem to highlight certain aspects of their emotional communication with children, in the same way that "baby talk" spontaneously simplifies the structure of language and directs the infant's attention to important features.

But although adults typically exaggerate their emotional responses somewhat with young children, it is important that these responses not be falsified or distorted. Honest expression of adult emotion is often hard to come by in institutional settings. As Hochschild argued in *The Managed Heart* (1983), the so-called service professions sell emotion as a product. Customers in restaurants, in stores, or on airplanes are, in a sense, paying for the concern of their waiter, check-out clerk, or flight attendant. These emotions may have little relationship to the "true feelings" of the service worker. In relationships on a plane or in a restaurant, this lack of genuine emotion might be necessary and adaptive.

However, these brief, superficial relationships are very different from the more intimate and developmentally significant relationships that should exist between caregivers and children in early childhood settings. Yet here, too, many adults assume a bland, affectively neutral persona (Katz, 1977) or exhibit emotions that are unrelated to children's real needs. Suransky's book, *The Erosion of Childhood* (1982), reports her observations of a number of child care classrooms over a 2-year period. Teachers frequently responded to children in emotionally false ways. Suransky cites one example in which a child deliberately and provocatively turned over a basket containing hundreds of beads. The teacher's response was to say, rather sadly and regretfully, that the child had had an accident. According to Suransky, both teacher and child knew perfectly well that it was no accident. The child was apparently trying to elicit some kind of genuine, personal emotional response from the teacher, but instead her behavior was met with a reaction that was almost bizarrely unrelated to her intentions and actions.

"Appropriateness"

Conflict sometimes exists between the teacher's desire to model *genuine* emotion and her desire to model the *appropriate* expression of emotion. At times, being appropriate means hiding or disguising one's true feelings. One of the most difficult tasks of teaching in an emotion-centered program is to balance emotional honesty with emotional appropriateness.

In the "weekend news" activity, Christine had decided to assign children to partners by having them match halves of puzzles she had made. Christine anticipated that some children might not be eager to do the activity with their assigned partner, and she humorously used this possibility to model appropriate responses. "What if I don't get the partner I want?" she said to the class in mock exasperation. "What if I don't get my best friend? What if I get *Patty* [the hapless student teacher] instead?" Christine wrinkled her face in an exaggerated expression of disgust. "Do I say, 'Eeeooww, not *Patty*! I don't want *Patty* for my partner!'?" Patty and the children giggled. "No," Christine continued, "I'm not going to say that, because Patty is my classmate, and I don't want to hurt my classmate's feelings. So I match my puzzle piece to Patty's"—here Christine demonstrated with a smile and an arm draped over Patty's shoulder—"and we tell our weekend news to each other."

In this example, Christine's modeling emphasized appropriateness over emotional genuineness. However, her modeling acknowledged that children might dislike their assigned partner, and she implicitly validated their right to their own feelings. Christine did not preach an emotionally dishonest message that "we all love one another in this class." Instead, her humorously modeled demonstration emphasized the hurtful consequences of expressing dislike for another child and stressed children's solidarity with their "classmates" (a term Christine uses frequently throughout the year). This group solidarity includes avoiding actions that will deliberately hurt classmates' feelings.

This example shows one way that one teacher dealt with the genuineness/appropriateness dilemma, in one situation. Influenced by a number of factors, including the age of the children, educational philosophy, personal style, and even the time of year, other early childhood professionals might choose a different balance between modeling genuineness and modeling appropriateness.

Anger Modeling

Managing anger constructively is an important developmental task for young children. One of the ways children accomplish this task is by observing how adults express and talk about anger. Outside of the early childhood program, many children are exposed to inappropriate models for anger expression. Some may have parents who often express anger by shouting, throwing objects, and hitting. Alcohol and drug abuse may further increase the violence of anger expression in these families. Others may have parents who never show anger themselves (or who unpredictably blow up after repressing their anger for long periods of time) and who disapprove of or may actively punish any expression of anger by their children. Through modeling, early childhood teachers can provide important, constructive alternatives to these extremes.

However, modeling the expression of anger is a complex, difficult task. Although conscientious teachers avoid deliberately frightening children with excessive displays of anger, it is not easy to maintain a balance between allowing children to experience a model of honest anger and overwhelming them with inappropriate, poorly controlled emotion.

Some early childhood teachers assiduously avoid any show of anger, believing that it is inappropriate and potentially harmful in early childhood programs. Others are more relaxed about expressing anger and feel that a certain amount of "letting loose" tends to clear the air (Hyson & Lee, 1992).

Whatever their beliefs, all adults who work with young children

become genuinely angry at times. In order to model anger constructively, teachers need to prevent excessive, inappropriate outbursts of
anger. Identifying situations that may trigger excessive anger is a helpful first step. Some teachers recognize that whining children cause
them to lose patience. Some feel themselves becoming irrationally
angry when a small child defies them; others find that unprovoked aggression arouses aggressive feelings. Teachers who are meticulous
planners may find that they react angrily when children reject the activities they carefully set up.

Teachers also report that certain times of the day may find them
with shorter fuses than usual. Clean-up and the transition to nap time
are often mentioned. Holiday periods, with special events and school-
wide assemblies, may tax patience even further, especially for teachers
with family responsibilities.

Simplifying the classroom environment helps some teachers maintain an appropriate level of emotional control. For example, materials
that need little supervision and that are calming for children, such as
play dough or simple collage work, may reduce tension. Allowing
longer blocks of time for activities may decrease the need to hurry children and may prevent outbursts of adult anger when children adhere
to their own timetable.

Because many early childhood classrooms have several teachers,
it is possible for staff temporarily to remove themselves from anger-
provoking situations. However, if early childhood professionals repeatedly find themselves unable to control their angry feelings while working with young children, they may need to discuss these feelings with
someone professionally or consider working with children and families
in a different kind of role.

Despite these prevention efforts, almost all teachers of young children will admit that they have occasionally expressed anger more directly and intensely than they wanted to. One teacher admits screaming at her four-year-olds; another describes banging a book down on
her desk, frightening the first graders into stunned silence. Another
person remembers grabbing the arm of a child who had frequent tantrums and squeezing harder than was really necessary as she led him
to the "quiet corner." Still another recalls hissing furiously at a one-
year-old child who had tried to bite her, "You little monster!"

These outbursts were undoubtedly noticed and remembered by the
children who observed them, in part because they were so out of character for these teachers. This does not mean that children were permanently damaged by these events, however, or that they will model their
own anger expression on that of the adult in this situation. Children

appear to model their behavior not on single observations, but on "prototypes" that they construct from many encounters with adult models (Maccoby & Martin, 1983).

Furthermore, if these teachers discussed their inappropriate behavior with the children after it occurred, they could partially counter its effects with more positive, appropriate models. "You know, I was really angry at the noise during story time this morning, and I yelled at you. I yelled too loud, and I think it was scary for some children. I'm sorry that I did that. Teachers shouldn't yell at children. I think there are other ways that I could have let you know how I felt. Maybe I could have closed the book and waited, or maybe I could have said, 'I am really upset about all this noise. No one can hear this story.' If I had done that, you would have known that I was angry but no one would have been scared by the yelling." This kind of honest discussion provides children with a model of how to talk about anger, how to distinguish between appropriate and inappropriate expressions of anger, and how to consider the consequences of different kinds of anger-related behavior.

CONCLUSION

This chapter has discussed modeling as an important strategy in helping children learn about emotions. Adults in early childhood programs are significant models for young children. In an emotion-centered program, adults consciously select aspects of emotion to model for children, and they integrate this emotion modeling into every aspect of the program. Teachers can increase the impact of their modeling by adopting the characteristics of effective adult models and by ensuring that children attend to their behavior, that children are developmentally able to produce the responses, and that children are praised for adopting the desired dispositions and behaviors.

The last section of the chapter discussed some particular difficulties and complexities of emotion modeling in early childhood programs. It examined what it means to express "genuine" emotion to young children, and it discussed how teachers decide whether to model honest, open emotions or whether to model appropriate inhibition of emotion expression. Because children have strong needs to learn how to express and cope with anger, and because anger is a fact of life in early childhood programs, teacher modeling of anger was given special attention. Differences in teacher beliefs about adult expression of anger were discussed, and strategies for preventing inappropriate anger modeling were presented.

This chapter has portrayed the adult as a powerful, active force in influencing children's adoption of desired emotional patterns. However, children are not photographic plates, passively reproducing whatever flashes before them. And the goal of an emotion-centered program is not to create pint-sized clones of adult models, even if those models are as creative and personable as Christine. Emotional development is more than copying others' behavior. *Emotional regulation* includes a variety of processes children can use to modify their emotions and emotion-related behavior. Modeling is only one component in this critically important, complex task. In Chapter 9, we will watch Denise's group of two- and three-year-olds as they move toward developmentally and culturally appropriate regulation of emotions.

Chapter 9

Supporting Children's Regulation of Emotions

It's late afternoon at the child care program where Denise teaches a group of two- and three-year-olds. Although the enrollment at this urban center is large, a family atmosphere prevails.

A small girl wraps both arms around another child in an exuberant hug. She pulls her friend with her on a tour of the playground, as her friend smiles tentatively. "Yes, she's your friend,

Tywana," Denise says quietly, as she loosens Tywana's grip on Arlette.

Four children are seated on a large tire swing, giggling. Rose, the director, has been showing a visitor the facilities. She comes over to play with the children for a moment. "Swing us, swing us!" the children call excitedly. Rose has everyone put their arms around each other; small hands grip T-shirts and wrists, and legs kick excitedly. As the tire swing starts to rotate and sway, Daria shakes her head doubtfully; she wants to leave. "Let's go slowly till Daria gets off," Rose tells the children, "and then we'll go a little faster. Leandra *needs* to hold on to you, Michelle (as Leandra grabs Michelle's arm and Michelle looks at her in alarm). Hold on tight, everyone!"

A little later, Denise's children are back indoors. This end-of-day activity period is low key and calming. Music plays on a tape recorder. Tables are set with manipulative toys brought out just at this time of day, including dollhouses with small figures and furnishings. The sand table is equipped with scoops and cups, and the low blackboard in the corner has brightly colored chalks for scribbling. A carpeted area has room to play with trucks and cars. Denise helps each child get started at one activity area.

"Miss Denise!" calls Charlotte from the sand table. "He frow' it in my face!" Denise walks to the group and sits down companionably. "You need to tell him not to do that. You need to ask him politely, 'Can you put it down?'"

"Lemme pour it out, Harold, okay? Okay, Harold?" Charlotte repeats several times, pushing her face into Harold's. "No," says Harold, but he yields to Charlotte's insistence, finally letting her take his sifter. As Harold notices what everyone else is playing with, his face crumples and he starts to cry, looking pleadingly at Denise. His hand shoots out and he grabs a spoon that Eddie has been using. "Is that how you do it?" Denise asks Harold, in a tone of patient explanation. "Now what do you need to say to get it?" "Can I have that spoon, Eddie?" Harold asks. Eddie hands it over. "Now do you need a thank-you, Harold?" Denise prompts. Meanwhile, the boys in the rug area are crashing cars. "Vroom!" roars Alexander in his fiercest tone. "We're crashing up! Oh, man, you crashed! Watch out, here it comes!" The crashes become louder as voices rise. Denise moves toward the rug area, where Alexander is now banging two cars together wildly. She touches his shoulder. "You need to calm down, Alexander. Do you want to play cars some more, or do you want to do something else?" Almost

with relief, Alexander allows Denise to walk with him from the
rug area. They circle the room and end up at the chalkboard,
where Alexander settles down to draw for a while.

Like all children their age, Denise's group expresses feelings with
intensity and vigor. A central issue for Denise and other early childhood professionals is the extent to which they should encourage or restrict children's open expression of emotions.

At one extreme, some would emphasize the emotional benefits of
encouraging children to "let their feelings out." According to this view,
angry exchanges, rough crashing, and direct expression of negative and
positive feelings allow emotional catharsis. By draining off powerful,
repressed impulses, children shed their affective burdens and can develop healthier personalities.

At the other extreme are those who regard any emotions as disturbing and troublesome. They worry about children losing control and
becoming victims of their own feelings. They believe children have little
ability to channel their own feelings and behavior in appropriate directions. Adults, they think, have the job of suppressing emotion expressions that violate social conventions or that make adults uncomfortable.

Neither of these extremes is good for children, neither reflects contemporary research findings, and neither is the approach adopted by
Denise and many other emotion-focused early childhood professionals.
This chapter does not advocate either catharsis or suppression. Rather,
its focus is on the *regulation* of emotions, a process by which children
come to have increasing control over their own feelings and their effects
on others, and by which children increasingly take on the emotional
standards or norms of their culture.

This chapter will emphasize that emotion regulation is indeed a
delicate balance that includes a number of important skills and dispositions. We will see that practitioners have many possible functions in
helping children develop regulatory competence and that practitioners
differ in their beliefs about appropriate roles in this process. Using a
variety of strategies, early childhood professionals can begin to construct an environment that supports appropriate emotion regulation.
Without offering simplified recipes, we will consider how practitioners
can helpfully intervene at some especially difficult times. Finally, I will
summarize the benefits that children receive as they become increasingly competent in regulating their own emotions and in influencing
others' feelings in positive ways.

EMOTION REGULATION: THE DELICATE BALANCE

"The emotions did not evolve to be regulated. They evolved because of their inherently adaptive qualities." With these words, Izard and Kobak (1991, p. 305) remind us that human emotions have important purposes; they are not merely annoying, uncivilized impulses. As we have seen, even negative emotions like anger, sadness, and fear serve to motivate purposeful behavior and have helped to ensure the survival of the human species. But these functions do not require unbridled expression. In fact, Izard and Kobak go on to argue that "anything as powerful as emotion requires regulation" (p. 318).

Like emotions themselves, emotion regulation has important adaptive functions in children's lives. And, as this chapter will show, regulation comes from within children as well as through external adult influences. Emotion regulation is far more than the elimination of "bad" feelings; children use emotion regulation to maintain or enhance their positive emotions and to alter their negative emotional states. Both positive and negative feelings can be heightened or suppressed through processes of emotion regulation (Cassidy, in press).

Emotion regulation includes a number of crucial skills and dispositions (Dunn & Brown, 1991; Katz & Gottman, 1991). Children who are developing competence in the regulation of emotions are able to

- Inhibit inappropriate behavior related to strong positive or negative emotion
- Soothe themselves or calm themselves down when they become highly emotionally aroused
- Use emotional states to focus or regulate their attention
- Coordinate their feelings, thoughts, and actions in the service of important goals
- Use emotions to influence others' feelings and actions
- Follow cultural standards for the display of emotions.

PRACTITIONERS' ROLES AND BELIEFS

Although emotion regulation starts in infancy, the preschool years are critically important in developing emotion regulation and emotional control (Maccoby, 1980). During these years, children spend increasing amounts of time in group settings. These settings require children to balance their own wishes against those of others, to wait for things, to conform to routines, and to deal with others' strong emotional responses. Denise and other early childhood professionals play a central role in this process.

However, no matter how skilled she is, Denise is not the sole regulator of her children's expression of emotions. Children's success or difficulty in emotion regulation has already been shaped by many factors even before the two-year-olds enter Denise's class. As described in earlier chapters, maturation of the brain and nervous system helps children to inhibit emotion expressions and to delay gratification of impulses. Denise's children are better at waiting for turns on the tire swing than they were last year, in part because they are maturationally able to do so. For better or worse, children's early family experiences have already affected their regulatory competence. Poverty, family violence, and instability of care have made it especially difficult for some of Denise's children to express their anger and sadness in flexible, adaptive ways. Some children have disabilities that have already caused them to adopt certain strategies for coping with their own and others' emotional states.

Furthermore, children have their own resources to assist in regulating their emotions. Even as infants, children soothe themselves and modulate their emotional arousal, although some children use these resources more effectively than others. Babies can turn their heads away or even fall asleep if caregivers overstimulate them with talk and play. Infants can use thumbs and pacifiers as calming devices, allowing them to focus attention on a rattle or mobile. Many older infants and toddlers adopt a blanket or soft toy as a "transitional object" to soothe their distress or allay anxiety at separation (Gay & Hyson, 1976; Jalongo, 1987).

Within these already existing patterns, what exactly *is* the role of the early childhood professional in fostering emotional regulation in young children? Little consensus exists. In surveying American and Korean teachers and program directors, Hyson and Lee (1992) found great variations in practitioners' endorsement of statements about certain emotion-related beliefs and strategies, such as, "When a child is upset, I try to put it in words"; "Teachers should 'let their feelings out' in class"; and "Children should be encouraged to display feelings openly." These variations existed within cultures as well as between cultures.

Rather than attempting to identify one "best" role in supporting children's emotion regulation, it may be better to examine an array of possible roles. As discussions of appropriate practices are now emphasizing (Bredekamp & Rosegrant, 1992), early childhood professionals need a broad repertoire of strategies to help young children learn. Possessing skill in these strategies, practitioners can be flexible in selecting those that are best suited to children's individual needs, cultural expectations, and educational purposes. When Alexander's car crashing became wild and uncontrolled, Denise had many options to choose from. Her gentle distraction and guidance to a new activity worked effectively, but other choices were possible. Another child (or even Alexander on a different day) might have been able to regain control with a look from Denise. Simply moving closer to Alexander and the other boys might have been sufficient. On the other hand, at times Denise may need to take over the regulatory function completely, physically removing Alexander from the area and holding him firmly until his excitement and anger subside.

As practitioners try to enhance children's skills in regulating emotions, they might be said to assume three kinds of roles: the *smorgasbord host,* the *scaffold,* and the *cultural guide.*

The Smorgasbord Host

The activities and materials in Denise's early childhood program offer children many avenues to express feelings in constructive, challenging ways. Pretend play, manipulative activities, creative arts, physical activity—these and other program features are like items on a smorgasbord laid out for children's selection (Howes, 1992, has used this and the following metaphor in a slightly different context). Like the host at this feast, Denise has arranged the selection to appeal to her "guests," and like a good host, she welcomes the children to the feast and describes its specialties. She invites children to sample whatever they like, pointing out their favorites but urging them to try new items. She encourages them to return again and again to the "table," pacing themselves to ensure enjoyment without overstuffing.

The Scaffold

Sometimes children need more than a host. Another role that Denise and others frequently assume is that of a helpful scaffold. The concept of "scaffolding" has been used in discussions of adults' roles in supporting cognitive development through close interaction and support as children work on emerging skills (Vygotsky, 1978; Wertsch, 1985). However, the concept is equally useful in reflecting on early emotional development. Like a framework around a new building, Denise's individual interactions with children support their emerging attempts at emotion regulation. With Denise's support, children are able to maintain a higher level of emotional control than they can manage on their own. At the sand table, Denise's presence and close interaction help the children sustain positive affect and reduce angry exchanges. Rather than building dependency on Denise, these scaffolding interactions establish emotional competencies that children are later able to use independently (Denham, Mason, & Couchoud, 1993).

The Cultural Guide

> "If he's in your seat, what do you need to say?" Denise firmly addresses Sanika, who has grabbed Julius's shirt and tries to pull him off the chair.
>
> Marcus reaches for a picture that Gloria has been examining. "You ask her, 'Gloria, can I see it? Can I see that, Gloria?' That's the way you ask her, Marcus," says Denise as Marcus looks up at her.

When Denise assumes this role, she is providing children with what Piaget might have called conventional knowledge. She calmly but directly instructs children about appropriate, socially acceptable behavior: asking permission to take things, saying please and thank you and excuse me, apologizing for hurting others. Frequently during the day, Denise will remind children of norms for the expression of emotions.

These are not understandings that children can acquire simply through maturation. Through observation and direct instruction, children learn what kind of emotion expressions and emotional controls are expected in various situations. Gradually, they begin to internalize these standards and behave in culturally consistent ways (Saarni, 1985). "Don't say that word!" says Eddie to Alexander. "That's right," says Denise. "It's not nice to talk to your friends that way."

Compared with some other teachers of this age group, Denise places an especially high priority on acquiring cultural display rules for emotions and on adopting culturally approved patterns of emotion-related behavior. This emphasis is consistent with the values of the community served by her program. In studies of parents' beliefs and attitudes (Hale-Benson, 1986; Hyson & DeCsipkes, 1993; McAdoo, 1992), African-American families have consistently valued children's early adherence to adult social conventions. In her calm, encouraging style, Denise is guiding her children not just toward general cultural standards, but into patterns of emotion regulation that are consistent with specific family and community expectations. Yet she does so in the context of a classroom environment where children are kissed hugged, and encouraged to express their feelings in a lively, physical way.

AN ENVIRONMENT FOR EMOTION REGULATION

Using the roles of smorgasbord host, scaffold, and cultural guide, early childhood professionals can begin to construct an environment within which children can strengthen their abilities to regulate their own emotions and to respond appropriately to others' feelings.

Establishing the Interpersonal Climate

Many of the strategies presented in earlier chapters are also relevant to building regulatory skills: Creating a secure emotional environment, helping children understand their own feelings and those of others, and serving as a model of genuine, appropriate emotion expressions. In addition, research suggests other interpersonal features that will support the development of emotion regulation.

Children who are in "good moods" are more likely to tune in to others' feelings, to be generous to others, and to help those in trouble (Moore, 1985). Denise's class and many other high quality programs strike the observer as happy places for children and adults. Despite conflicts among children and occasional reprimands for misbehavior, the dominant mood is positive and loving. Rose, the director of Denise's program, says that the first thing many visitors comment on is how happy everyone seems to be. Staff turnover is low. Foster grandparents, parent helpers, and other volunteers enjoy being around the center; children who have graduated to public school come back to visit. Children bask in the warmth of the center's nurturing, extended family.

Although she instructs children in culturally valued patterns of regulation, Denise matter-of-factly and openly accepts children's expression of a wide variety of emotions. She assumes that young children will express anger, excitement, and distress; they will cry, hit each other, grab toys, and squeal with joy. Denise does not express horror or dismay at any of this; rather, she works within children's present level of behavior to move them toward desired patterns of appropriate expression. This open affective exchange has been found to create favorable conditions for the development of empathy and healthy emotion regulation (Eisenberg, Fabes, Carlo, & Karbon, 1992).

We have already seen that talking about emotions helps children understand their own and others' feelings. Feeling-talk is equally important in predicting competent patterns of emotional regulation. Children who do not learn to use emotion language have a difficult time making connections with their own feelings and accurately identifying how others feel; this deficit places them at increased risk for emotion regulation problems (Cicchetti, Ganiban, & Barnett, 1991). Denise weaves emotion language into many of her interactions: "You need to calm down," she comments, as Alexander roars and crashes his cars. Later, in a concerned tone Denise observes, "You're hurting your babies," as two children bang dolls on the floor. However, not all talk about feelings is conducive to healthy emotion regulation. Cicchetti and colleagues (1991) observe that some adults use language to overintellectualize or defend against their own and others' feelings, and that their children may end up with maladaptive patterns of emotion regulation.

Adults can create a climate that supports the regulation of emotion if they help children see that they can change their own negative feelings or can help others feel better. When Harold was upset because he wanted Eddie's spoon, Denise showed him how he could control his distress and negotiate the situation in a satisfying way. Such experiences build children's feelings of self-efficacy (Bandura, 1977b).

Emotion regulation is supported in a climate where children focus on other people. Coordinating one's own desires with those of others is impossible unless one is aware of others' feelings and unless one genuinely cares about the effect one's behavior has on others. Children like the two- and three-year-olds in Denise's class do not automatically come to this awareness. Adult involvement is essential (Eisenberg et al., 1992). Denise has the qualities that researchers have shown to be effective in creating this awareness of others' feelings and needs; she is highly nurturant in her interactions with children, and she uses induction or reasoning as a discipline strategy, explicitly directing children's attention to the consequences of their behavior for others. "He doesn't like it when you ask him that way," Denise said gently, with a restraining hand on Eddie.

Some may feel these techniques are too directive. However, research strongly supports the need for adult scaffolding if young children are to develop empathy and prosocial behavior. In a laboratory study, Denham, Mason, and Couchoud (1993) found that the most effective way to encourage helping behavior among preschoolers was for the adult who needed help to explicitly label her own emotional state ("Ow, that really hurt!") and to ask the child to do something to assist her ("Will you help me?").

Promoting Peer Interactions

So far we have focused on the adult–child interpersonal climate. But as Kopp (1989) points out, peer interactions give children an especially potent setting to learn about regulating emotions, because other children are often less tolerant than adults of unpleasant emotional displays. Often, classmates will simply refuse to play with children who lack emotional control. This is a powerful though painful incentive for children to gain skill at modulating their anger, distress, and excitement.

Peer interactions also help children learn how to influence or regulate others' emotional states. In Denise's class, Raymond has become skilled at raising other children's interest in his games: "Come on, doggy," he begs, panting and hanging his tongue out of his mouth as he wheedles two other children to join in his play. "We're the doggies, right?" Enticed by his expressions and playful actions, the others woof enthusiastically and join in.

In a less benign vein, toddlers also learn to elicit negative emotional reactions through teasing or deliberate provocations (Dunn & Brown, 1991). Although they use these interactions to find out more about others' displays of emotion, children also need to learn how to control these teasing tendencies in order to preserve their friendships.

Friendship ties offer especially rich sources of emotion regulation. Fabes, Smith, Murphy, and Eisenberg (1993) have found that children are better able to regulate their anger during quarrels with friends than in quarrels with nonfriends. In Denise's group, Tywana and Arlette have been close friends for 2 years. Their arguments are frequent, but they moderate the intensity of their emotion because they know each other well and they both want to maintain their friendship. In creating a climate for emotion regulation, then, early childhood professionals should allow ample time for children to develop close friendships and to let children work through disagreements. With children older than those in Denise's class, self-chosen cooperative learning groups (such as Hope uses with her multi-age primary class) are an effective way to ensure this kind of experience.

Providing Activities

The emotion-centered teacher is aware that classroom activities can help children learn to heighten, dampen, redirect, and otherwise regulate their expressive behavior. Many of the best activities allow children to symbolize or represent their experiences, encouraging feelings of efficacy or control. It is also important to keep in mind that few of these activities are "about" emotions. As in other aspects of an emotion-centered curriculum, activities that have many other purposes can be effective avenues toward emotion regulation.

Observing Denise's children, one can see how they use the program's activities to build emotion regulation skills. Just as it supports emotional understanding, pretend play is essential for the regulation of emotions. Dunn and Brown (1991) found that toddlers used more emotion language and were more engaged in expressing emotions during make-believe play than at any other time. Howes (1992) argued that issues of trust and intimacy become the core of social pretend play in the preschool years. In pretend play, children can experiment with intense feelings.

> In Denise's room, Tywana and Arlette lay on their backs, pretending to sleep, eyes squinched tight. Teasingly, Eddie rolled a truck into them. In mock fear, they "woke up," shrieked loudly, and fled to the book corner, where they huddled with their arms around each other, smiling gleefully.

These kinds of episodes give children practice in expressing a great range of emotions through words, gestures, and symbolic actions, turning them on and off at will.

Like pretend play, painting and other creative activities not only provide emotional outlets (the catharsis perspective), but also give children access to additional, culturally valued ways of expressing feelings. Denise makes particularly effective use of music throughout her program. During a period when the children are in small groups using manipulative materials, Denise turns on a lively, familiar tape. As they stand at small tables working on puzzles and Lego structures, most of the children move in time to the music, performing little spontaneous dances. At one point, Bradley takes Whitney's hand and dances on the rug, returning to his table a few minutes later. Rather than distracting them from their "work," the emotional and physical satisfactions of music seem to focus the children's attention and heighten their enjoyment.

All these activities extend children's capacities for emotion regulation. Through pretending, drawing, dancing, building, swinging, and many other symbolic and physical activities, children build a repertoire of options for expressing, exaggerating, and minimizing emotions, and for coordinating their feelings with others. This broad repertoire sets the stage for emotional competence.

INTERVENTIONS AT DIFFICULT TIMES

Certain situations present added difficulty for children's regulation of emotions. Although simple recipes for intervening at these times are few, research offers some suggestions that are consistent with approaches that Denise and others have found successful.

When Children Face Another's Anger

Children differ greatly in their responses to another child's anger or aggression. Some quickly seek revenge, while others shrink back and avoid any conflict. Many practitioners agree that an assertive response is the most desirable—standing up for one's rights without losing control completely. Eisenberg and Fabes (1992) found that adults' responses to children's negative emotions predicted how children would react to other children's anger. As one might expect, those who punish their children's negative emotion, or who minimize its importance, are more likely to have children who seek revenge when angered or who avoid the aggressor completely. Adults who respond to their children's distress by taking it seriously (but not punishing it) tend to have children who can regulate their own anger better in response to peer aggression. Although the adults in this study were parents, not teachers, the results have implications for early childhood professionals. Denise does not ignore or laugh off children's anger and distress, but neither does she react in shock and anger. Her attitude may help explain the low levels of aggression observed among her young children, despite their frequent conflicts.

When Children Hurt Others' Feelings

One of Denise's children has a physical disability resulting from a birth defect. Phylicia's arms and hands look different. In Denise's class, staring and teasing about Phylicia's appearance are not allowed, although questions at the beginning of the year were answered calmly and matter-of-factly. Some practitioners may believe that natural expressions of emotion should never be discouraged and that children will come to think curiosity is a bad thing if they are discouraged from staring and commenting. But studies of the development of prosocial behavior indicate that Denise's prohibitions are helpful. Parents who explicitly instruct their children to control emotional displays that could be hurtful to others (such as staring at a person with a disability) tend to have more sympathetic children (Eisenberg et al., 1992). Such prohibitions do not restrict children from any and all emotional dis-plays—only those that hurt others' feelings.

When Children Are Anxious

All children have fears (Hyson, 1979). Adults can easily under-stand some of these fears (fear of injections, hospitals, violence), while others are harder to comprehend (fear of Halloween masks, balloons, new hairdos). Helping children deal with anxiety-producing situations is a complex process. Some children's fears are intense and disabling enough to require expert consultation. However, research offers helpful suggestions for more "routine" fears. Adults need to assist children in two areas: coping with the event and regulating their level of fear and anxiety.

In Denise's class, a grandparent once hired someone to dress up as the television character Big Bird to help celebrate a child's birthday. To the grandparent's surprise, many children were distressed by the unexpected appearance of their formerly favorite character. In this kind of situation, simply loading children with information about the feared event can actually increase anxiety. As adults, we often want children to face up to issues squarely. But emotion regulation may be better served with a more gradual, indirect process. Useful techniques may include concrete demonstrations or modeling (e.g., a puppet demon-stration), or even focusing the child's attention away from the situation or onto aspects of the situation that are more benign. All these ap-proaches can aid the child in regulating his negative emotional re-sponse to the situation through increased control and distraction (Miller & Green, 1985).

When Children Have to Wait

Denise's young preschoolers have a hard time waiting for their snack. Seated at tables and hearing food carts being trundled to other classrooms, they can quickly lose control, with contagious whining filling the room. Denise, like other effective early childhood teachers, minimizes useless waiting time as much as she can, but in any group setting some waiting is unavoidable. Waiting is another task that calls on children's ability to control or manage their emotional states, and the ability to "delay gratification" is an important index of emotional competence.

Many laboratory studies have explored the factors that make it eas-ier for young children to tolerate the frustration of waiting for a desired reward. Moore's (1985) review of these studies concluded that children cope most effectively with these kinds of situations when they can avoid thinking about what they are waiting for or when they can imaginatively transform it in some way. Giving children something else to occupy their time while they wait is especially effective; Denise has found that simply giving each child a sheet of paper and a crayon creates a distraction that helps them keep their pre-snack distress under control (and produces some wonderful scribbles besides).

Children's emotional states have also been found to affect their ability to delay gratification. Positive emotions seem to increase children's tolerance for delays in getting what they want. Once again, the happy mood of Denise's classroom creates advantages in the development of emotion regulation.

BENEFITS OF REGULATION

All children gain from increasing their ability to regulate their own emotions and to influence others' emotional states in positive, flexible, culturally accepted ways. Thinking back over Denise's class and other groups of young children, one can identify at least five benefits of increased competence in emotion regulation.

1. *Children Reach the Goals They Desire.* Getting what one wants, whether it is a snack, a friend, or completion of a task, requires successful emotion regulation. Emotions can motivate children to move toward their goals, but some emotional states can interfere with goal achievement. Excessive distress or fearfulness, for example, can interfere with exploration and restrict later cognitive and social development. Emotion regulation puts children's feelings in the service of children's goals.
2. *Children Feel Better.* Overwhelming emotion, both negative and positive, can cause confusion and a scary sense of being out of control. Children feel better when they know that they have some control over how they feel and how they express it (sometimes with a lot of adult scaffolding), and when they are confident that others will take their feelings seriously.
3. *Children Experience Mastery.* Healthy development requires a generalized sense of competence and mastery. Many accomplishments contribute to this sense, but an especially important one is children's confidence that they can heighten, minimize, and redirect

their emotions in ways of their choosing and in ways that others value.

4. *Children Become Part of the Culture.* Because norms for regulating emotions are culturally defined, children who are skilled in emotion regulation become increasingly integrated into their culture. They are accepted as functioning members of the community, who share the standards others have set.

5. *Children Become More Socially Competent.* Emotion regulation contributes to peer acceptance and social competence. In families and in early childhood programs, children constantly encounter others whose affective thresholds and emotional needs differ from their own. Therefore it is essential for children to learn to modify their own expressions of emotion and to direct their attention to others' feelings.

CONCLUSION

This short discussion has not been able to convey how complex the process of developing emotion regulation is, and how creative and flexible early childhood professionals must be if they are to help with this process. Denise and other teachers know that children need different kinds of support at different times. One child may need to experience a kind of emotional catharsis after a traumatic experience; another may need to regress for a while through pretend play. Many children simply need gentle guidance to extend and broaden their ways of expressing emotions. At times, others need explicit instruction in a warm atmosphere. But at the same time that we try to socialize children to conform to the norms of their culture, we need to recognize that there are developmental constraints on the extent to which young children can consistently adhere to those norms.

We also have alluded to but not fully explored individual differences in children's styles of expressing and regulating emotions. Differences in temperament and individual expressiveness can strongly influence how easily children become emotionally aroused and how easily they can adjust or modify their emotional responses. In Chapter 10, I will return to Hope's class to describe ways that early childhood professionals can recognize and honor these expressive styles.

Chapter 10

Recognizing and Honoring Children's Expressive Styles

Hope has made copies of a poem for her multi-age primary class. It is titled "tiger":

> The tiger
> Has swallowed
> A black sun.
>
> In his cold
> Cage he
> Carries it still:
>
> Black flames
> Flicker through
> His fur,

Black rays roar
From the centers
Of his eyes.
—Valerie Worth, *Small Poems Again,* ©1975, 1986

As Hope passes out copies of the poem, she says to the children, "This poem has been very controversial at my house. My
son Will, who is 17, said to me, 'Your class will *never* understand
this.'" At that, Serena rolls her eyes at Will's obtuseness. Hope continues. "And one of the other teachers looked at the poem when I
was copying it. She said to me, 'Wow, that's an exciting poem, but
it's pretty *dark,* isn't it?' But, you know, I think there are some interesting ideas in this poem—about animals' feelings and about
our respect for animals."

Hope reads the poem aloud twice, as the children follow
along. Then, as they usually do with poems to be included in
their poetry notebooks, the children read the poem by themselves, using markers to highlight the words they are sure of.

As the children work, Hope moves around the room, watching what the children are doing, answering questions, and providing help. She leans over Frederico, who is sitting looking at his
paper. Hope points to the first line. "Frederico, I bet you know
this word." "*The,*" Frederico whispers, picking up his marker.
"And how about that word?" Hope questions. "*Sun,*" says
Frederico with a stronger voice.

After the children work individually on the poem, they each
draw a picture to illustrate it. Azra laboriously copies a picture
from a nature book on the shelf. "You found a good book to help
you there, Azra," Hope says. Serena's tiger has bold stripes, large
pointed teeth, and a fierce expression. "Now *that's* a tiger,
Serena!" Hope exclaims. Serena grins and nods proudly.

As the morning goes on, the children work in small groups
reading "tiger" and old favorite poems to each other. Xavier waits
alone on the rug. "Xavier," Hope says with gentle humor and confidence, "I think you have to get up and be a little more active, to
find someone who wants you for a partner. Somebody will!" As
the children read poems together, Hope listens in. Some children
read fluently and exuberantly; others hesitate over each word as
if worried about making a mistake. Some children quickly select
poems to read, while others leaf slowly through their notebooks
before making a decision.

Later, the class gathers on the rug to read their own writing and to talk with Hope about the "tiger" poem and other stories with tiger themes. At the end of the discussion, Hope sums up: "You have all worked really hard this morning." "Whew!" calls Mario loudly. "Can we have recess?" Hope and the others laugh and nod in shared satisfaction.

During the morning, the children in Hope's class worked on some common tasks: They read a poem, they drew pictures, they found partners to work together in "paired reading," they wrote stories, and they discussed one another's work-in-progress. Yet despite the fact that they all were working on the same things, the children showed striking individual differences in how they approached these tasks and how they showed their feelings about their work, themselves, and their classmates.

If you ask any early childhood teacher to describe the children in her class, the chances are that she will use emotion words. Frederico is "quiet" and "shy"; Serena is "exuberant" and "proud"; Xavier is "cautious" and "hesitant." To create an emotion-centered program, teachers must recognize and honor these individual differences in children's emotional expressiveness. Most good teachers already know that children have unique personal styles, but this chapter will provide some help in focusing more closely on emotion-related individual differences. We will also identify some strategies that teachers can use to allow them to observe these differences more carefully and to keep track of their observations. Then we will underscore the importance of respecting and honoring children's unique expressive styles. Finally, we will acknowledge some obstacles to teachers' acceptance of these emotional patterns.

WHAT IS EXPRESSIVENESS AND WHERE DOES IT COME FROM?

Defining Expressiveness

Expressiveness can be defined as a persistent individual style of emotional response (Halberstadt, 1991). In earlier chapters, we emphasized that emotions are universal: Children and adults all over the world experience and express basic emotions such as joy, anger, sadness, and interest. However, the children in Hope's class—and people everywhere—also have uniquely different patterns or styles of emotional responsiveness. For example, as the children worked on their illustrations of the tiger poem, they all seemed to experience the emotion of interest. But individual children showed their feelings in very different ways. Serena's whole body reflected her absorption in the task, and she eagerly sought others with whom to share her pleasure at her accomplishment. Peter, in contrast, shut others out, hunching over his drawing in solitary absorption. Azra's interest was sporadic and diffused. Once she found a book to copy from, she involved herself in the task, but before that she sat at the table gazing off into the distance and wandered around the room, looking at what others were doing.

Sources of Expressive Styles

These individual differences, like other aspects of emotional development, are the product of many interrelated influences. They are neither entirely innate nor entirely learned. Halberstadt (1991) argues that expressive styles are actually complex individual patterns of emotional communication. As such, they develop gradually over time, as a product of biological, cultural, and social influences. Thus, children become more different from one another the older they get. Frederico and Serena were probably more similar as babies than they are today. But if one had known Serena as an infant, one might already have seen some indications of the expressive style she displays as an eight-year-old. Her genetic inheritance may have predisposed her to a highly sociable disposition and to an easy readiness to smile and laugh.

However, the precise direction taken by Serena's individual expressive style was also shaped by her family environment. Her family, although warm and loving, is not highly expressive. Like many young children from "low expressive families" (Halberstadt, 1991), Serena readily expresses positive emotions but is slow to express anger. Serena's parents have little tolerance for children's expressions of anger. In contrast to the more economically advantaged families of some other children in Hope's class, Serena's parents do not go along with the idea that children should "let their feelings out" (Halberstadt, 1991). Rather, they actively discourage the expression of negative emotions, including anger and sadness, although they reward Serena's older brothers for participation in aggressive sports such as football and hunting.

By the time Serena reached Hope's class, then, her expressive style was well formed. Over the past year, Serena has further developed her unique style, in part as a result of opportunities afforded by Hope's program. As one of the oldest children in this mixed-age class, Serena has had many opportunities to view herself as a guide and model for the younger children. This has certainly influenced her way of expressing her feelings and has shaped her emotional responses to classroom activities.

Finally, we need to recognize that these unique individual patterns show themselves differently in different situations. When Serena is on the playground or helping her father work on their house, she shows essentially the same expressive patterns as she does when she is working on a tiger picture in the classroom. However, these social contexts pull forth different aspects of Serena's emotional style. Even as a primary-grade child, she is already learning the display rules of her culture, and she is able to modify her own expressive style to meet the expectations of varied social settings.

HOW TO RECOGNIZE CHILDREN'S EXPRESSIVE STYLES

The more attuned a teacher is to the unique emotional response patterns of young children, the better able she will be to use this information in building a positive, emotion-centered program.

Identifying Basic Emotions

Before early childhood professionals are able to create detailed pictures of individual children's expressive styles, they need to be sure they are able to make accurate judgments about basic emotion expressions and emotion-related behavior. Most current researchers have relied on facial expressions as the most reliable indicators of emotional states (although, as we will see, children differ greatly in how easy it is to "read" their emotion expressions). The studies usually have been based on laborious review of videotapes, doing second-by-second coding of children's expressions and classifying them into specific emotion categories using objective criteria.

For example, a researcher looking at a tape of Frederico would probably judge that Frederico was feeling both sad and a little shy. The judgment would be based on several observations: Frederico's mouth is downturned, his eyes are not as bright as usual, and his face and body seem droopy. He seems to be comforting himself by thumbsucking. As Hope approaches, Frederico's shyness may be evident when he turns his head away and avoids looking at his teacher. As Hope helps Frederico to become more confident about identifying the words he knows in the tiger poem, signs of interest appear: Frederico's brows are lifted, his eyes brighten, and his mouth relaxes and opens slightly. His posture shifts from its helpless slump, and he picks up the marker, exploring the paper with his hand and his eyes.

Most early childhood educators would have little interest in conducting such complex microanalytic coding of facial expressions. However, some familiarity with these methods, and with the criteria generally used for identifying emotion expressions (Izard, 1991), will make practitioners more aware of the basic facial and bodily expressions of emotion and will help them appreciate differences among children's expressive styles.

Dimensions of Difference: What to Look for

In trying to put one's finger on the unique qualities of children's emotional responses, it is sometimes difficult to know exactly what to look for. Halberstadt (1991) describes six dimensions on which children's expressiveness may differ:

1. *Balance of Positive and Negative Emotions.* Everyone experiences both positive and negative emotions, but people differ in how frequently they experience and express these feelings. Frederico's general mood, for example, is much more frequently negative than is Phoebe's. Serena's expressive style is consistently positive; on the rare occasions when she shows sadness or anger, Hope wonders if she is coming down with a cold or if some problem has occurred at home.
2. *Frequency of Specific Emotion Displays.* In addition to differing in positive versus negative expressions, children have consistent differences in how often they show more specific emotions. Xavier frequently displays fear and shyness, being inhibited in new situations, especially social ones. Phoebe is notable for her frequent expressions of joy; of all the children in Hope's class, she is the one who most often claps her hands, giggles in delight, and smiles broadly at any pleasurable experience.
3. *Intensity of Emotion Expressions.* Two children who are alike in their *frequency* of expressing an emotion such as anger may be very different in the *intensity* with which they show these feelings. Neither Peter nor Azra is often angry, but when Peter is upset he explodes in a rage, stomping about and yelling at anyone who gets in his way. Azra, on the other hand, shows her anger in a more muted way: She may sit at her desk, hands clenched and eyes narrowed, glaring at the person who has offended her. When Hope surprised the children with a new math game, Serena's eyes widened slightly and she drew

in her breath in anticipation, while Randall struck himself on the forehead and flopped on the rug in an exaggerated pantomime of astonishment.

4. *Duration of Specific Emotion States.* In Hope's class as in other early childhood settings, some children shift quickly from one emotion state to another. Upset by a classmate's rejection, their tears quickly turn to smiles when another child invites them to play. Other children, like Peter, are more likely to persist in sadness or anger. At the end of the day, Peter stood at the door, shaking his head disconsolately. When Hope asked him what was the matter, she finally found out that he was still thinking about an incident on the playground at morning recess, when Adam would not let him have the ball.

5. *Pure versus Mixed Emotion Expressions.* Children's faces are fascinating to watch. Although all children use more blended emotion expressions as they get older, there are strong individual differences in how often children display these "mixed feelings" in comparison to more direct, "pure" emotion expressions. In Hope's class, everyone always knows exactly how Leo is feeling. His face is a mirror of basic emotions. When he is happy, his expression is almost a classic vision of joy, and when he is angry, there are no two ways about it: Every line on his face and body shows that single emotion. In contrast, Frederico's face and body typically reflect more complicated combinations of feelings. His happiness is often mixed with shyness, and interest and sadness seem to alternate on his face as he tackles the challenges of schoolwork.

6. *Speed of Emotion Onset.* Finally, expressive differences are seen in how quickly children's emotions are activated. The whole class laughed at Mario's demand for recess, but the children did not all start laughing at once. Rachel's giggles were heard first (as they usually are in Hope's room), while it took a little time for Leo to join in. Similarly, when Hope began reading "tiger," some children were immediately fascinated by the poem, leaning forward in a posture of complete emotional engagement. Others took longer to be drawn in, their interest expressions only becoming evident during Hope's second reading.

TOOLS FOR IDENTIFYING EMOTION STYLES

Unlike emotion researchers, early childhood teachers have many other responsibilities to distract them from the task of identifying children's unique "emotion profiles." There are a number of ways that teachers can help themselves to focus on these important aspects of children's development.

Classroom Organization and Activities

The organization of the early childhood classroom can make it much easier for teachers to learn about children's expressive styles. To do this, teachers must be free to step back occasionally and just "kid-watch." A program like Hope's makes this possible. From the very beginning of the year, Hope has encouraged children to do things for themselves. Long periods each day are spent in independent work. Classroom helpers ("Recess Equipment Manager," "Chalkboard Specialist") take care of many routine housekeeping chores. Supplies are readily available. Older children help their younger classmates with reading and math work. Besides building security and self-esteem, these management strategies give Hope some solid blocks of time in which she can really look at what children are doing and how they are doing it.

In addition, the kinds of activities that Hope offers in her program make children's individual expressive styles much more apparent. In laboratory settings, researchers have often devised experimental situations that elicit varied patterns of individual emotional responses. For example, they have observed children's reactions to events such as a brief separation from mother, the appearance of a strange-looking toy robot, or having to solve a frustrating puzzle.

Hope's classroom affords more natural but equally revealing opportunities for children to show their unique emotional styles. Because children have many choices, their selections can tell Hope and other observers a great deal. Even when all the children are doing the same activity, the activity can usually be done in many different ways. In planning a drawing activity, some teachers might give children a dittoed tiger picture to fill in with prescribed colors. Hope chose a different and more productive strategy. Before the children drew their pictures, Hope talked with the class about the poem, encouraging quieter children to contribute: "Kathy, what ideas do you get when you hear this poem?" She then invited the children "to draw a picture of how the poem makes you feel." The children's comments about the poem ("Maybe the tiger doesn't want anyone to look at him in the zoo") and their individual drawings provided a fascinating glimpse of their unique emotional styles.

Some activities are almost guaranteed to highlight differences in expressive styles. Inspired by spring weather, robins, and a recent rainy spell, Hope's class has been studying worms. One afternoon was spent inspecting worms that Hope had obtained for the class. After a group discussion (including the development of humane guidelines for handling the worms), each child was given a worm to observe closely, using a magnifying glass. The children were encouraged to write notes for their science notebooks. Every emotion in the researcher's lexicon could be observed on children's faces, in their voices, and in their bodies. Azra gently touched her worm, stroking it and smiling as the worm moved across the paper. Leo stretched out a tentative finger, yanking it back before even touching his worm, and looking anxiously at his friend Jeremy, who attended to his worm with scientific precision, writing his notes in careful printing.

Observation Methods

Early childhood educators have traditionally valued well-recorded observations of children's behavior. Recently, many psychologists who are interested in early emotional development have followed this tradition, observing naturally occurring behavior in home, community, and school settings. Surprisingly, however, not many researchers have studied emotional development in day care centers or other early childhood programs. One exception is the work of Lewis and Michalson (1983), who observed children in a day care center to find out what kinds of situations elicited various expressions of emotion, and described the many facial, bodily, and verbal channels children used to express their feelings in this naturalistic setting. Some of the techniques used by research observers can be adapted by early childhood professionals who wish to learn more about young children's expressive styles.

Notetaking. Many early childhood educators have been trained in writing anecdotal records. The problem is not how to do it; rather, the challenge is to make the time to do it. Hope has devised a notetaking system that uses the large blank address labels that come on a long continuous paper roll. She has found that these are easy to jot notes on as she moves around the room visiting small groups of children and as children conference with her about their reading and writing. She uses these sticky labels to note many aspects of children's behavior, including their emotional responses to classroom activities. The labels can then be peeled off their backing and added to the individual folders Hope keeps for the children in the class.

The recent growth of interest in naturalistic or "authentic" approaches to assessing children's progress has spurred the development of numerous resources. These offer teachers realistic suggestions for taking notes in the classroom and for organizing these observations (Bredekamp & Rosegrant, 1992; Clay, 1979, 1982; Grace & Shores, 1991). No one system is best; the point is to find one that works and use it regularly.

Videotaping Children. Because so much of children's emotional life is communicated through facial expression, gesture, and body movement, videotape offers a medium that is well matched to the teacher's need for appropriate observational tools. Our expanded knowledge about early emotional development can be attributed in part to researchers' use of sophisticated video technology to record and review examples of children's expression of feelings.

Like researchers, early childhood practitioners are becoming more adept at the use of video equipment. A growing number of schools and child care programs have access to portable video cameras. Teachers can learn a great deal about children by watching them on videotape. Subtle patterns of emotion that are lost in the bustle of the classroom may take on new significance when they are reviewed at the end of the day or in a weekly staff meeting.

Videotaping is not as complicated as the newcomer may fear. The hardest thing is getting started. If there are two adults in the room (or if a parent volunteer can be recruited), one teacher can videotape on a regular basis (perhaps once a week). Even with only one adult, programs organized like Hope's have some periods of time when children can easily work independently.

What should be videotaped? Almost anything will provide useful information, but tapes of children working on open-ended, emotion-laden activities are especially revealing. A visitor to Hope's class happened to videotape the children's worm observations; the resulting tape offers an inexhaustibly rich resource for understanding individual children's emotions. One school enlists a parent volunteer to tape each child twice a year, during several kinds of activities. The tapes are saved for the 3 or 4 years that most children are enrolled, providing a fascinating archive of developmental and individual information for staff and parents.

Emotion-Related Scales and Checklists. Another useful observational tool is an emotion-related scale or checklist. Until recently, it was easier to find measures of children's cognitive or physical development than to identify instruments that provided information about emotion-related characteristics. However, because there has been so much recent research on early emotional development, a number of researchers have now devised rating scales or checklists that can be used by classroom teachers.

Many teachers have an automatically negative reaction to the checklist concept, associating these measures with testing or labeling children's emotional competence. However, these kinds of scales do not have to be used to score the adequacy of children's emotional development. Rather, they can focus the teacher's attention on children's emotion-related characteristics. Certainly teachers can devise their own sets of items to use in observing children. Before doing so, however, it may be useful to examine several already developed measures.

In the early 1980s, Lewis and Michalson developed the "Scales of Socioemotional Development." Their goal (Lewis & Michalson, 1983) was to develop a research instrument to measure everyday manifestations of emotions in young children, so as to trace age-related and individual differences. Their scales were developed in child care settings, using common situations encountered during extensive observations (e.g., "When the child is left at day care by the parents . . . " or "When the child wants something that is out of easy reach . . . " or "When the child notices a stranger in the room . . ."). For each of these situations, Lewis and Michalson developed a checklist of possible emotion-related responses: for example, "watch intently"; "squeal"; "refuse help"; "decrease activity."

Lewis and Michalson (1983) collected data on individual differences in five emotion-related areas: fear, anger, happiness, social affiliation (that is, tendency to approach or be sociable with family, peers, and other caregivers), and competence (that is, a tendency to participate in age-appropriate tasks with positive emotions). Their goal was not to identify what is "normal," but rather to describe individual children's characteristic responses.

For the early childhood professional, Lewis and Michalson's (1983) work has a great deal of merit. Although teachers would be unlikely to use the time-consuming methods employed in the original study, the items make intuitive sense and could easily be adapted for classroom use. There is nothing sacred about Lewis and Michalson's set of items; staff in any early childhood program could come up with a different set of situations that interested them (for example, "child is presented with new material to read" or "child is asked to finish a task") and could create a list of possible responses based on their informal observations of children in the program. Then, staff could use the checklist when observing individual children, creating a picture of individual differences in emotion-related responses.

A second promising measure is the Preschool Socioaffective Profile (LaFreniere, Dumas, Capuano, & Dubeau, 1992). Unlike the Lewis and Michalson instrument, this measure was designed specifically to be used by preschool teachers. Its focus is on helping teachers identify possible adjustment difficulties or behavior problems. Nevertheless, the measure seems appropriate even if early childhood professionals simply want to obtain a clear picture of individual children's emotion-related characteristics. The measure aims to identify children's emotion expressions "in social interaction with peers and adults, as well as expressions of characteristic emotion in a nonsocial context" (LaFreniere et al., 1992, p. 443). This measure differs from the Lewis and Michalson instrument because, rather than responding to a checklist, teachers rate children on each of a number of statements, using a six-point scale ranging from "Very unlike this child" to "Very much like this child." Items on the list represent several domains, including Anxiety-Withdrawal (e.g., "Inhibited or uneasy in group" or "Maintains neutral facial expression; doesn't smile or laugh") and Anger-Aggression (e.g., "Irritable, gets mad easily" or "Forces other children to do things they don't want to do"). The measure, which is available from the authors, seems well suited to the goals of an emotion-focused early childhood program.

Finally, an instrument called the Emotion Prototype Questionnaire has been developed to obtain parents' reports about their toddlers' expression of 12 emotions, including shame, anxiety, jealousy, and empathy (Nikkari, Gilbert, Emde, & Campos, 1993). The questionnaire describes causes and behaviors typically associated with each emotion, and the parent rates each one on how frequently and intensely the child has expressed it.

This measure, which is also available from the authors at the University of Colorado Health Sciences Center, might be adapted for use by programs for toddlers. Its strengths are its precise focus on the second and third year of life and its description of a set of crucially important "social emotions."

USING KNOWLEDGE OF EXPRESSIVE STYLES

Knowledge is of little value unless it can be used. Teachers who take the time to organize their classroom environment to elicit emotional responses, and who systematically observe their children, need to be sure that this information is used in constructive ways.

Anticipate Individual Difficulty or Enjoyment

One way that teachers can use their observations is to help them anticipate what situations may present either special difficulties or special pleasure for individual children. From her observations and notes, Hope knows that Xavier worries about new situations. She knows that Phoebe will eagerly plunge into any activity that involves pretending and creating. With this kind of knowledge, Hope can anticipate her children's likely responses to the activities she has planned, although fortunately children always have a few surprises in store.

Individualize to Fit Children's Emotion Styles

Knowing about the special characteristics of children's emotional responses and patterns of emotion communication, early childhood teachers can modify their program to build on individual children's preferences and strengths. For example, Hope has many highly expressive children in her class, who display their feelings quickly, intensely, and (usually) with much positive emotion. Her program meets their needs through a rich array of activities that allow children to express their feelings immediately and vividly. Children talk about their opinions, they draw pictures, they engage in lively debate over whether the tiger in the poem was happy or angry, whether he should be let out of his "cold cage," and how it might feel to be a tiger locked in a cage. Hope encourages this lively emotional climate but keeps it on track through clear ground rules for discussions and through well-planned transitions from one activity to the next. And because the program allows time for individual work as well as whole and small group activities, those children who have a lower-key style feel comfortable in the classroom.

Honor Children's Individuality

An emotion-centered program respects and honors individual differences. Hope refers to children's emotional states in a respectful way: "Phoebe, you're sitting there looking serious. What kind of ideas do you have?" To lively, impulsive Leo she says, "Can you wait for that until we read the poem as a group?"—acknowledging his eagerness while steering him toward postponing his outburst of excitement.

Wendy closes her notebook after starting to draw her tiger picture. Hope notices this, moves closer, and says quietly, "Are you not feeling too good about that picture, Wendy?" When Serena stumbles over her words in her eagerness to explain her ideas about the tiger poem, Hope says, "Just a minute, Serena. Try to tell me again; I want to be sure I understand your idea." Watching Hope with her primary grade class, it is clear that she delights in their individuality.

There is no limit to the ways that emotion-centered teachers can honor children's individual expressive styles. The notebooks that Hope's children keep have certain standard contents, but each is given a unique stamp by its owner. The walls of Hope's classroom are covered with children's artwork and writing. Unlike classrooms in which each piece of artwork seems produced from the same factory, these products reflect the distinctive characteristics of each child in the class. Other teachers may display close-up photographs of each child engaged in a favorite activity, showing Linda's serious attention, David's happy grin, and Latoya's astonished gaze.

OBSTACLES TO RESPECT FOR INDIVIDUALITY

It is easier to declare a belief in honoring children's emotional individuality than to act on that belief. All of us are products of our individual and cultural histories. Although at times these histories create empathy and support for children's patterns of expressive behavior, at other times they create obstacles to understanding and respect.

Research by Halberstadt (1991) and others has shown that people tend to develop friendships with those who have the same expressive style that they do. Most of us feel more comfortable with those who share our ways. Early childhood teachers who express their feelings openly, quickly, and directly may be drawn to those children who do the same thing, and may view less expressive "deadpan" children more negatively. In contrast, adults whose own style is to keep some emotional distance and to hide both positive and negative emotions may feel uncomfortable with those children whose expressive style is very intense and direct.

Cultural patterns play a significant part in these feelings. As we have seen in earlier chapters, there are strong cultural differences in expressive behavior. Many writers have noted that African and African-American groups tend to value a high level of emotional expressiveness and physical contact, while European Americans and many Asian cultures may not (Halberstadt, 1985; Lynch & Hansen,

1992). When teachers are from different cultural groups than the children they teach, these differences may create obstacles to genuine respect for children's expressive styles.

CONCLUSION

Respect for children's individual emotional qualities is an essential component of an emotion-centered early childhood program. However, respect does not necessarily imply approval or encouragement. Every early childhood teacher can think of children whose emotional responses create difficulty and unhappiness for the child and for others. Hope may respect Frederico's shyness and uncertainty in new learning situations, but she may also see that Frederico would benefit from increased confidence in his own abilities. Likewise, Hope may respect Nathaniel's impassioned defense of his rights, but she may urgently need to help him find ways of resolving playground disputes other than wrestling other children to the ground.

There's a poster that says, "I am the only me I can be right now." The purpose of this chapter has been to help early childhood professionals describe and respect that "me," as seen in each child's unique pattern of emotional responsiveness and emotion communication. The "me" displayed by Leo, Azra, Serena, Phoebe, Frederico, and other young children is the unique manifestation of a unique genetic, familial, cultural, developmental, and social context. It represents that child's best attempt to cope with the challenges of his or her life right now, with the tools that he or she has available.

In Chapter 11 we will return to Christine's kindergarten classroom to look at some of the ways that early childhood teachers can create emotionally and intellectually positive learning communities for young children, continuing to respect the "me" within each child while guiding children along pathways that are satisfying and educationally valuable.

Chapter 11

Uniting Children's Learning
With Positive Emotions

Half a dozen of Christine's kindergartners are settled on the rug
looking at books and magazines that they have selected from a
nearby display shelf. Several children are lying on their stom-
achs, heads propped on their hands. Others are flopped in bean-
bag chairs. Matt and Ricky huddle side by side, shoulders touching, paging through magazines. Voices rise and fall as children
share their books with each other and as they call out to children
working in other parts of the room. "Martina! Martina!" Sean
laughs excitedly and waves a book in the air. "I found your
name!"

   As she crosses the room, Christine pauses beside Matt and
Ricky. She bends down. "Oh, Matt—you have my magazine about
the Mayan people." Christine watches companionably as Matt continues to leaf slowly through the magazine. "If you turn the page,
I think there's a picture of one of their gods." Matt turns

the page, nodding with recognition as he finds the picture. "Remember when we saw a picture of where they went swimming?" Christine comments. Matt smiles broadly and nods again. Christine joins a group of children at another table. Matt turns to Ricky and tugs at Ricky's arm. He shoves the picture under Ricky's nose, pointing urgently. "Awesome!" exclaims Ricky, his eyes widening in amazement.

Christine's kindergarten classroom embodies the emotion-centered teacher's emphasis on linking positive emotions to children's learning. In this chapter, we will reflect on the way that feelings of interest and joy can motivate, sustain, and enhance children's intellectual development. Conversely, we will note that anxiety and fear may undermine learning and diminish young children's usually positive feelings about school. The chapter will outline the basic characteristics of experiences that are most likely to produce interest and joy. It will illustrate some of the many ways that early childhood professionals can use to support and extend children's interests. Finally, we will see how active teacher intervention can remove roadblocks to interest development and set children on the path to new, challenging intellectual experiences.

EMOTIONS AND EARLY LEARNING

The emphasis in this chapter differs from the simplistic belief that "learning should be fun." Teachers who place a thoughtful focus on emotions select appropriate, educationally worthwhile experiences and use them to generate positive feelings in children. Furthermore, emotion-centered teachers like Christine do not manipulate children into a state of superficial excitement (which can actually interfere with learning). Rather, they try to build patterns of sustained interest and effort, while affording opportunities for children to experience the joy of mastery.

Interest and Intellectual Development

As we have seen, many theorists hold that specific emotions motivate specific kinds of adaptive behavior. *Interest* has been identified as the primary emotion that motivates exploration and problem solving (Izard, 1991). At first, it may be hard to think of "interest" as an emo-

tion with strong motivational value. It is easier to see how anger motivates resistance, or fear motivates escape. However, some reflection will
provide many examples of times when feelings of curiosity have guided
our attention to new sights and have kept us working at tasks even
when we are tired, hungry, or discouraged. When we are interested, we
feel alert and focused. We feel a keen desire to explore and learn more
about the object of our fascination. Feelings of curiosity make us ready
to tackle a problem or pursue a question until a satisfactory conclusion
is reached (Izard, 1991).

Research on interest has also shown that it enhances memory,
comprehension, and selective attention (Renninger, Hidi, & Krapp,
1992). For all these reasons the emotion of interest plays a key role in
children's intellectual development.

The Effects and Sources of Joy

Like interest, joy and happiness also foster learning and development. Researchers have found that people are more empathic, more
generous, and more creative when they are feeling joyful. Feelings of
joy are accompanied by confidence, vigor, and self-esteem. Joy opens
our minds and hearts to new experiences, making our mental processes
more creative and flexible. When people feel joyful, they are motivated
to share their thoughts and feelings with others (Izard, 1991). Toddlers
often engage in "affective sharing," joyfully showing their special treas-
ures to parents and teachers (Waters, Wippman, & Sroufe, 1979). In
Christine's kindergarten, Matt happily shows his friend Ricky the "awesome" picture, and Sean shares his discovery with Martina.

Play is one of the most reliable sources of joy for young children.
In fact, play researchers find that observers depend on children's expressions of happiness (smiling, laughter) to help them decide whether
children's activities are playful or not. One of the reasons that children
"learn through play" may be that play generally occurs in such a positive emotional climate, fostering attention, memory, and creative problem solving. Like many emotion-centered teachers, Christine organizes
her program around rich opportunities for many kinds of play, including pretend play, manipulative play, and games with rules.

One of the most frequent occasions of joy is mastery of some kind
of challenge. Children who have experienced the deep happiness that
results from mastering a difficult skill or reaching an important goal
are motivated to seek out experiences that will produce that feeling
again. Sean, the child in Christine's class who found his friend Martina's name in a book, reacted to his discovery with smiles and laugh-

ter. These joyful feelings, experienced as a result of effort, will help to motivate Sean to tackle other challenges in figuring out the printed word.

Negative Emotions and Children's Learning

Just as positive emotions support learning, negative emotions can interfere with and even permanently disrupt normal intellectual development. Children who seldom experience feelings of interest may fail to develop essential skills and competencies because they lack the emotional foundations of exploration and practice (Case, Hayward, Lewis, & Hurst, 1988). As we have seen, the emotion of fear motivates action to avoid or escape from a fear-producing situation. Children who are presented with academic tasks that they must complete because of fear of punishment or fear of failure may complete the tasks because they want to avoid embarrassment or punishment. However, they are likely to avoid similar tasks in the future, or they may go through the motions of completing the tasks while avoiding genuine engagement.

Laboratory studies have repeatedly shown that (in contrast to the positive effects of feelings of interest) feelings of anxiety serve to limit the ability to focus attention and recall information. Mental processes are generally less efficient when people are feeling anxious. Case, a cognitive developmental psychologist influenced by neo-Piagetian theory, argues that the level of cognitive development that children attain is partly influenced by the sheer amount of time they are able to devote to what he calls "epistemic activities" — exploration, imitation, and problem solving (Case et al., 1988). Case points out that negative emotions such as anxiety may sharply reduce children's investment in epistemic, intelligence-building activities.

Emotions and Reactions to School

Thus, positive emotions about learning are crucially important if children are to benefit from educational programs. We know that most children begin school with very positive feelings. However, in general, children feel less positive about their abilities and their school experiences with every year they spend in school. This decline is not inevitable, however. In our study of early academic experiences, children whose preschools and parents had provided them with child-focused, developmentally appropriate experiences had more positive attitudes toward school at the end of kindergarten (Hirsh-Pasek, Hyson, & Rescorla, 1990). Early childhood programs can build long-term dispositions to engage in challenging learning activities, to derive pleasure from mastering intellectual tasks, and to share knowledge and skill with others.

ENGAGING CHILDREN'S POSITIVE EMOTIONS: CRITICAL FEATURES

What learning activities and experiences will engage young children's interest and joy? The specific answer depends on children's ages, experiences, and individual preferences. However, interest- and joy-producing experiences do have some general features. Christine's classroom makes good use of these features in strengthening children's positive dispositions about learning.

Change

Change is a reliable elicitor of interest, as shown in numerous studies of attention from infancy through adulthood. Children's interest is captured by occasional variations on a familiar theme. Christine's classroom embodies the use of change-within-familiarity. As children enter the room each day, they look around for "what's new," curious about what may be awaiting them in the room's well-defined interest areas. Before the daily free-choice time begins, Christine describes the activities that are available. Often, small variations will rekindle children's curiosity. For example, all this week the dramatic play area has been the site for a take-out restaurant where children write down orders, make pizzas, and deliver them. Today, Christine has added some carbon paper and new order pads to the area, extending interest in the dramatic play. Graphs have occupied the attention of many children over the past weeks; today, Christine tells the children that they will be making a new kind of graph, to let Mrs. Madison know how many children want to have marshmallows in their hot chocolate. The wall above the chalkboard is already covered with graphs of many kinds. The graphs are the result of children's representations of personally meaningful information. Each one is different, and each one is the product of sustained attention and effort. One graph proclaims MY FEMLES FAVRT FRUTS, with pictures of fruits drawn above the names of family members. Other graphs are equally personal and varied.

By spring of the kindergarten year, Christine occasionally injects larger variations into the class routine. This week, for example, was spontaneously designated as "Science Week." The week before, a child happened to bring a book of science experiments to school. Many children became fascinated with trying out these experiments, and this informal interest grew into an official "Science Week," featuring numerous science activities available during free-choice time.

It is important to emphasize that both adults and children create interest-producing variations in the early childhood program. The previous section may sound as though adults are responsible for initiating all variations. Although the focus of this chapter is on adult contributions, in a high quality program children frequently initiate activities, vary the way activities are done, and continually contribute ideas to the life of the program.

Movement

Researchers find that animation or *movement* heightens children's interest in visual stimuli. Moving displays are inherently fascinating to children. The emotion-centered teacher does not have to become Walt Disney to tap into this source of interest, however. Christine engages children's interest with many movement-related activities and materials. The classroom aquarium, often dotted with signs directing children's attention to interesting sights, is a continual source of motion.

Every Thursday, Christine and her staff perform skits dramatizing classroom issues in a visually compelling way. On this day, two student teachers presented a brief, humorous skit about a current problem: although some children have been working hard at cleaning up, others have not. The adults' vivid pantomime, as they stacked blocks, gestured indignantly, and stomped out of the room, fully engaged the children's interest and stimulated lively discussion of possible fair solutions.

Besides watching others' movements, Christine's kindergartners are intensely interested in producing movement of their own. Whether making and swinging a sand pendulum, dressing up in seasonal clothing and prancing down a fashion runway, or observing and recording the speed at which objects hit the floor when dropped from a height, movement-related activities capture the sustained attention of the class.

Faces

Human *faces* are the earliest and most powerful elicitors of interest and joy. While intense interest in the human face peaks in infancy, faces—and the relationships they represent—remain sources of pleasure and curiosity in later years. Christine uses this interest effectively, getting down close to children, looking them in the eye, and using her own facial expressions as clear communicative signals. This interest in faces may also account for the children's fascination with some new computer software that has been programmed to display photographs of the children in the class. On this morning, Lily, Anna, and Pauline spent 15 minutes intensely focused on the computer, identifying the children in the pictures and manipulating various features of the program.

Mastery

Mastery and control are features of many experiences offered in Christine's classroom. Researchers find that these features consistently bring forth interest and joy in infants and young children. In fact, opportunities for control can change an unpleasant, negative experience to a positive one. Gunnar (1980) found that young children who feared a toy robot responded with pleasure when they were able to guide its movements. And children can control their own actions as well as those of objects or other people. Despite their reputation for negativism, in one study many toddlers showed great enjoyment at complying with commands from an adult, as if saying, "See, I can do that!" (Rheingold, Cook, & Kolowitz, 1987)

It is difficult to know where to begin in describing the many opportunities for child control and mastery available in Christine's kindergarten class. At group time, Christine calls one child to her side and poses a "question of the day" in a game-like format. These questions, which are a regular feature of morning meetings, are invariably related to classroom activities and encourage reflection and recall. Today, the question to Danny was, "In our pizza shop, can you name two kinds of toppings available to our customers?" (Whispered hints from Christine are sometimes needed, and the rest of the children have no objection, since the point is success, not competition.) When Danny—with no hints today—comes up with pepperoni, cheese, and mushrooms, the class cheers and Danny grins delightedly at his mastery of the day's question.

Mastery opportunities during group time form only a small part of Christine's curriculum. As in all developmentally appropriate programs, children select most of their own activities. Within these activities, there are many ways for children to be "in charge." In the pizza shop, for example, children choose roles they will assume. They write down the customers' orders, make the pizzas with play dough and construction paper, and deliver them with a flourish. Interest and joy are evident on the faces of the children who are involved in this activity.

The day's graphing activity offered children another source of control. By stating their individual preferences and communicating them to the cook, the children could influence what they received for snack. Children in Christine's class know that they can approach problems in a variety of ways. The graph Christine had set up had two columns: "Marshmallows" and "No Marshmallows." However, Aaron declared, "I don't care whether I have marshmallows or not." Christine responded, "Whoops—I should have written three columns on our graph: Marshmallows, No Marshmallows, and Don't Care. Maybe next time I will do that."

Another class discussion further illustrates how opportunities for control stimulate children's interest. Christine explained to the class that the tape recorder had broken because children were pushing the buttons incorrectly (apparently this had been discussed before with no effect). Now, Christine said, the class had no tape recorder, and the director was not sure they should buy another one right away because the same thing might happen again. This kind of discussion often turns into a teacher-directed scolding for past mistakes. However, Christine then asked the children how they thought the director might be persuaded to buy another tape recorder. "We could promise not to hit the buttons so hard," one child suggested. "We could make a sign telling kids not to push two buttons at the same time," was another suggestion, countered with, "But I can't read." "A picture sign!" suggested yet another child. Finally the class agreed that they would all try to remember to be careful using the new tape recorder and that a large pictorial reminder would be posted in the listening area. Christine said that she would discuss the children's ideas with the director and see whether the arguments would convince her to try the tape recorder again. This whole dialogue was intensely interesting to the children, since they could see that they had the opportunity to influence the outcome of events that were important to them.

JUMP-STARTS FOR CHILDREN'S INTEREST

Emotion-centered teachers recognize that children will usually seek out activities and materials that stimulate their interest and that hold out the possibility of mastery. To a great extent, teachers can rely on children's intrinsic motivation to help them notice these interest-producing features of the program and to sustain their interest over long periods of time. Teachers can also be reasonably confident that, as children develop, most of them will broaden their interests and extend them into areas that are important for later academic success and full personal development.

Roadblocks to Interest Development

However, for many reasons this is not always the case. Many children come into the early childhood program having had little encouragement of their interests and having had few opportunities to feel the joy of mastery. Fearful of scorn or punishment, they may avoid most learning activities. Other children may be temperamentally inhibited (Kagan, Reznick, Clarke, Snidman, & Garcia-Coll, 1984), reluctant to try anything new. Some children's family environment or culture may discourage attempts at mastery or may confine mastery to group rather than individual success. Many Native American, Latino, or Asian children may hesitate to try anything that will force them to compete or set them above other children. These cultural standards should be respected but may present challenges to success in "mainstream" educational settings (Lynch & Hansen, 1992).

In addition to these individual variations, teachers may also find that children do not always "naturally" gravitate toward the skills that our culture requires them to master. As Spodek (1991) and others have noted, curriculum is defined by sociocultural values (what the society deems worth knowing) as well as by children's spontaneous interests and needs. This issue becomes particularly pressing by first and second grade, when our society expects children to master basic literacy and mathematical concepts and to begin to acquire conventional knowledge of historical events and places. Although the "emergent literacy" literature suggests that children are intrinsically motivated to master many of these skills, the process is not as seamless or painless as some case study descriptions (Bissex, 1980) would lead us to believe.

Teachers' "Interest Interventions": Falling Objects

For all these reasons, emotion-centered teachers frequently intervene to broaden the range of experiences that children will respond to with interest and joy. A science activity that Christine organized highlights some of these techniques.

Christine began the activity by calling the group together on the rug. "This is another one of the experiments from Martina's book," Christine explained. "This one is *a lot* of fun; I think you may really like it. It's a "Falling Objects" experiment, and we'll try it out first with everyone here. If you don't get a chance to do it right now, you can try it during free-choice time."

The children scooched closer on the carpet. "Now," said Christine, "we are going to need someone to be the recorder." Juliette waved her hand eagerly. "Your job, Juliette, is going to be to write down what people find out about the falling objects. Here's your recording notebook." (The children had been re-cording the results of other experiments earlier in the week and liked the job of recorder very much.) Next, Christine had two chil-dren volunteer to be the "scientific observers" of the falling ob-jects. In hard hats, the two observers lay on the floor. Above them, Quentin stood on a table. He selected two objects from a basket and held them up.

"What we have to do," Christine declared, "is to figure out which object will hit the ground first." Quentin held up a whiffle ball and a soccer ball. "Which one do you think will hit the ground first?" Christine asked the group in an interested tone. "I think the whiffle ball," said Tracy. "Why do you think that?" asked Christine, again in a sincerely curious tone of voice. "Well," reflected Tracy, "the whiffle ball has air in it and the soccer ball doesn't." "But the soccer ball is heavier," Matt interrupted. "Heav-ier things go faster." "No they *don't*, Matt," Sean patiently ex-plained. "I think Matt's right," Ricky said loyally. "The soccer ball *should* go faster. But I don't know if it *will.*"

"Let's see," said Christine. "Quentin can drop the balls at the same time and the observers can watch to see which one hits the ground first. How many times should we try it?" The class agreed on three tries. Everyone watched intently as the balls were dropped, cheering if their "favorite" was the winner. Juliette re-corded the results in her notebook, deciding to use "F" for "Faster" under a picture of the balls Quentin was dropping.

This activity is described in detail, not because it is necessarily a model for teaching a scientific concept, but as an example of how teach-ers can intervene to broaden the sources of interest and joy for young children. Many aspects of Christine's guidance of this activity contrib-uted to its emotion-engaging power.

Christine's own affective engagement in scientific pursuits invests the activity with significance for children. As we saw in an earlier chap-ter, Christine spontaneously models the kinds of emotional responses she hopes children will develop in their kindergarten learning. Her enthusiasm for this activity and her curiosity about the outcome do not seem contrived. Teachers sometimes fake curiosity—"Goodness, boys and girls, I *wonder* what will happen when we put a brick into the tub of water. Will it sink or will it float? I just can't wait to see!" Such contrived interest is fundamentally disrespectful and is readily penetrated by perceptive children. In contrast, Christine's involvement in the activity is spontaneous and genuine. The children's attachment to Christine (Pianta, 1992) also increases the likelihood that children will become interested in activities and skills that Christine values.

Christine has definite goals for this and other science activities. One is to help the children to view themselves as scientists, capable of engaging in scientific work. Children's feelings of control and mastery are highlighted by this activity. Children—boys and girls—get to enact scientific roles, observing, recording, making, and verifying predictions. But they can choose what roles they prefer to play, including just watching for a while if they prefer. Juliette's earlier interest in writing and in making little books is now being applied in a new domain. Matt and Ricky's friendship and love of pretend play are extended to a new role—being the hard-hatted observers for the experiment.

Christine plays a very active role in this first go-around of the Falling Objects experiment. Without controlling every aspect of the activity, she guides the class through the activity, posing questions, encouraging children to explain their predictions, highlighting features of the objects being dropped, reminding children of their "jobs" in the experiment ("Did you remember to write down which was faster that time, Juliette? We can put the book on our science shelf later."). At the conclusion of the whole-class portion of the experiment, Christine invites the children to try the activity during free-choice time and organizes another group of children to start it off. From time to time, Christine checks back with the children to see how they are using the materials.

This description shows how emotion-centered teachers can extend the range of educationally worthwhile experiences that give children satisfaction and pleasure. Christine links these new experiences in scientific experimentation with earlier emotionally positive experiences. In the science experiment and in casual conversation with children, Christine frequently makes reference to children's previous successes and their enjoyment of other, similar activities. "Remember when we saw the picture of them swimming?" she commented to Matt as he attempted to read the magazine. Matt's smile showed that this was an emotionally positive memory for him. The math graphs on the wall had to do with pleasurable topics of personal relevance for children; for example, their family's favorite foods, their own hair color, and their cookie preferences.

EXTENDING CHILDREN'S INTERESTS

Besides "jump starting" children's interest in new intellectual pursuits through active interventions such as the science project just described, Christine and other early childhood professionals have numerous ways to support and extend children's positive engagement in learning.

Honoring Preferences

As children get older they increasingly develop individual activity preferences. Although these preferences—which occasionally become brief obsessions—may restrict children's willingness to try new experiences, those same preferences also may be used as bridges from the familiar to the new. One of the strengths of the project approach to curriculum (Katz & Chard, 1989) is that children may participate in a class project in a variety of ways. Science Week activities were designed to appeal to the interests of children who "specialize" in drawing, writing, ball playing, and so on. The emphasis on small-group, cooperative investigations allowed each child to move into a new area of learning within a framework of comfortable, preferred activities.

Providing Time

Another feature of Christine's program that helps children extend their emotional range is that children are provided with enough time to explore new learning experiences. Hutt's experiments (1966) showed that most children go through a predictable sequence when confronted with a new, unfamiliar apparatus. After perhaps hanging back for a bit, they begin to explore the strange device, at first in a random sort of way. After a time of "aimless" exploration, children shift intellectual gears, so to speak, and become deeply focused on serious systematic investigation of what the apparatus can do, followed by more playful, creative variations. This kind of sequence is likely to lead to feelings of mastery and to the development of positive dispositions to encounter new experiences. However, the sequence is often short-circuited when early childhood teachers rush children from one "exciting" new activity to another. In her science experiment, Christine went beyond a one-shot, teacher-led demonstration. Rather, she engaged the entire group in an initial exploration and guided children to return to the activity throughout the day.

Other activities in Christine's room also encourage this sequence of exploration and systematic investigation. The writing center is always available for children to draw, scribble, copy, compose letters or stories. Free exploration is balanced with times when Christine prompts children to attempt specific writing tasks.

Conveying Confidence

A crucial factor in broadening children's positive emotional responses to learning is the teacher's attitude that children are capable of tackling new and possibly difficult material. "High expectations" can receive a bad name because some early childhood educators believe that children should not have too much pressure put on them. However, there is a difference between expectations that are pressuring and an emotionally supportive belief that children are capable of doing great things. "You can be good observers," Christine comments to Matt and Ricky, the first two volunteers. "You have good eyes, and you notice a lot of things." "Juliette, you are a good recorder because you like to write things down." Sometimes Christine will refer to children that she taught at another school, saying, "I don't know if you guys can do this. My children in New York had a really hard time with it." This is usually followed by a loud chorus of "We can do it!" On the printed page, these words may suggest an overemphasis on competition. However, as spoken in Christine's classroom, they sound a different note. Through these kinds of playful challenges, Christine conveys to her children that she admires them, that she thinks it is interesting and fun to try hard activities, and that it is okay to try something and have it not work out.

Scaffolding and Support

Christine and other emotion-centered teachers also recognize that certain children may require a higher degree of teacher "scaffolding" as they move into new educational challenges, if they are to come out of the experience with positive feelings. This may mean actually holding a young child on one's lap while the child tries a difficult puzzle. Hesitant older children may require physical closeness and a tactful hint now and then. Young children with disabilities often need more actively interventionist strategies than nondisabled children (Bredekamp & Rosegrant, 1992). However, many children without disabilities also enter the early childhood program lacking confidence in their own skills. For all these children, the emotion-centered teacher must achieve a thoughtful balance between two extremes: just waiting for the child to try new activities on his or her own, and rushing the child into challenges that may create anxiety and undermine the child's positive learning dispositions.

CONCLUSION

In *Bread and Jam for Frances* (Hoban, 1964), the little badger's parents yield to her food fussiness and give her a steady diet of her favorite bread and jam. As time goes by, what Frances had longed for becomes dull and unappetizing. When Frances finally asks for some of the family's spaghetti and meatballs, her parents "naively" comment that they thought Frances did not like spaghetti. Frances' lament—"How do you know what I'll like if you won't even try me?"—captures children's need for the teacher-activist approach described in this chapter.

Teachers of young children need to do more than give children a sweet, steady, intellectually shallow diet of things they already like. Being offered new experiences—and being supported in trying them out—provides children with a chance to develop new likes, new enthusiasms, and new areas of competence. Teachers sometimes hesitate to be too activist out of fear of pushing children. Although this fear is well founded, the other extreme is also risky. Some children automatically assume that they will hate any new experience. Sometimes this declaration covers their fears that they will fail or look silly. Some children may be temperamentally inhibited and simply need a longer period of familiarization.

In broadening children's intellectual diet, teachers can help by expressing confidence that children could have a different feeling about things later on. "When I was a little girl, I remember that I didn't want to go to the gym. I thought I might fall when I had to climb the rope. But my teacher held me and I practiced and finally I learned to climb up the rope." Sometimes it is appropriate to require that children "taste" new experiences—not just once, but repeatedly—to give themselves a chance to explore and investigate. A great advantage of mixed age groups, such as the one in Hope's primary class, is that children can observe and work side by side with older, more skilled children—but still children close in age—who are taking on new educational challenges and experiencing interest, pride, and joy in their efforts.

The conclusion of this chapter brings us full circle. None of Christine's efforts to create curious, joyful learners would be possible without an emotion-centered philosophy of education, firmly grounded in theory and the wisdom of practice. As they investigate Mayan gods and falling whiffle balls, the children are supported by the secure emotional environment Christine has created. They work well together because they are gaining understanding of how they and others feel, in part through Christine's modeling of authentic, appropriate emotions. They are able to sustain their engagement in these challenging activities because of their growing competence at emotional regulation. And each of Christine's children feels that his or her unique emotional style is a valued part of the class. Like the children who experience the loving care and education given by Natalie, Ilene, Leslie, Hope, Terry, Denise, and all emotion-focused early childhood professionals, these children thrive because feelings are at the very center of their early childhood program.

References ——————————————————————

Ainsworth, M.D.S., Blehar, M.C., Waters, E., & Wall, S. (1978). *Patterns of attachment*. Hillsdale, NJ: Erlbaum.

American Association for the Advancement of Science. (1989). *Project 2061: Science for all Americans*. Washington, DC: Author.

Ayers, W. (1989). *The good preschool teacher*. New York: Teachers College Press.

Bandura, A. (1977a). *Social learning theory*. Englewood Cliffs, NJ: Prentice-Hall.

Bandura, A. (1977b). Self-efficacy: Toward a unifying theory of behavior change. *Psychological Review, 84,* 191–215.

Baratta-Lorton, M. (1976). *Mathematics their way*. Menlo Park, CA: Addison-Wesley.

Bartlett, J.C., Burleson, G., & Santrock, J.W. (1982). Emotional mood and memory in young children. *Journal of Experimental Psychology, 34,* 59–76.

Bates, J. (1987). Temperament in infancy. In J.D. Osofsky (Ed.), *Handbook of infant development* (2nd ed., pp. 1101–1149). New York: Wiley.

Beane, J.A. (1990). *Affect in the curriculum: Toward democracy, dignity, and diversity*. New York: Teachers College Press.

Bereiter, C., & Engelmann, S. (1966). *Teaching disadvantaged children in the preschool*. Englewood Cliffs, NJ: Prentice-Hall.

Bertenthal, B., & Campos, J.J. (1990). A systems approach to the organizing effects of self-produced locomotion during infancy. In C. Rovee-Collier & L. Lipsitt (Eds.), *Advances in infancy research* (pp. 1–60). Hillsdale, NJ: Erlbaum.

Biber, B. (1984). *Early education and psychological development*. New Haven: Yale University Press. (Original work published 1942)

Bissex, G.L. (1980). *GNYS AT WRK: A child learns to read and write*. Cambridge, MA: Harvard University Press.

Bloom, L., & Beckwith, R. (1989). Talking with feeling: Integrating affective and linguistic expression in early language development. *Cognition and Emotion, 3,* 313–342.

Bornstein, M.H., Gaughran, J.M., & Homel, P. (1986). Infant temperament: Theory, tradition, critique, and new assessments. In C.E. Izard & P.B. Read (Eds.), *Measuring emotions in infants and children* (Vol. II, pp. 172–199). New York: Cambridge University Press.

Bower, G.H. (1981). Mood and memory. *American Psychologist, 36,* 129–148.

Bowlby, J. (1969). *Attachment and loss* (Vol. 1). London: Hogarth.

189

Braun, S., & Edwards, E. (1972). *History and theory of early childhood education.* Worthington, OH: Charles A. Jones.

Brazelton, T.B. (1992). *Touchpoints: Your child's emotional and behavioral development.* Reading, MA: Addison-Wesley.

Bredekamp, S. (Ed.). (1987). *Developmentally appropriate practice in early childhood programs serving children from birth to age 8* (exp. ed.). Washington, DC: NAEYC.

Bredekamp, S., & Rosegrant, T. (Eds.). (1992). *Reaching potentials: Appropriate curriculum and assessment for young children* (Vol. 1). Washington, DC: NAEYC.

Bretherton, I., Fritz, J., Zahn-Waxler, C., & Ridgeway, D. (1986). Learning to talk about emotions: A functionalist perspective. *Child Development, 57,* 529–548.

Bretherton, I., & Waters, E. (Eds.). (1985). Growing points of attachment theory and research. *Monographs of the Society for Research in Child Development, 50*(1–2, Serial No. 209).

Buhler, C.M. (1974). *The first year of life.* Westport, CT: Greenwood Press. (Original work published 1930)

Bullock, M., & Russell, J.A. (1986). Concepts of emotion in developmental psychology. In C.E. Izard & P.B. Read (Eds.), *Measuring emotions in infants and children* (Vol.II, pp. 203–237). New York: Cambridge University Press.

Burts, D., Hart, C.H., Charlesworth, R., Fleege, P.O., Mosley, J., & Thomasson, R.H. (1992). Observed activities and stress behaviors of children in developmentally appropriate and inappropriate kindergarten classrooms. *Early Childhood Research Quarterly, 7,* 297–318.

Buss, A.H., & Plomin, R. (1984). *Temperament: Early developing personality traits.* Hillsdale, NJ: Erlbaum.

Bussis, A.M., & Chittenden, E.A. (1972). Toward clarifying the teacher's role. In E.B. Nyquist & G.R. Hawes (Eds.), *Open education* (pp. 117–136). New York: Bantam.

Campos, J.J., Barrett, K.C., Lamb, M.E., Goldsmith, H.H., & Stenberg, C. (1983). Socioemotional development. In M. Haith & J.J. Campos (Eds.), P.H. Mussen (Series Ed.), *Handbook of child psychology: Vol. 2. Infancy and developmental psychobiology* (pp. 783–915). New York: Wiley.

Camras, L.A. (1988, April). Darwin revisited: An infant's first emotional facial expressions. In H. Oster (Chair), *Emotional expressions in infants: New perspectives on an old controversy.* International Conference on Infant Studies, Washington, DC.

Camras, L.A. (1985). Socialization of affect communication. In M. Lewis & C. Saarni (Eds.), *The socialization of emotions* (pp. 141–160). New York: Plenum.

Camras, L., Grow, G., & Ribordy, S. (1983). Recognition of emotional expressions by abused children. *Journal of Clinical and Child Psychology, 12,* 325–328.

Carey, S., & Gelman, R. (Eds.). (1991). *The epigenesis of mind: Essays on biology and cognition.* Hillsdale, NJ: Erlbaum.

Caring for our children. National health and safety performance standards: Guide-lines for out-of-home child care programs. (1992). Washington, DC: Ameri-can Public Health Association and American Academy of Pediatrics.

Case, R., Hayward, S., Lewis, M., & Hurst, P. (1988). Toward a neo-Piagetian theory of affective and cognitive development. *Developmental Review, 8,* 1–51.

Cassidy, J. (in press). Emotion regulation: Influences on attachment relation-ships. In N. Fox (Ed.), Biological and behavioral foundations of emotion regulation. *Monographs of the Society for Research in Child Development.*

Cassidy, J., Parke, R., Butkovsky, L., & Braungart, J. M. (1992). Family–peer connections: The roles of emotional expressiveness within the family and children's understanding of emotions. *Child Development, 63,* 603–618.

Castillo, G.A. (1974). *Left-handed teaching: Lessons in affective education.* New York: Praeger.

Chapman, M., Zahn-Waxler, C., Cooperman, G., & Iannotti, R. (1987). Empa-thy and responsibility in the motivation of children's helping. *Develop-mental Psychology, 23,* 140–145.

Cicchetti, D., & Carlson, V. (Eds.). (1989). *Child maltreatment: Theory and re-search on the causes and consequences of child abuse and neglect.* Cam-bridge: Cambridge University Press.

Cicchetti, D., Ganiban, J., & Barnett, D. (1991). Contributions from the study of high-risk populations to understanding the development of emotion regulation. In J. Garber & K.A. Dodge (Eds.), *The development of emotion regulation and dysregulation* (pp. 15–48). New York: Cambridge Univer-sity Press.

Cicchetti, D., & Hesse, P. (1983). Affect and intellect: Piaget's contributions to the study of infant emotional development. In R. Plutchik & H. Kellerman (Eds.), *Emotion: Theory, research, and experience: Vol. 2. Emotions in early development* (pp. 115–170). New York: Academic Press.

Clay, M.M. (1979). *The early detection of reading difficulties.* Portsmouth, NH: Heinemann.

Clay, M.M. (1982). *Observing young readers.* Exeter, NH: Heinemann.

Cohen, S. (1966). The problem with Piaget's child. *Teachers College Record, 68,* 211–218.

Cowan, P.A. (1978). *Piaget with feeling: Cognitive, social, and emotional dimen-sions.* New York: Holt, Rinehart & Winston.

Cummings, E.M. (1987). Coping with background anger in early childhood. *Child Development, 58,* 976–984.

Cummings, E.M., Iannotti, R.J., & Zahn-Waxler, C. (1985). The influence of conflict between adults on the emotions and aggression of young children. *Developmental Psychology, 21,* 495–507.

Cummings, E.M., Zahn-Waxler, C., & Radke-Yarrow, M. (1981). Young chil-dren's responses to expressions of anger and affection by others in the family. *Child Development, 52,* 1274–1282.

Darwin, C.R. (1872). *The expression of the emotions in man and animals.* Lon-don: John Murray.

Demos, E.V. (1986). Crying in early infancy: An illustration of the motivational function of affect. In T.B. Brazelton & M. Yogman (Eds.), *Affect and early infancy* (pp. 39–73). New York: Ablex.

Denham, S.A. (1986). Social cognition, prosocial behavior, and emotion in preschoolers: Contextual validation. *Child Development, 57,* 194–201.

Denham, S.A. (1989). Maternal affect and toddlers' social-emotional competence. *American Journal of Orthopsychiatry, 59,* 368–376.

Denham, S., Mason, T., & Couchoud, E. (1993). Scaffolding young children's prosocial responsiveness: Preschoolers' responses to adult sadness, anger, and pain. Manuscript submitted for publication.

Derman-Sparks, L., & the A.B.C. Task Force. (1989). *Anti-bias curriculum: Tools for empowering young children.* Washington, DC: NAEYC.

Deutsch, M. (1967). *The disadvantaged child.* New York: Basic Books.

Dix, T. (1991). The affective organization of parenting: Adaptive and maladaptive processes. *Psychological Bulletin, 110,* 3–25.

Dodge, K.A., & Garber, J. (1991). Domains of emotion regulation. In J. Garber & K.A. Dodge (Eds.), *The development of emotion regulation and dysregulation* (pp. 3–11). New York: Cambridge University Press.

Duckworth, E. (1987). *"The having of wonderful ideas" and other essays on teaching and learning.* New York: Teachers College Press.

Dunn, J. (1988). *The beginnings of social understanding.* Cambridge, MA: Harvard University Press.

Dunn, J., Bretherton, I., & Munn, P. (1987). Conversations about feeling states between mothers and their young children. *Developmental Psychology, 23,* 132–139.

Dunn, J., & Brown, J. (1991). Relationships, talk about feelings, and the development of affect regulation in early childhood. In J. Garber & K.A. Dodge (Eds.), *The development of emotion regulation and dysregulation* (pp. 89–108). New York: Cambridge University Press.

Dunn, J., Brown, J., & Beardsall, L. (1991). Family talk about feeling states, and children's later understanding of others' emotions. *Developmental Psychology, 27,* 448–455.

Dunn, J., & Munn, P. (1985). Becoming a family member: Family conflict and the development of social understanding. *Child Development, 56,* 480–492.

Eisenberg, N. (1992). *The caring child.* Cambridge, MA: Harvard University Press.

Eisenberg, N., & Fabes, R.A. (Eds.). (1992). *Emotion and its regulation in early development.* San Francisco: Jossey-Bass.

Eisenberg, N., Fabes, R.A., Carlo, G., & Karbon, M. (1992). Emotional responsivity to others: Behavioral correlates and socialization antecedents. In N. Eisenberg & R.A. Fabes (Eds.), *Emotion and its regulation in early development* (pp. 57–73). San Francisco: Jossey-Bass.

Ekman, P. (1972). Universals and cultural differences in facial expressions of emotion. In J.K. Cole (Ed.), *Nebraska symposium on motivation* (Vol. 19, pp. 207–283). Lincoln: University of Nebraska Press.

Ekman, P., Friesen, W.V., & Ellsworth, P. (1972). *Emotion in the human face: Guidelines for research and an integration of findings.* New York: Pergamon Press.

Ekman, P., Levenson, R.W., & Friesen, W.V. (1983). Autonomic nervous system activity distinguishes among emotions. *Science, 221,* 1208–1210.

Elicker, J., Englund, M., & Sroufe, L.A. (1992). Predicting peer competence and peer relationships in childhood from early parent–child relationships. In R. Parke & G. Ladd (Eds.), *Family–peer relationships: Modes of linkage* (pp. 77–106). Hillsdale, NJ: Erlbaum.

Emde, R.N. (1980). Toward a psychoanalytic theory of affect. II. Emerging models of emotional development in infancy. In S. Greenspan & G. Pollock (Eds.), *The course of life: Psychoanalytic contributions toward understanding personality development* (pp. 63–83). Washington, DC: U.S. Government Printing Office.

Erikson, E.H. (1950). *Childhood and society.* New York: Norton.

Erikson, E.H. (1959). *Identity and the life cycle.* New York: Norton.

Erikson, E.H. (1977). *Toys and reasons.* New York: Norton.

Evans, E. (1975). *Contemporary influences in early childhood education* (2nd ed.). New York: Holt, Rinehart & Winston.

Fabes, R.A., Smith, M., Murphy, B., & Eisenberg, N. (1993, March). *Peer relationships and the regulation of young children's anger.* Paper presented at biennial meeting of the Society for Research in Child Development, New Orleans.

Fischer, K.W., Shaver, P.R., & Carnochan, P. (1990). How emotions develop and how they organise development. *Cognition and Emotion, 4,* 81–127.

Fogel, A., & Reimers, M. (1989). On the psychobiology of emotions and their development. In C.Z. Malatesta, C. Culver, J.R. Tesman, & B. Shepard (Eds.), The development of emotion expression during the first two years of life (pp. 105–113). *Monographs of the Society for Research in Child Development, 54*(1–2, Serial No. 219).

Fogel, A., & Thelen, E. (1987). Development of early expressive and communicative action: Reinterpreting the evidence from a dynamic systems perspective. *Developmental Psychology, 23,* 747–761.

Fox, N.A., & Davidson, R.J. (1986). Psychophysiological measures of emotion: New directions in developmental research. In C.E. Izard & P.B. Read (Eds.), *Measuring emotions in infants and children* (Vol. II, pp. 13–47). New York: Cambridge University Press.

Fox, N.A., & Davidson, R.J. (1988). Patterns of brain electrical activity during facial signs of emotion in 10-month-old infants. *Developmental Psychology, 24,* 230–236.

Fraiberg, S. (1979). Blind infants and their mothers: An examination of the sign system. In M. Bullowa (Ed.), *Before speech.* New York: Cambridge University Press.

Freud, S. (1959). Analysis of a phobia in a 5-year-old boy. In A. Strachey & J. Strachey (Ed. and Trans.), *Collected papers* (Vol. 3, pp. 149–289). New York: Basic Books. (Original work published 1909)

Freud, S. (1964). New introductory lectures on psycho-analysis. In J. Strachey (Ed. and Trans.), *The standard edition of the complete psychological works of Sigmund Freud.* (Vol. 22). London: Hogarth Press. (Original work published 1933)

Freud, S. (1964). *An outline of psycho-analysis.* In J. Strachey (Ed. and Trans.), *The standard edition of the complete psychological works of Sigmund Freud.* (Vol. 23). London: Hogarth Press. (Original work published 1940)

Garber, J., & Dodge, K.A. (Eds.). (1991). *The development of emotion regulation and dysregulation.* New York: Cambridge University Press.

Gay, E., & Hyson, M. (1976). Blankets, bears, bunnies: Studies of children's contacts with treasured objects. In T. Shapiro (Ed.), *Psychoanalysis and contemporary science* (Vol. 5, pp. 271–316). New York: International Universities Press.

Genishi, C. (Ed.). (1992). *Ways of assessing children and curriculum: Stories of early childhood practice.* New York: Teachers College Press.

Goldsmith, H.H., & Campos, J.J. (1982). Toward a theory of infant temperament. In R.N. Emde & R.J. Harmon (Eds.), *The development of attachment and affiliative systems* (pp. 161–193). New York: Plenum.

Goldsmith, H.H., & Campos, J.J. (1990). The structure of temperamental fear and pleasure in infants: A psychometric perspective. *Child Development, 61,* 1944–1964.

Goodlad, J.I. (1973). *Early schooling in the United States.* New York: McGraw-Hill.

Goodlad, J.I. (1984). *A place called school: Prospects for the future.* New York: McGraw-Hill.

Gordon, S.L. (1989). The socialization of children's emotions: Emotional culture, competence, and exposure. In C. Saarni & P.L. Harris (Eds.), *Children's understanding of emotion* (pp. 319–340). New York: Cambridge University Press.

Grace, C., & Shores, E.F. (1991). *The portfolio and its use: Developmentally appropriate assessment of young children.* Little Rock, AR: Southern Association on Children Under Six.

Greenspan, S.I. (1989). *The development of the ego.* Madison, CT: International Universities Press.

Greenspan, S.I. (1991). *Infancy and early childhood: The practice of clinical assessment and intervention with emotional and developmental challenges.* Madison, CT: International Universities Press.

Greenspan, S.I., & Greenspan, N.T. (1985). *First feelings: Milestones in the emotional development of your baby and child.* New York: Viking.

Griffin, E. (1982). *Island of childhood: Education in the special world of the nursery school.* New York: Teachers College Press.

Gunnar, M. R. (1980). Control, warning signals, and distress in infancy. *Developmental Psychology, 16,* 281–289.

Gunnar, M.R., Mangelsdorf, S., Larson, M., & Hertsgaard, L. (1989). Attachment, temperament, and adrenocortical activity in infancy: A study of psychoendocrine regulation. *Developmental Psychology, 25,* 355–363.

Halberstadt, A.G. (1985). Race, economic status, and nonverbal behavior. In A. Siegman & S. Feldstein (Eds.), *Nonverbal communication and interpersonal relations* (pp. 227–266). Hillsdale, NJ: Erlbaum.

Halberstadt, A.G. (1991). Toward an ecology of expressiveness: Family socialization in particular and a model in general. In R.S. Feldman & B. Rime (Eds.), *Fundamentals of nonverbal behavior* (pp. 106–160). New York: Cambridge University Press.

Hale-Benson, J.E. (1986). *Black children: Their roots, culture, and learning styles.* Baltimore: Johns Hopkins University Press.

Hancock, J., & Hill, S. (Eds.). (1988). *Literature-based reading programs at work.* Portsmouth, NH: Heinemann.

Harkness, S., & Kilbride, P.L. (1983). Introduction: The socialization of affect. *Ethos, 11,* 215–220.

Harkness, S., & Super, C.M. (1985). Child-environment interactions in the socialization of affect. In M. Lewis & C. Saarni (Eds.), *The socialization of emotions* (pp. 21–36). New York: Plenum.

Harlow, H. (1958). The nature of love. *American Psychologist, 13,* 673–685.

Harris, P. (1989). *Children and emotion: The development of psychological understanding.* New York: Blackwell.

Hart, C.H., Charlesworth, R., Burts, D.C., & DeWolf, M. (1993, March). *The relationship of attendance at developmentally appropriate or inappropriate kindergarten classrooms to first and second grade behavior.* Paper presented at biennial meeting of the Society for Research in Child Development, New Orleans.

Harter, S., & Buddin, B. (1987). Children's understanding of the simultaneity of two emotions: A five-stage developmental sequence. *Developmental Psychology, 23,* 388–399.

Harter, S., & Whitesell, N. (1989). Developmental changes in children's emotion concepts. In C. Saarni & P. Harris (Eds.), *Children's understanding of emotion.* New York: Cambridge University Press.

Hartley, R.E., Frank, L.K., & Goldenson, R.M. (1952). *Understanding children's play.* New York: Columbia University Press.

Hartup, W.W., Laursen, B., Stewart, M.I., & Eastenson, A. (1988). Conflict and the friendship relations of young children. *Child Development, 59,* 1590–1600.

Harwood, R. (1992). The influence of culturally derived values on Anglo and Puerto Rican mothers' perceptions of attachment behavior. *Child Development, 63,* 822–839.

Haviland, J.M., & Malatesta, C.Z. (1981). The development of sex differences in nonverbal signals: Fallacies, facts, and fantasies. In C. Mayo & N. Henley (Eds.), *Gender and non-verbal behavior* (pp. 183–208). New York: Springer.

Heath, S.B. (1983). *Ways with words: Language, life and work in communities and classrooms.* New York: Cambridge University Press.

Hendrick, J. (1992). *The whole child: Developmental education for the early childhood years.* New York: Macmillan.

Hills, T.W. (1992). Reaching potentials through appropriate assessment. In S. Bredekamp & T. Rosegrant (Eds.), *Reaching potentials: Appropriate curriculum and assessment for young children* (Vol. 1, pp. 43–63). Washington, DC: NAEYC.

Hirsh-Pasek, K., Hyson, M.C., & Rescorla, L. (1990). Academic environments in early childhood: Do they pressure or challenge young children? *Early Education and Development, 1,* 401–423.

Hoban, R. (1964). *Bread and jam for Frances.* New York: Harper & Row.

Hochschild, A. (1983). *The managed heart.* Berkeley: University of California Press.

Hoffman, M. (1982). The measurement of empathy. In C.E. Izard (Ed.), *Measuring emotions in infants and children* (Vol. 1, pp. 279–296). New York: Cambridge University Press.

Honig, A.S. (1981). *Infant caregiving: A design for training.* Syracuse, NY: Syracuse University Press.

Howes, C. (1988). Peer interaction of young children. *Monographs of the Society for Research in Child Development, 53*(1, Serial No. 217).

Howes, C. (1992). *The collaborative construction of pretend: Social pretend play functions.* Albany: State University of New York Press.

Howes, C., & Hamilton, C.E. (1992). Children's relationships with caregivers: Mothers and child care teachers. *Child Development, 63,* 859–866.

Hutt, C. (1966). Exploration and play in children. *Symposia of the Zoological Society of London, 18,* 61–81.

Hymes, J. (1947). *A pound of prevention: How teachers can meet the emotional needs of young children.* New York: Teachers Service Committee on the Emotional Needs of Children.

Hyson, M. (1979). Lobster on the sidewalk: Understanding and helping children with fears. *Young Children, 37,* 49–60.

Hyson, M. (1983). Going to the doctor: A developmental study of stress and coping. *Journal of Child Psychology and Psychiatry, 24,* 247–259.

Hyson, M. (1985, March). *Emotion–behavior relationships during brief separations.* Paper presented at biennial meeting of the Society for Research in Child Development, Toronto.

Hyson, M., & DeCsipkes, C. (1993, March). *Educational and developmental belief systems among African-American parents of kindergarten children.* Paper presented at biennial meeting of the Society for Research in Child Development, New Orleans.

Hyson, M.C., Hirsh-Pasek, K., & Rescorla, L. (1990). The Classroom Practices Inventory: An observation instrument based on NAEYC's Guidelines for Developmentally Appropriate Practices for 4- and 5-Year-Old Children. *Early Childhood Research Quarterly, 5,* 475–494.

Hyson, M.C., & Izard, C.E. (1985). Continuities and changes in emotion expressions during brief separation at 13 and 18 months. *Developmental Psychology, 21,* 1165–1170.

Hyson, M.C., & Lee, M. (1992, November). Building a professional knowledge base for an emotion-centered early childhood curriculum. Paper presented at annual conference of the National Association for the Education of Young Children, New Orleans.

Hyson, M.C., Whitehead, L.C., & Prudhoe, C. (1988). Influences on attitudes toward physical affection between adults and children. *Early Childhood Research Quarterly, 3,* 55–75.

Isaacs, S. (1963). *Intellectual growth in young children.* New York: Schocken Books. (Original work published 1930)

Izard, C.E. (1977). *Human emotions.* New York: Plenum.

Izard, C.E. (1991). *The psychology of emotions.* New York: Plenum.

Izard, C.E., Hembree, E.A., & Huebner, R.R. (1987). Infants' emotion expressions to acute pain. *Developmental Psychology, 23,* 105–113.

Izard, C.E., & Kobak, R.R. (1991). Emotions system functioning and emotion regulation. In J. Garber & K.A. Dodge (Eds.), *The development of emotion regulation and dysregulation* (pp. 303–321). New York: Cambridge University Press.

Izard, C.E., & Malatesta, C. (1987). Perspectives on emotional development I: Differential emotions theory of early emotional development. In J.D. Osofsky (Ed.), *Handbook of infant development* (2nd ed.) (pp. 494–554). New York: Wiley.

Jalongo, M. (1987). Do security blankets belong in preschool? *Young Children, 42,* 3–8.

Johnson, H.M. (1928). *Children in the nursery school.* New York: John Day.

Kagan, J. (1970). The determinants of attention in the infant. *American Scientist, 58,* 298–306.

Kagan, J., Reznick, J.S., Clarke, C., Snidman, N., & Garcia-Coll, C. (1984). Behavioral inhibition to the unfamiliar. *Child Development, 55,* 2212–2225.

Kagan, J., Reznick, J.S., & Snidman, N. (1988). Biological bases of childhood shyness. *Science, 240,* 167–171.

Kamii, C., Manning, M., & Manning, G. (Eds.). (1991). *Early literacy: A constructivist foundation for whole language.* Washington, DC: National Education Association.

Katz, L. (1977). *Talks with teachers.* Washington, DC: NAEYC.

Katz, L., & Chard, S. (1989). *Engaging children's minds: The project approach.* Norwood, NJ: Ablex.

Katz, L.F., & Gottman, J.M. (1991). Marital discord and child outcomes: A social psychophysiological approach. In J. Garber & K.A. Dodge (Eds.), *The development of emotion regulation and dysregulation* (pp. 129–155). New York: Cambridge University Press.

Katz, M.B. (1971). *Class, bureaucracy, and schools: The illusion of educational change in America.* New York: Praeger.

Klinnert, M.D., Campos, J.J., Sorce, J.F., Emde, R.N., & Svejda, M. (1983). Emotions as behavioral regulators: Social referencing in infancy. In R. Plutchik & H. Kellerman (Eds.), *Emotion: Theory, research, and experi-*

ence: Vol. 2. Emotions in early development (pp. 57–86). New York: Academic Press.

Klinnert, M.D., Sorce, J., Emde, R.N., Stenberg, C., & Gaensbauer, T.J. (1984). Continuities and changes in early affective life: Maternal perceptions of surprise, fear, and anger. In R.N. Emde & R.J. Harmon (Eds.), *Continuities and discontinuities in development* (pp. 339–354). New York: Plenum.

Kobak, R., & Sceery, A. (1988). Attachment in late adolescence: Working models, affect regulation, and representations of self and others. *Child Development, 59,* 135–146.

Kohlberg, L., & Mayer, R. (1972). Development as the aim of education. *Harvard Educational Review, 42,* 449–496.

Kopp, C.B. (1989). Regulation of distress and negative emotions: A developmental view. *Developmental Psychology, 25,* 343–354.

Kopp, C.B. (1992). Emotional distress and control in young children. In N. Eisenberg & R.A. Fabes (Eds.), *Emotion and its regulation in early development* (pp. 41–56). San Francisco: Jossey-Bass.

Krogh, S. (1990). *The integrated early childhood curriculum.* Highstown, NJ: McGraw-Hill.

Kuczynski, L., Zahn-Waxler, C., & Radke-Yarrow, M. (1987). Development and content of imitation in the second and third years of life: A socialization perspective. *Developmental Psychology, 23,* 276–282.

LaFreniere, P.J., Dumas, J.E., Capuano, F., & Dubeau, D. (1992). Development and validation of the preschool socioaffective profile. *Psychological Assessment, 4,* 442–450.

Leavitt, R.L., & Power, M.B. (1989). Emotional socialization in the postmodern era: Children in day care. *Social Psychology Quarterly, 52,* 35–43.

Lewis, C.C. (1988). Cooperation and control in Japanese nursery schools. In G. Handel (Ed.), *Childhood socialization* (pp. 125–142). New York: Aldine deGruyter.

Lewis, M. (1987). Social development in infancy and early childhood. In J.D. Osofsky (Ed.), *Handbook of infant development* (2nd ed., pp. 419–493). New York: Wiley.

Lewis, M., & Michalson, L. (1982). The socialization of emotions. In T. Field & A. Fogel (Eds.), *Emotions and early interaction* (pp. 189–211). Hillsdale, NJ: Erlbaum.

Lewis, M., & Michalson, L. (1983). *Children's emotions and moods.* New York: Plenum.

Lindahl, K.M., & Markman, H.J. (1993, March). Regulating negative affect in the family: Implications for dyadic and triadic family interactions. Paper presented at biennial meeting of the Society for Research in Child Development, New Orleans.

Lutz, C. (1983). Parental goals, ethnopsychology, and the development of emotional meaning. *Ethos, 11,* 246–262.

Lutz, C. (1985). Cultural patterns and individual differences in the child's emotional meaning system. In M. Lewis & C. Saarni (Eds.), *The socialization of emotions* (pp. 37–53). New York: Plenum.

Lynch, E.W., & Hansen, M.J. (1992). *Developing cross-cultural competence: A guide for working with young children and their families.* Baltimore: Paul H. Brookes.

Maccoby, E.E. (1980). *Social development: Psychological growth and the parent–child relationship.* New York: Harcourt Brace Jovanovich.

Maccoby, E.E., & Martin, J.A. (1983). Socialization in the context of the family: Parent–child interaction. In P.H. Mussen (Ed.), *Handbook of child psychology* (Vol. 4, pp. 1–101). New York: Wiley.

Mahler, M., Pine, F., & Bergman, A. (1975). *The psychological birth of the human infant.* New York: Basic Books.

Malatesta, C.Z. (1981). Infant emotion and the vocal affect lexicon. *Motivation and Emotion, 5,* 1–23.

Malatesta, C.Z. (1988). The role of emotions in the development and organization of personality. In R.A. Thompson (Ed.), *Socioemotional development.* (pp. 1–56). Lincoln: University of Nebraska Press.

Malatesta, C.Z., Culver, C., Tesman, J.R., & Shepard, B. (1989). The development of emotion expression during the first two years of life. *Monographs of the Society for Research in Child Development, 54*(1–2, Serial No. 219).

Malatesta, C.Z., & Haviland, J.M. (1982). Learning display rules: The socialization of emotion expression in infancy. *Child Development, 53,* 991–1003.

Manstead, A.S.R. (1992). Gender differences in emotion. In M.A. Gale & M.W. Eysenck (Eds.), *Handbook of individual differences: Biological perspectives.* Chichester, England: Wiley.

Matas, L., Arend, R., & Sroufe, L.A. (1978). Continuity of adaptation in the second year: The relationship between quality of attachment and later competence. *Child Development, 49,* 547–556.

McAdoo, H.P. (Ed.). (1992). *Black families* (2nd ed.). Newbury Park, CA: Sage Publications.

Miller, S.M., & Green M.L. (1985). Coping with stress and frustration: Origins, nature, and development. In M. Lewis & C. Saarni (Eds.), *The socialization of emotions* (pp. 263–314). New York: Plenum.

Mitchell, R. (1992). *Testing for learning: How new approaches to evaluation can improve America's schools.* New York: Free Press.

Miyake, K., Chen, S-J., & Campos, J. (1985). Infant temperament, mother's mode of interaction, and attachment in Japan: An interim report. In I. Bretherton & E. Waters (Eds.), *Growing points of attachment theory and research* (pp. 276–297). *Monographs of the Society for Research in Child Development, 50*(1–2, Serial No. 209).

Moore, B.S. (1985). The behavioral consequences of affect. In M. Lewis & C. Saarni (Eds.), *The socialization of emotions* (pp. 213–237). New York: Plenum.

Murphy, L.B. (1962). *The widening world of childhood: Paths toward mastery.* New York: Basic Books.

Mussen, P.H. (Ed.). (1970). *Handbook of child psychology* (3rd ed.). New York: Wiley.

National Association of Early Childhood Specialists in State Departments of

Education. (1987). *Unacceptable trends in kindergarten entry and placement.* Unpublished document.

National Association for the Education of Young Children. (1988). Position statement on standardized testing of young children 3 through 8 years of age. *Young Children, 43,* 42–47.

National Commission on Testing and Public Policy. (1990). *From gatekeeper to gateway: Transforming testing in America.* Chestnut Hill, MA: Author.

National Council of Teachers of Mathematics. (1989). *Curriculum and evaluation standards for school mathematics.* Reston, VA: Author.

New, R. (1992). The integrated early childhood curriculum: New interpretations based on research and practice. In C. Seefeldt (Ed.), *The early childhood curriculum* (pp. 286–322). New York: Teachers College Press.

Nikkari, D.S., Gilbert, J., Emde, R.N., & Campos, J.J. (1993, March). *The Emotion Prototype Questionnaire: A new parental report instrument for assessing emotional development in toddlers.* Paper presented at biennial meeting of the Society for Research in Child Development, New Orleans.

Nyquist, E.B., & Hawes, G.R. (Eds.). (1972). *Open education.* New York: Bantam.

Pianta, R. (Ed.). (1992). *Beyond the parent: The role of other adults in children's lives.* San Francisco: Jossey-Bass.

Plutchik, R. (1991). *The emotions* (rev. ed.). Lanham, MD: University Press of America.

Radke-Yarrow, M., & Zahn-Waxler, C. (1984). Roots, motives, and patterns in children's prosocial behavior. In E. Staub, D. Bar-Tal, J. Karylowski, & J. Reykowski (Eds.), *Development and maintenance of prosocial behavior: International perspectives on positive behavior* (pp. 81–98). New York: Plenum.

Ramsey, P. (1987). *Teaching and learning in a diverse world.* New York: Teachers College Press.

Rapaport, D. (1967). *Emotions and memory.* New York: International Universities Press.

Renninger, K.A., Hidi, S., & Krapp, A. (Eds.). (1992). *The role of interest in learning and development.* Hillsdale, NJ: Erlbaum.

Renninger, K.A., & Wozniak, R. (1985). Effect of interest on attentional shift, recognition, and recall in young children. *Developmental Psychology, 21,* 624–632.

Rheingold, H.L., Cook, K.V., & Kolowitz, V. (1987). Commands activate the behavior and pleasure of 2-year-old children. *Developmental Psychology, 23,* 146–151.

Ricks, D. (1979). Making sense of experience to make sensible sounds. In M. Bulowa (Ed.), *Before speech* (pp. 245–268). Cambridge: Cambridge University Press.

Roberts, W., & Strayer, J. (1987). Parents' responses to the emotional distress of their children: Relations with children's competence. *Developmental Psychology, 23,* 415–422.

Russell, J.A. (1989). Costumes, scripts, and children's understanding. In C. Saarni, & P.L. Harris (Eds.), *Children's understanding of emotion* (pp. 293–318). New York: Cambridge University Press.

Saarni, C. (1979). Children's understanding of display rules for expressive behavior. *Developmental Psychology, 15,* 424–429.

Saarni, C. (1985). Indirect processes in affect socialization. In M. Lewis & C. Saarni (Eds.), *The socialization of emotions* (pp. 187–209). New York: Plenum.

Saarni, C. (1990). Emotional competence: How emotions and relationships become integrated. In R.A. Thompson (Ed.), *Socioemotional development* (pp. 115–182). Lincoln: University of Nebraska Press.

Saarni, C., & Harris, P.L. (Eds.). (1989). *Children's understanding of emotion.* New York: Cambridge University Press.

Scherer, K.R. (1979). Nonlinguistic vocal indicators of emotion and psychopathology. In C.E. Izard (Ed.), *Emotions in personality and psychopathology* (pp. 495–529). New York: Plenum.

Schweinhart, L.J., Weikart, D.P., & Larner, M.B. (1986). Consequences of three preschool curriculum models through age 15. *Early Childhood Research Quarterly, 1,* 15–45.

Seifert, K.L. (1993). Cognitive development and early childhood education. In B. Spodek (Ed.), *Handbook of research on the education of young children* (pp. 9–23). New York: Macmillan.

Shapiro, M.S. (1983). *Child's garden: The kindergarten movement from Froebel to Dewey.* University Park: Pennsylvania State University Press.

Shaver, P., Schwartz, J., Kirson, D., & O'Conner, C. (1987). Emotion knowledge: Further exploration of a prototype approach. *Journal of Personality and Social Psychology, 52,* 1061–1086.

Sigel, I.E., McGillicuddy-Delisi, A.V., & Goodnow, J.J. (Eds.) (1992). *Parental belief systems: The psychological consequences for children.* (rev. ed.). Hillsdale, NJ: Erlbaum.

Sigman, M.D., Kasari, C., Kwon, J., & Yirmiya, N. (1992). Responses to the negative emotions of others by autistic, mentally retarded, and normal children. *Child Development, 63,* 796–807.

Spodek, B. (1991). Early childhood curriculum and cultural definitions of knowledge. In B. Spodek & O. Saracho (Eds.), *Issues in early childhood curriculum* (pp. 1–20). New York: Teachers College Press.

Spodek, B. (Ed.). (1993). *Handbook of research on the education of young children.* New York: Macmillan.

Sroufe, L.A., & Fleeson, J. (1986). Attachment and the construction of relationships. In W.W. Hartup & Z. Rubin (Eds.), *Relationships and development* (pp. 51–71). Hillsdale, NJ: Erlbaum.

Sroufe, L.A., Schork, E., Motti, E., Lawroski, N., & LaFreniere, P. (1984). The role of affect in social competence. In C. Izard, J. Kagan, & R. Zajonc (Eds.), *Emotions, cognition, and behavior* (pp. 289–319). New York: Cambridge University Press.

Stein, N.L., & Jewett, J.L. (1986). A conceptual analysis of the meaning of negative emotions: Implications for a theory of development. In C.E. Izard & P.B. Read (Eds.) *Measuring emotions in infants and children* (Vol. II, pp. 238–267). New York: Cambridge University Press.

Stenberg, C., & Campos, J. (1990). The development of anger expressions in infancy. In N. Stein, B. Leventhal, & T. Trabasso (Eds.), *Psychological and biological approaches to emotion* (pp. 247–282). Hillsdale, NJ: Erlbaum.

Stipek, D. (1991). Characterizing early childhood education programs. In L. Rescorla, M.C. Hyson, & K. Hirsh-Pasek (Eds.), *Academic instruction in early childhood: Challenge or pressure? New Directions for Child Development* (pp. 47–55). San Francisco: Jossey-Bass.

Stipek, D. (1992). Characterizing early childhood programs for poor and middle class children. *Early Childhood Research Quarterly, 7,* 1–19.

Stoller, S.A., & Field, T. (1982). Alteration of mother and infant behavior and heart rate during a still-face perturbation of face-to-face interaction. In T. Field & A. Fogel (Eds.), *Emotion and early interaction* (pp. 57–82). Hillsdale, NJ: Erlbaum.

Strickland, D.S., & Morrow, L.M. (Eds.). (1989). *Emerging literacy: Young children learn to read and write.* Newark, DE: International Reading Association.

Suransky, V.P. (1982). *The erosion of childhood.* Chicago: University of Chicago Press.

Thompson, R.A., & Lamb, M.E. (1983). Individual differences in dimensions of socioemotional development in infancy. In R. Plutchik & H. Kellerman (Eds.), *Emotion: Theory, research, and experience: Vol. 2. Emotions in early development* (pp. 87–114). New York: Academic Press.

Trevarthen, C. (1984). Emotions in infancy: Regulators of contact and relationships with persons. In K.R. Scherer & P. Ekman (Eds.), *Approaches to emotion* (pp. 129–157). Hillsdale, NJ: Erlbaum.

Tronick, E., Ricks, M., & Cohn, J. (1982). Maternal and infant affective exchange: Patterns of adaptation. In T. Field & A. Fogel (Eds.), *Emotion and interaction: Normal and high-risk infants.* Orlando, FL: Academic Press.

U.S. Congress, Office of Technology Assessment. (1992). *Testing in America's schools: Asking the right questions.* Washington, DC: U.S. Government Printing Office.

U.S. Department of Health, Education, and Welfare, Office of Child Development. (1973). *Head Start program performance standards* (Head Start Policy Manual, OCD Notice N-30–364–1). Washington, DC: U.S. Government Printing Office.

Vygotsky, L.S. (1978). *Mind in society: The development of higher mental processes.* Cambridge, MA: Harvard University Press.

Waters, E., Wippman, J., & Sroufe, L.A. (1979). Attachment, positive affect and competence in the peer group: Two studies in construct validation. *Child Development, 50,* 821–829.

Watson, J.B. (1919). *Psychology, from the standpoint of a behaviorist.* Philadelphia: Lippincott.

Weber, E. (1969). *The kindergarten: Its encounter with educational thought in America.* New York: Teachers College Press.

Weber, E. (1984). *Ideas influencing early childhood education: A theoretical analysis.* New York: Teachers College Press.

Wertsch, J. (1985). *Vygotsky and the social formation of mind.* Cambridge, MA: Harvard University Press.

Whitebook, M., Howes, C., & Phillips, D. (1989). *Who cares? child care teachers and the quality of care in America* (Final report, National Child Care Staffing Study). Oakland, CA: Child Care Employee Project.

Wieder, S., & Greenspan, S.I. (1993). The emotional basis of learning. In B. Spodek (Ed.), *Handbook of research on the education of young children* (pp. 77–87). New York: Macmillan.

Worth, V. (1975/1986). Tiger. *Small poems again.* NY: Farrar, Straus, & Giroux.

Zahn-Waxler, C., Cummings, E.M., Iannotti, R.J., & Radke-Yarrow, M. (1984). Young offspring of depressed parents: A population at risk for affective problems. In D. Cicchetti & K. Schneider-Rosen (Eds.), *Childhood depression* (pp. 81–105). San Francisco: Jossey-Bass.

Index

About the Author

Marion C. Hyson is Associate Professor of Individual and Family Studies at the University of Delaware. She received her Ph.D. in child development and early childhood education at Bryn Mawr College's Department of Human Development. She has taught preschool and kindergarten children and has directed a college-affiliated child care center. As a member of the Higher Education Consortium, she has worked with child care advocates in the state of Delaware to design and implement a comprehensive system of professional development. Her research projects and publications have emphasized early emotional development, attitudes toward adult–child affection, and the causes and effects of early academic pressures. With Leslie Rescorla and Kathy Hirsh-Pasek, Professor Hyson is co-editor of the *New Directions for Child Development* volume *Academic Instruction in Early Childhood: Challenge or Pressure?*. She is Associate Editor of *Early Education and Development* and serves as a Consulting Editor for *Early Childhood Research Quarterly*. She is a member of the Board of Examiners of the National Council for Accreditation of Teacher Education. Currently, she is engaged in research examining teachers' emotion-related beliefs in American and Korean early childhood programs.